# THE ILLUSTRATED ENCYCLOPEDIA OF

# WILDLIFE

## VOLUME 13

## The Invertebrates

## Part III

Wildlife Consultant

MARY CORLISS PEARL, Ph. D.

**Distributed by Encyclopaedia Britannica
Educational Corporation**                    **Grey Castle Press**

Published by Grey Castle Press, 1991

Distributed by Encyclopaedia Britannica Educational Corporation, 1991

THE ILLUSTRATED ENCYCLOPEDIA OF WILDLIFE
Volume 13: THE INVERTEBRATES—Part III

Library of Congress Cataloging-in-Publication Data
The Illustrated encyclopedia of wildlife.
     p.     cm.
       Contents: v. 1–5. The mammals—v. 6–8. The birds —
v. 9. Reptiles and amphibians — v. 10. The fishes —
v. 11–14. The invertebrates — v. 15. The invertebrates
and index.
       ISBN 1–55905–052–7
       1. Zoology.
QL45.2.I44 1991                              90–3750
591—dc20                                     CIP


ISBN 1–55905–052–7 (complete set)
      1–55905–049–7 (Volume 13)


Printed in Spain

Photo Credits
Photographs were supplied by: *Archivio IGDA*: 2569, 2571; (L. Andena) 2640; (Barletta) 2677; (Bertola) 2616; (Bevilacqua) 2671; (Boieri) 2663t; (Bucciarelli) 2517, 2519, 2633; (F. Cirillo) 2525t, 2535; (Donnini) 2674; (Ferrais) 2525b, 2559t, 2562, 2563, 2589t, 2589b, 2620; (M. Giovanoli) 2529b, 2533, 2554, 2574b, 2590r, 2602, 2608b, 2614l, 2664; (G. Giovenzanna) 2586r; (La Palude) 2537, 2581, 2589c, 2612, 2668b, 2641; (M. Pilloud) 2621; (M. Pizzarani) 2541, 2561, 2610, 2632, 2635; (C. Rives) 2675t, 2676; (C. Salvadeo) 2599, 2662; *Ardea*: (I. Beames) 2579; (J.L. Mason) 2577; *G. Bartella: Bavestrelli*: (Bevilacqua; Prato) 2551; *Bruce Coleman*: (J. Burton) 2549, 2560; (D. Green) 2618, 2619; (G. McCarthy) 2630, 2631; (H. Reinhard) 2578, 2548r; (F. Sauer) 2582b, 2625t; (K. Taylor) 2540; (P. Ward) 2611; *H. Chaumeton*: 2625b, 2631, 2672, 2678, 2679, 2680, 2682, 2689, 2692; (Lanceau) 2675b; *Jacana*: (Champroux) 2553; (H. Chaumeton) 2586l; 2598, 2627, 2628, 2665; (F. Danrigal) 2584l, 2681, 2688; (P. Dormangeat) 2534; (R. Dulhoste) 2613, 2657; (B. Hawkes) 2606; (J.P. Hervy) 2607, 2623; (Konig) 2526t, 2542l; (L. Lacoste) 2591t, 2636; (P. Lorne) 2530, 2545b, 2653b, 2666; (C. & M. Moiton) 2521, 2526t, 2527, 2572, 2585, 2590l, 2600, 2605, 2608t, 2614r, 2615, 2625b, 2626, 2629, 2637, 2642, 2648, 2651, 2660; (Nardin) 2609, 2647; (Noailles) 2544, 2545t; (P. Petit) 2591b; (P. Pilloud) 2529t, 2542r, 2574t, 2655; (K. Ross) 2532, 2538, 2566, 2653t; (Rouxaime) 2565, 2575, 2576, 2578, 2645; (P. Varin) 2547t, 2552l, 2547t, 2552l; 2558; (Varin-Visage) 2594lr, 2622, (F. Winner) 2516, 2524, 2546, 2547b, 2656; *S. Lombardi*: 2571b; *A. Margiocco*: 2559b; *NHPA*: (ANT) 2603; (A. Bannister) 2661; (G.I. Bernard) 2687; (J. Carmichael) 2601; (S. Dalton) 2530l, 2549, 2568, 2582t, 2592, 2649; (J. Shaw) 2523; *Orion Press*: 2643; *Oxford Scientific Films*: (G. Thompson) 2654; *Planet Earth Pictures*: (K. Lucas) 2683, 2684, 2685; (M. Mattock) 2531.

FRONT COVER: A swallowtail butterfly (Ardea/Ian Beames)

# CONTENTS

# SOCIABLE AND SOLITARY

Wasps, bees and ants represent a pinnacle of insect evolution.
Many species have evolved complex societies, while solitary wasps
are some of the most cunning parasites in the insect world

ABOVE **The front view of a hornet's head reveals its large, composite eyes. The hornet is Britain's largest and rarest wasp. It is greatly feared because of its size, but is actually a docile species. Hornets are larger than common wasps, and have red and yellow coloring, rather than black and yellow.**

PAGE 2515 **Swarms of bees congregate on top of the cells of their hive. Ants and bees have the most organized of insect societies. A single queen governs the society, and female workers maintain it. Males make a brief appearance to fertilize new queens, and they die soon after mating.**

## INSECTS CLASSIFICATION: 16

### Wasps, bees and ants (1)

The order Hymenoptera is the second-largest division of insects (after beetles) with about 290,000 species. It is divided into two major suborders—the Symphyta and the Apocrita. The suborder Symphyta contains about 10,000 species of "primitive" hymenopterans in 14 families. They include the Siricidae (horntails or wood wasps, such as the giant wood wasp, *Uroceros gigas*); and the Tenthredinidae (sawflies), which contains the pear-tree sawfly, *Caliroa limacina*, and the pine sawfly, *Diprion pini*, of Europe.

The suborder Apocrita contains two divisions—the Parasitica (parasitic wasps) and the Aculeata (wasps, bees and ants). The division Parasitica contains approximately 200,000 species in six superfamilies and 51 families. These include the Cynipidae (gall wasps) containing the oak gall wasp, *Biorrhiza pallida*, the rose gall wasp, *Diplolepis rosae*, and the genus *Neuroterus*; and the Agaonidae (fig wasps, such as the *Blastophaga psennes*) of the superfamily Chalcidoidea; the Ichneumonidae (ichneumon flies) contains the species *Rhyssa persuasoria* of Europe and North America; the Braconidae (bracon flies) has the tiny *Apanteles glomeratus*; and the Proctotrypidae (proctotrypid wasps, such as *Inostemma pyricola*).

The 290,000 species of the order Hymenoptera include bees, wasps and ants. They are second only to the beetles in numbers of species and range throughout the world, except for Antarctica. They are highly specialized insects and form several types of highly developed social organization. In certain species, for example, some individuals form social castes and others receive and transmit messages. Certain species are able to "memorize" where they have stored food so that they can return to it later.

The order Hymenoptera includes some of nature's most important pollinators. They play an important role in maintaining much of the world's vegetation. Parasitic species, such as parasitic wasps, exert tremendous pressure on their insect hosts and many species prey on other types of plant-eating insects, maintaining biological balances within the insect kingdom. Indeed, predaceous hymenopterans are used as biological control agents against pests. Although there are a few plant-eating species, the members of the order Hymenoptera are generally beneficial to humans, producing wax and honey.

The earliest fossil hymenopterans date from the sawflies of the superfamily Xyeloidea, which lived 225-195 million years ago in the Triassic epoch. The insects with which the hymenopterans share the most common ancestors are the scorpion flies (Mecoptera), dating from the Permian epoch 280-225 million years ago.

### Stalks and stings

The order Hymenoptera divides into the suborders Symphyta and Apocrita. Members of the suborder Apocrita have distinctive, pedunculated abdomens—they have a narrow, stalk-like connecting part between their first and second abdominal segments. The members of the suborder Symphyta lack this feature. The suborder Apocrita further divides into two subdivisions—Parasitica, which have sword-shaped ovipositors, and Aculeata, in which the ovipositor has become a defensive sting.

## Membranous wings

The hymenopterans receive their name (the Greek *hymen* meaning "membrane" and *pteron* meaning "wing") from their two pairs of transparent, membranous wings. Their front wings are usually larger than the rear wings; the front and rear wings on each side couple together with a row of hooks (hamili) during flight to form a single, strong wing surface. When the insect is stationary, the wings either rest horizontally over the abdomen or hang down the sides of their bodies.

The head is separate from the body in hymenopterans, and bears two large, compound eyes, each of which consists of hundreds of tiny eyes (ommatidia). The mouthparts vary from one species to another according to their diet. They are either specialized for chewing, or for sucking and chewing.

## Poisonous sting

All female hymenopterans have a well-developed ovipositor, which they use to insert eggs into plant tissue or into the body of a host insect. In some species, the ovipositor has been transformed into a sting with poison glands attached. Most hymenopterans reproduce sexually, although there are cases of parthenogenesis, where the male is not required to fertilize the egg. The larvae undergo a series of changes, turning first into pupae, then into adults in a process called holometabolism, or complete transformation.

## Horntails

The horntails of the family Siricidae are medium to large in size with robust bodies and large, strong wings. Their white, grub-like larvae are characteristically xylophagous (wood-eating), and spend most of their time digging long, winding tunnels in the wood that forms their homes. One of the commonest horntails is the giant wood wasp, *Uroceros gigas*, a species that has pronounced differences between the sexes, especially in body coloration. The male has a dark abdomen with red segments in the middle, while the female has a reddish yellow abdomen with a dark center.

## Dead wood

During midsummer, the female giant wood wasp takes to the woods immediately after mating, and searches for dead tree trunks in which to lay her eggs (the adult female is capable of laying up to 1000 eggs). She then extends a darkened, drill-like structure from

ABOVE **A female giant wood wasp lays her eggs in the trunk of a tree. She frequently chooses a tall conifer such as a larch or fir. Using her long, pointed ovipositor, she perforates the wood and deposits her eggs inside. The larvae take up to three years to mature, and the trees in which they live may be sawn into planks and used as building materials while they are still inside. Once mature, male giant wood wasps may reach 1.2 in. in length; females can reach up to 1.6 in.**

ABOVE *Tenthredopsis sp.*, a member of the largest sawfly family, can be a major agricultural pest. It uses its saw-shaped ovipositor to cut slits in plant stems and leaves.

BELOW *Caliroa limacina* of the sawfly family lays its eggs in leaf tissue, thus providing a place for the larvae to grow. The small-legged larvae resemble black slugs.

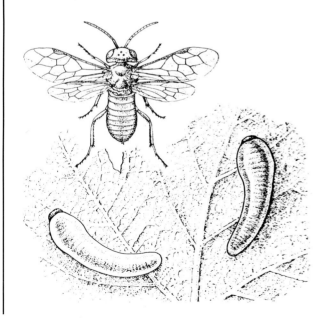

her long ovipositor, points it vertically and starts to burrow slowly into the wood, laying her eggs one at a time as she proceeds. It takes the female a quarter of an hour to penetrate about 0.4 in. into the wood.

## Strong mandibles

After a few days, the larvae hatch out of their eggs. They have strong mandibles, and each larva immediately begins to bore into the wood, digging a long, tortuous tunnel. As the larvae grow, the diameter of the tunnel that they occupy begins to expand correspondingly. Because they transmit a fungus that can kill the tree, the larvae are seen as pests.

The fungus and the horntail larvae form a mutually beneficial partnership—the fungus gains access to wood that it uses as a food substrate, and the larvae gain nutrients liberated by the fungus. In some cases, the tree is carved into furniture before the larvae turn into adults; the owners then have the unpleasant surprise of discovering that their house has become infested with adult horntails.

## Sawflies

The 14 families of sawflies are so called because the female sawfly has saw-like blades along her ovipositor, with which she bores into plant tissue to insert eggs. As members of the group Symphyta, they lack the wasp waist that characterizes other hymenopterans. In most sawfly species, the short-lived adults are active in spring and early summer. Some species do not feed, but most visit flowers for nectar and some eat small insects.

About three-quarters of all sawfly species belong to the family *Tenthredinidae*, many of which are major agricultural pests. They are medium to small in size, and the females lay their eggs in the stems of flowers, leaves or wood. As a result, the larvae must tunnel their way out when they hatch. The larvae of most sawflies resemble the caterpillars of moths and butterflies; they differ in having only one pair of simple eyes (ocelli) and more than five pairs of abdominal forelegs.

Members of the family Tenthredinidae include the sawflies of the genus *Hoplocampa*, which attack apple, plum and pear trees as well as other types of fruit trees. They include the apple sawfly, a major pest in European orchids, where their larvae burrow into

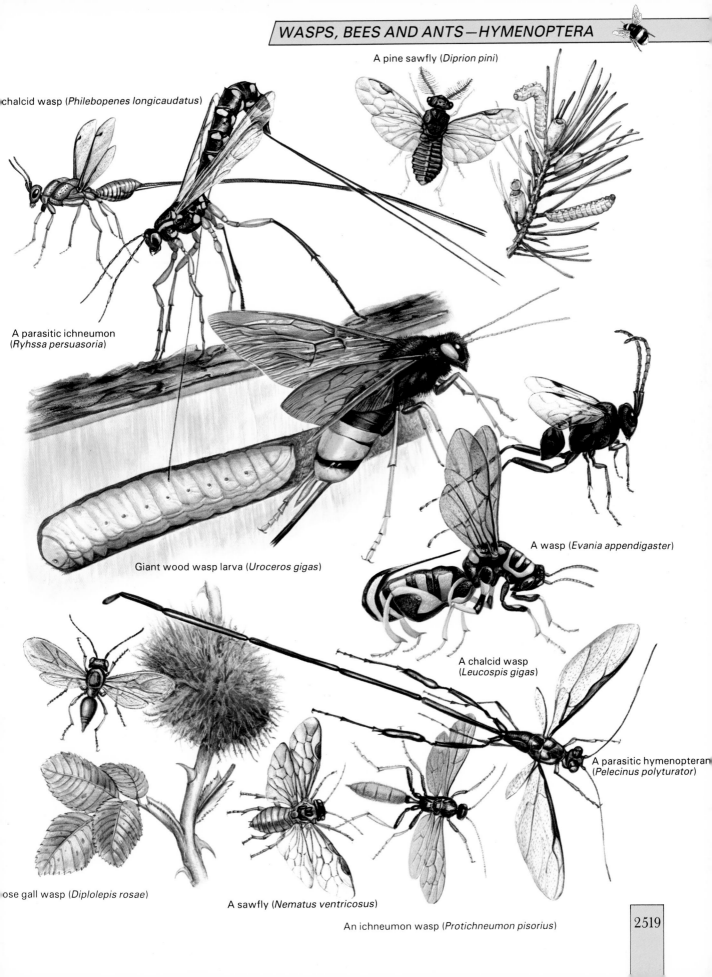

A pine sawfly (*Diprion pini*)

chalcid wasp (*Philebopenes longicaudatus*)

A parasitic ichneumon
(*Ryhssa persuasoria*)

Giant wood wasp larva (*Uroceros gigas*)

A wasp (*Evania appendigaster*)

A chalcid wasp
(*Leucospis gigas*)

A parasitic hymenopteran
(*Pelecinus polyturator*)

ose gall wasp (*Diplolepis rosae*)

A sawfly (*Nematus ventricosus*)

An ichneumon wasp (*Protichneumon pisorius*)

ABOVE The rose gall wasp of the family Cynipidae is a plant parasite. It lays its eggs inside the stem of a wild rose bush, which causes characteristic pin-cushion galls to form on the plant. The wasps are so small that a microscope is needed to identify them. It is often easier to identify them by the shape of the gall they produce.

ABOVE RIGHT The inside of the gall of a rose gall wasp, showing the larvae. The plant tissues behaved abnormally and produced the gall because of the activity of the larvae, which feed directly from the gall.

young fruitlets to feed. The species *Blennocampus pusilla* is familiar to rose cultivators everywhere. The larvae usually roll themselves up in the small leaves of the rose plant.

Sawflies of the family Diprionidae are much feared because of the damage they cause to plants; they are particularly notorious in Canada as defoliators of forestland. The pine sawfly species *Diprion pini*, which is widespread throughout much of Europe, is a typical member of the family. Measuring 0.3-0.4 in. in length, it is a small creature with a squat, black body. The tip of the abdomen is red in males and yellow with black spots in females.

After mating takes place, the female pine sawfly flies up into pine trees and lays about 10-20 eggs on a single needle. After about three weeks, the first larvae appear, collecting on the branches and chewing away voraciously at the pine needles. They are agile insects and secrete irritants to deter would-be predators.

## Gall wasps

Commonly known as gall wasps, members of the family Cynipidae usually lead a parasitic life-style at the expense of other insects; other species feed entirely on plants. For example, the species *Biorrhiza pallida*, or oak gall wasp, is a small creature that produces characteristic oval-shaped tunnels on the roots and buds of oak trees.

There are alternate generations in the biological cycle of oak gall wasps. The first generation reproduces by parthenogenesis, and the second reproduces sexually. The parthenogenetic female is wingless. It grows and develops inside a small tunnel in the roots of the tree. As soon as it leaves the shelter of the tunnel, it climbs up the trunk until it reaches the leaves. There, the female perforates a young bud with its ovipositor and lays at least a dozen eggs in the center. Having completed her work, the female then dies.

When the larvae hatch out, they secrete a special substance that causes a proliferation of the cells of the vegetable tissue. Consequently, when the bud opens out, the new leaves have small, rounded galls, known as oak apples, on their upper surface. The galls have a hardened outer shell, but inside they are soft and rich in nutrients, such as grains of starch and oily substances. The gall provides both food and shelter for the young.

By late spring the larvae are fully grown and leave the gall. They flit around for a short while and then mate. Afterward, the females descend to ground level and burrow into the roots of the oak tree to lay their eggs. The larvae that hatch from these eggs will form the next parthenogenetic generation. They grow and develop inside irregularly shaped galls which they induce themselves in the cells of the roots.

The rose gall wasp, *Diplolepis rosae*, produces "pincushion" galls on rose bushes, another species induces rounded galls on the branches of oak trees, and the members of the genus *Neuroterus* produce disk-shaped galls on the leaves.

# SOCIABLE AND SOLITARY

## Parasitic wasps

The superfamily Chalcidoidea consists of about 20 families and 80,000-100,000 species of parasitic wasps in the suborder Apocrita. Most are parasites of other insects, and some are hyperparasites—parasitizing insects that are themselves parasitic. Since many species prey on insects that damage agricultural crops, they are widely used in biological control programs. However, it is only the larvae of parasitic wasps that live off the eggs and larvae of various other types of insect. The adults are free-living and have an exclusively vegetarian diet.

One species of chalcid wasp is widely used in the fight against a species of scale insect that attacks mulberry trees. In the spring, as soon as the female wasp reaches adulthood, it settles on a mulberry tree and sits beside the tiny white shields that protect the scale insect. Using its sharp ovipositor, the wasp makes a deep hole in each shield and lays an egg inside each of the holes. When the larvae hatch, they grow at the expense of the scale insect host, gradually devouring it completely. As soon as the wasps reach adulthood, they fly off in search of new prey.

## Pollinating fig insects

Fig insects, or Agaontidae, are among the most remarkable of the nonparasitic members of the Chalcidoidea superfamily. They live in symbiosis (a mutually beneficial partnership) with the wild fig tree, developing in galls within the figs and successfully pollinating the tree so it bears fruit. The males are wingless and remain permanently inside the fruit. The females, on the other hand, fly about freely. Before they leave the gall, they mate and become inadvertently dusted with pollen, so they are able to fertilize other figs that they enter to lay their eggs.

The best-known fig insect is the species *Blastophaga psennes*. The females of the species lay their eggs in the "flowers" of the fig tree. The wild fig does not have true flowers. Instead, the tree's floral parts—known as syconia—occur inside the immature fig fruit. During the course of summer, three different types of syconia appear. The first type comes out when the tree is just beginning to sprout leaves and consists of both male and female flowers. The second type appears when the first type has reached maturity, and contains a small

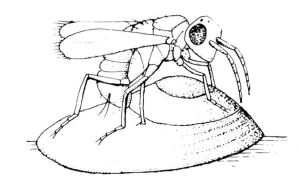

TOP The large ichneumon wasp, *Rhyssa persuasoria*, uses its long ovipositor to deposit eggs inside the bodies of sawfly larvae. The female wasp first locates the sawfly larvae within the wood and then drills a hole through the wood to reach the larvae.

ABOVE A chalcid wasp lays an egg inside the body of the scale insect, *Diaspis pentagona*, which attacks mulberry trees. Many species of chalcid wasp are used to control agricultural pests, reducing the need for chemical pesticides.

number of male flower parts near the mouth and many female flower parts. The third type, mainly female flower parts, lies dormant throughout the winter and reaches maturity the following spring. Consequently, the fig insect, *B. psennes*, produces three generations a year, one for each type of syconium.

When fig insects lay their eggs in the "flowers" of the fig tree, galls develop and the insect larvae grow inside the galls. In early spring, only the first type of syconium contains eggs. The males emerge first. They seek out galls containing females, open them and then mate. Later, the fertilized females leave the syconium and, in doing so, cover themselves in pollen. They fly off in search of other syconia (by now the tree bears only the second kind), and when they find one they climb inside and move around, laying eggs as they go and inadvertently distributing pollen from the fig tree flower. The flowers containing this generation of eggs also develop galls, thus giving shelter to the larvae.

## Repeating the cycle

When the fig insect larvae reach adulthood, they repeat the cycle, behaving in the same way as the previous generation. The males are born first. They fertilize the females inside their galls and die soon afterward. Then the fertilized females emerge from the galls and the syconium. They, too, brush against the male flowers as they leave the syconium and receive a dusting of pollen.

The females fly around in search of other flowers in which to lay their eggs, and only find the third type of syconium. They crawl inside and deposit both eggs and pollen on the female flowers, thus repeating the cycle for the third time. The flowers containing the eggs develop galls containing both males and females. But, in this case, the larvae hibernate inside the syconia until they reach maturity the following spring. The males hatch first and fertilize the females inside the galls. The females emerge and again become covered in pollen as they leave the flowers. As they search the fig tree, they find only the first type of syconium, and so the whole cycle begins again.

In a few countries, the symbiosis between *B. psennes* and the wild fig is put to agricultural use. In accordance with an ancient practice performed in Roman times, a few of the first type of syconia from a wild fig tree are placed among the branches of a cultivated fig. When the insects emerge, they enter the syconia of the cultivated fig. They try to lay their eggs there, but do not succeed because the flowers of the cultivated fig are different and prevent them from doing so. In the meantime, however, they fertilize the tree by scattering the pollen from the wild fig.

## Larvae-eating Ichneumonoidea

The Ichneumonoidea comprise another superfamily of Hymenoptera in the suborder Apocrita. They lead a parasitic life-style at the expense of other insects,

offering no benefits to their hosts. Typical of the 60,000 species in the family of ichneumon flies (Ichneumonoidae) is *Rhyssa persuasoria*, a large, black wasp that parasitizes the wood-eating larvae of horntails. It uses its long ovipositor—often one and a half times the length of its own body—to dig through wood to the larvae and embed its eggs within them.

*R. persuasoria* are distributed throughout America and Europe, and they are a common sight in summer as they fly around among the conifers in search of prey. Once a member of the species has located a tree trunk that contains a horntail larva, the insect settles and digs a hole in the trunk using its long, drill-like ovipositor. The task is long and laborious, and while the insect is drilling, it is completely at the mercy of potential predators since it is unable to remove its ovipositor from the tree quickly in order to defend itself.

As a rule, *R. persuasoria* completes its task successfully—reaching a horntail larva with its ovipositor, making a wound in its body and then laying an egg inside it. After a few days, the egg hatches into a tiny larva that immediately begins to feed on the internal tissues of its host. Once it has reached adulthood, the newly formed *R. persuasoria* digs a tunnel out of the tree trunk and begins life on its own.

## Butterfly and moth prey

*Pimpla investigator* is a species of ichneumon fly that lives at the expense of butterfly and moth larvae. The female of the species falls upon her chosen victim and quickly digs her ovipositor into its body so that she can lay an egg there. Then she flies away in search of new victims. The larva of *P. investigator*—like that of *R. persuasoria*—feeds on the internal tissues of its larval prey. When fully grown, it makes a small cocoon and undergoes the transition into adulthood. It then comes out into the open.

Within the superfamily Ichneumonoidea, the bracon flies comprise a family of about 40,000 species that parasitize other insects. However, unlike most Ichneumonoidea, they lay a number of eggs inside their prey. Furthermore, the females usually paralyze their victims by injecting poison into them.

RIGHT The female ichneumon wasp uses her needle-like ovipositor for two purposes—to drill into a tree to reach a beetle larva living inside, and to serve as the channel through which the wasp can lay an egg or eggs in the larva's body.

# SOCIAL INSECTS
## COLONIAL COMMUNICATION AND DEFENSE

The communal life-style of bees, ants and wasps is a fascinating aspect of nature. The congregation of thousands of insects with a limited number of behavioral responses has created advanced levels of social organization and behavior. Worker bees, for example, communicate information about food sources to their nest mates by performing elaborate dances. These show the distance and direction of the food source from the hive.

The congregation of insects into colonies occurs in response to the demands of the surrounding habitat and the need for defense. In the high temperatures and low rainfall of the African savannahs, for example, termites would only survive for a few minutes without the protection of their nests.

Colonial defense ensures the successful distribution of insect species and is a mark of highly evolved social behavior. In the bee genus Apis, worker bees secrete an alarm pheromone from glands at the base of their sting apparatus to warn other members of the community about attacks from their enemies.

### Nest-building

Ants, wasps and bees existed over 50 million years ago, but the evolution of nest-building behavior was a major evolutionary advance. Although the vast majority of bees still have a solitary life-style, they have inherited their nesting habit and certain physical structures, such as longer tongues that enable them to transport nectar and pollen from their sphecoid wasp ancestors. In some species of bees, such as the honeybee, nesting behavior has led to the development of societies where individuals cooperate in the gathering of food, care of offspring and defense.

### Stages of behavior

There are six stages of social behavior between solitary and social insects. Insects belonging to the first stage possess no social characteristics and are called solitary species. The second stage consists of subsocial insects, such as the primitive wasp family Ampulicidae. Adults prepare a simple

space in which they store food for their larvae and show rudimentary parental care for their eggs, larvae or pupae.

In the third stage of social behavior, groups of females act communally. Females of the Central American wasp Trigonopsis cameronni, *for example, cooperate in constructing a nest, but each stocks its own cell with food and they do not cooperate in taking care of the young. A more complex form of social behavior occurs in the fourth stage of social behavior. Females collect in group nests and share the task of rearing the young. Up to 11 females of the wasp* Microstigmus comes *share a single nest and provide their young with springtails on which to feed.*

Semisocial insects share the same characteristics as the fourth stage of social behavior, but also divide the individuals within the community into castes according to their reproductive role. Each caste performs specific tasks —for example, the sterile caste takes care of the offspring produced by the fertile caste. The highest level of sociability is achieved by the eusocial insects—these include the insect societies of bees, wasps, ants and termites. Several generations of insects live together, and the first generation of offspring assist in running the community.

**LEFT Worker bees feed their larvae and store their honey in the honeycomb that they construct within a hive or nest. When a worker first emerges, it cleans the nest and tends to the larvae. As it gains experience, it is promoted to other duties such as foraging for food for the other bees. ABOVE RIGHT Some "paper wasps" construct their nests from material that resembles paper, and they attach them to the undersides of rocks. RIGHT Ants of the species *Messor barbarus* transport larvae in their mandibles. Their society is similar to that of the bees, with the worker caste mainly responsible for running the colony—cleaning the nest, looking after the larvae and gathering food.**

ABOVE The larvae of small braconid wasps are much appreciated by horticulturalists because they prey on garden pests such as the larvae of cabbage white butterflies. BELOW The female velvet ant is a type of wasp that moves about with an ant-like gait. It has no wings and spends its life on the ground, often in leaf litter. It parasitizes the prepupa or pupal stages of insects, and most species attack wasps and bees. The male possesses wings and is larger than the female. It mates in flight, carrying the female.

The tiny species *Apanteles glomeratus* is a fierce enemy of butterflies, and justly famed for the positive contribution that it makes to agriculture by attacking and destroying the larvae of the cabbage white butterfly, *Pieris brassicae*. A fertilized female *A. glomeratus* will attack the larvae on sight, piercing their flesh with her ovipositor and filling them with eggs. After a while, the eggs hatch into tiny larvae that feed on the internal tissues of the caterpillar, without damaging any of its internal organs.

As yet unharmed, the cabbage white caterpillar continues to grow, and in some cases it even manages to reach the chrysalis stage. The parasitic larvae also continue to grow and develop. Once they reach maturity, they almost completely devour the inside of the caterpillar. They then pierce the covering of the host so that they can emerge and pupate. Once transformed into adults, they break open the walls of the cocoon in which they have metamorphosed and fly away.

## Nocturnal Proctotrupoidea

The Proctotrupoidea, or proctotrypid wasps, comprise another superfamily in the suborder Apocrita. They, too, are parasites, preying on many types of insect. The adults are all short-lived, predominantly nocturnal creatures, and some are useful in the control of plant pests. The species *Inostemma pyricola*, for example, is a small, shiny, black hymenopteran that plays an important role in the fight against gall midges—insect pests that seriously damage pear trees.

As soon as *Inostemma pyricola* has mated, the female flies away in search of her favorite victim—a gall midge. She finds its eggs in pear trees, so she settles on a pear blossom and digs her ovipositor into the tiny, developing fruit. Simultaneously, she penetrates the egg of the gall midge. She lays four or five eggs inside it, and then withdraws her ovipositor and flies away.

The *I. pyricola* eggs hatch out into minute larvae that remain inside the host egg but do not prevent it from developing. Consequently, when the gall midge larva hatches, the larvae of the parasite remain inside it. At first, they are located within the gall midge's nervous system, where they feed on nutrients absorbed by its system. Later on, they spread out and occupy its entire body. Only one *I. pyricola* larva survives to reach maturity. In the meantime, the gall midge larva continues to grow. The larvae that do not contain the parasite eventually descend to the ground to pupate.

Those that contain a surviving parasite are killed, and the parasite transforms itself into a pupa inside the remains of its host. It emerges as an adult and then repeats the cycle.

## Bethyloidea

The superfamily Bethyloidea contains at least 3500 species of predatory insects in nine families. Among them, the family chrysidid, commonly known as ruby-tailed wasps, contains some of the most attractive of the hymenopterans. They are characterized by beautiful fluctuating, metallic colors. One species in the family chrysidid is *Chrysis ignita*, a parasite that lives on various types of sand-dwelling hymenopterans. Found in many parts of Europe, the creature is a brilliant shade of metallic green and has a contrasting purplish red abdomen that gives the species its name.

The female of the species will watch a group of wasps carefully as they build their nest in the sand. When they have finished, she waits until one of them leaves the nest for a moment and then goes inside and lays an egg beside that of the host. Sometimes the host returns before she has finished. If that happens, she rolls herself up into a ball so that only the hard exoskeleton armor on her back is exposed, and lies motionless. Protected in this way, she can fend off the host. As soon as it gives up and goes away, the ruby-tailed wasp unfolds its wings and flies away to safety, leaving its offspring behind. Soon afterward, the host wasp places a paralyzed larva inside the nest to serve as food for its own young. The ruby-tailed wasp larva waits while its nest companion takes nourishment and grows; then it attacks and kills it. Having acquired sufficient food to grow and develop into an adult, it leaves the nest and —like the other parasitic wasps—repeats the cycle.

## Vespoidea

The superfamily Vespoidea contains 40,000-50,000 species of wasps in 12 families. They are characteristically yellow and black in color and include the potter or mason wasps, paper wasps, hornets and common wasps.

## Potter or mason wasps

Members of the family Eumenidae, commonly known as potter or mason wasps, lead solitary lives. They are excellent fliers and are only active during the day when they feed on sweet substances that they

**ABOVE** Unique among the hymenopterans, the ruby-tailed wasp has a fluctuating metallic sheen that resembles a coat of mail. Depending on the species, it is a brilliant blue-green, green or copper color. It flies close to sheltered walls and fences, searching for the nests of bees and other wasps that it parasitizes. The female lays her eggs side by side with those of her host, and her larvae feed upon the host larvae before they pupate and become adults.

gather from flowers. A common species of potter wasp, *Eumenes arbustorum*, appears in spring when it moves about from one flower to another in search of food. Using a mixture of dust, mud and pebbles bound together by saliva to form a kind of cement, the female potter wasp builds a vase-shaped nest, usually on the underside of a leaf, consisting of layers of individual cells. When she has completed the nest, she flies off in search of moth, butterfly or beetle grubs. She paralyzes the prey with her sting and carries them back to the nest, placing them inside each cell and laying an egg on top of them. Then, using the same cement-like mixture as before, she blocks up the entrance to the nest. As soon as the larvae hatch, they begin to feed on the live tissue of the victims and continue to do so until they reach maturity, when they transform into pupae and become adults.

The female potter wasp of the species *Eumenes coarctatus* uses similar materials to build her nest, but the pebbles vary in shape. The nest itself resembles a jar with a small rimmed opening at the top.

The female potter wasp of the species *Odynerus murarius* builds her nest in clay; she digs a small, round hole and surrounds it with clay walls that meet at the top and form a narrow, downward-pointing entrance. She then makes a number of small cavities in the bottom of the nest, packs them with paralyzed grubs and lays her eggs on top. Finally, she seals the entrance of the nest carefully and flies away. The potter wasp larvae grow and develop, feeding on the tissues of the paralyzed grubs. Once they have matured into adults, they leave the nest and fly away.

## Semisocial wasps

Members of the subfamily *Polistinae*, or paper wasps, belong to the family Vespidae and spend part of each year living in colonies. In winter the colonies break up, and the fertilized females lie dormant until the spring. The most common species, *Polistes gallicus*, is a slender, black wasp that has yellow stripes across its abdomen, and is harmless to man. After her winter rest, a fertilized female, or queen, begins to build her nest. It comprises wood fibers and saliva that she mixes to form a paste similar to cardboard. The queen polistine wasp takes this substance to a jutting rock, a branch of a tree or the roof of a building, and builds a stalk from which she hangs a small hexagonal, downward-facing cell. She adds more cells until the nest resembles an upside-down cup. She begins to lay her eggs before the nest is complete, depositing a single egg in each cell and fertilizing them using stored sperm. She attaches a small amount of honey to the cell as a safeguard against unfavorable conditions, when there may not be enough food for the larvae.

The polistine wasp larvae, positioned head downward in their cells, are unable to obtain food for themselves. The queen feeds them on a paste consisting of chewed-up caterpillars and other insects mixed with saliva. As a result of such care, the larvae grow quickly and soon become pupae. At this point, the queen seals the cells tightly with a papery substance. After a few days, the pupae undergo their final molt and the newly formed adults emerge. All emerge as sterile females, and take on the role of workers within the community. Straightaway they begin their life's work of raising new generations, building new cells and looking after the nest. The queen polistine wasp continues to reproduce.

The polistine wasp colonies are complex in both structure and in behavior. For example, if the temperature rises too high inside the nest, all the workers gather at the entrance and beat their wings rapidly, creating a draft that cools the nest down. If the heat is excessive, the wasps even fetch water and sprinkle it over the outer walls of the cells to cool the larvae down. Life in the community continues in this way until later in the season, when the temperature starts to fall. The queen then lays unfertilized eggs that hatch into sterile males, and she raises fertile females—that are to become the new queens—by feeding the larvae on a rich diet.

## The death of a colony

As the weather turns colder, the larvae die, probably because of a failing food supply. But before they do, the males and females set out on their mating flight. The males die shortly afterward and the females disperse and go in search of a suitable place to hibernate. The old queen and most of the workers cannot survive in temperate regions, and the colony slowly dies. In spring, when the young females re-emerge, new colonies flourish elsewhere. In tropical and subtropical regions, the workers hibernate through brief periods of bad weather and become active again when the weather improves.

Polistine colonies may be founded by either one female (haplometrosis) or several females (pleometrosis). Although female polistine wasps are similar in appearance and structure, one always emerges as the leader. Being the sole or major egg-layer, she rarely leaves the nest. The sexual organs of the other females degenerate, and the wasps function as workers. In some species of polistine wasp, the female that eats the greatest number of eggs laid by her nest mates eventually assumes dominance, and in other species the most aggressive female becomes the queen of the colony.

## Vespinae wasps

Members of the subfamily Vespinae—another group belonging to the family Vespidae—behave in much the same way as the polistine wasps, except that their colonies are always established by a single queen. She behaves as a solitary and then as a semisocial

## INSECTS CLASSIFICATION: 17

### Wasps, bees and ants (2)

The second division of the hymenopteran suborder Apocrita is the Aculeata, which contains an estimated 70,000-85,000 species of true or aculeate wasps, bees and ants in 41 families. The superfamily Bethyloidea includes the family Chrysididae (ruby-tailed wasps) that contains the parasitic *Chrysis ignita* of Europe. The superfamily Vespoidea contains 40,000-50,000 species in 12 families. They include the Eumenidae (mason or potter wasps, such as *Eumenes arbustorum* and *Odynerus murarius*); the Vespidae (hunting wasps and paper-making wasps) containing the subfamily Polistinae with its commonest species, *Polistes gallicus*, and the subfamily Vespinae containing the hornet, *Vespa crabro*, and the common wasp, *Vespula vulgaris*; the Mutillidae (velvet ants) containing some 4000 species, including the *Mutilla europaea* and *M. barbara*; and the Scoliidae (hairy-flower wasps, such as *Scolia flavifrons*).

The largest family within the superfamily Vespoidea is the Formicidae (ants) with about 14,000 species, including the leafcutter ants, *Atta sexdens*, and *A. cephalotta*; the weaver ant, *Oecophylla smaragdina*; the carpenter ant, *Camponotus herculaneus*; the tree-dwelling ant, *Crematogaster scutellaris*; the common wood ant, *Formica rufa*; army (or legionary) ants of the genus *Eciton* of South America and driver ants (genus *Anomma*) of Africa; and Amazon or slave-maker ants of the genus *Polyergus*.

TOP RIGHT *Scolia flavifrons*, a member of the hairy-flower wasp family, parasitizes the scarab beetle but is harmless to humans. It is one of the largest of the European hymenopterans, with the females measuring up to 1.6 in. long.

ABOVE RIGHT *Ammophila sabulosa*, a species of thread-waisted wasp, is also called a sand wasp because it often nests in sandy places. It is a small wasp found in many parts of Europe, and it feeds its larvae on nonhairy caterpillars.

RIGHT A female sand wasp captures a caterpillar and carries it off to its underground nest. It then lays an egg on top of the caterpillar. When the sand wasp larva emerges, it eats the caterpillar that awaits it. The adult female blocks the entrance to the nest with a pile of stones to protect the developing larva from intrusion by predators.

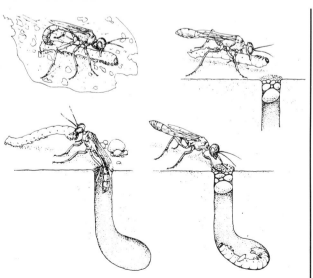

**ABOVE** *Philanthus triangulum* is a "pirate" species of wasp that waylays honeybees in flight and forces them to regurgitate their nectar for its own use. A pest to beekeepers, the wasp kills the honeybees and then feeds them to its larvae.

**BELOW** The female *Bembix variabilis* builds a nest in the sand. She covers the entrance (A) and then drags her abdomen across the surface to make a series of furrows (B). Finally, she digs a small false entrance to the nest to deceive predators (C).

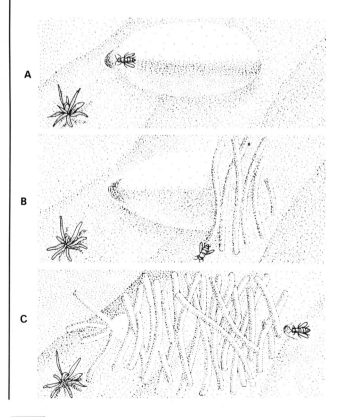

A

B

C

wasp until the first generation of workers appears. Vespine wasps build nests out of papery substances that are either suspended under branches or made in cavities in the ground. Their colonies are set up on an annual basis, appearing in the spring and declining as the weather starts to turn colder. Although vespine wasps are often a nuisance and are frequently pests of beehives, they are also beneficial insects as they kill a wide range of pest species for their larval food.

## Hornets

The European hornet, *Vespa crabro*, is a large, squat-bodied, social wasp that lives in Europe and occasionally in well-wooded districts of southern Britain. In North America a large native wasp, the white-faced hornet, and the introduced European species, both occur. The word "hornet" appears to have lost a precise meaning and is generally applied to any large, social wasp. However, the European hornet can be distinguished from a common wasp by its larger size and distinct coloring. Worker hornets are larger than queen wasps, and female hornets may be as long as 1.4 in. A hornet has a red head and black thorax. Part of its abdomen is red, and the rest is yellow with reddish spots. A hornet's sting can be dangerous to man, although it is a less aggressive insect than the common wasp and does not sting unless it feels in considerable danger.

## A paper nest

Hornets build "papery" nests from wood chewed to a paste. They usually site them in a hollow tree or occasionally in an unfrequented building. Wasps use hard, sound wood to make their paper, but hornets are less particular and content themselves with soft, decayed wood, sometimes mixing it with sand or soil. The resulting yellowish paper has a coarse texture. The nest hangs upside-down and comprises layers of hexagonal cells that open downward. Each layer hangs from the one above, supported on tiny columns. The top layer hangs from the tree by means of a stalk that varies in length. The cells in a hornet's nest are

**RIGHT** Common wasp workers feed on nectar and the juices of fruit, but are quickly attracted by other sources of sweet food such as the contents of this discarded honey jar. They feed the queen wasp and larvae on the juices of insects, such as bluebottle flies, that they have killed.

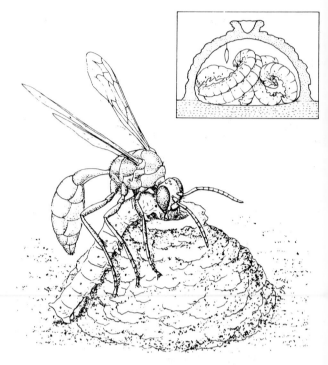

**ABOVE The female *Eumenes arbustrorum*, a solitary wasp, builds a nest the size of a hazelnut from pebbles and dust, binding them together with her saliva to form a clay-like mixture. She feeds her larvae on beetle and butterfly grubs.**

**ABOVE RIGHT A female potter or mason wasp brings a paralyzed caterpillar to her nest to feed to her offspring. The cross-section (top) shows the wasp egg hanging from a thread of silk, and the supply of food ready for when it hatches out.**

larger but less numerous than those in a wasp's nest, and the total population of a hornet colony is smaller.

The life history of a hornet is similar to that of a common wasp. The nest is initially built by a young fertilized female, just after the first warm rays of sunshine arouse her from her winter sleep. She lays eggs inside a few of the cells and attaches them with a sticky substance so that they cannot fall out.

The hornet larvae hatch head downward, and the queen feeds them. The larvae are carnivorous, so the queen has to hunt for prey. She grabs any insect that comes her way, then breaks it up and works it into a shapeless pap suitable for her offspring.

## Sterile workers

The close attention that the queen hornet pays to her larvae ensures that they develop quickly, grow to full size and pupate. She seals the entrances to the relevant cells tightly, so that the final metamorphosis can take place. Soon the pupae become adults and emerge from the cells. All individuals of this first generation are sterile females and become workers within the community. The queen abandons all previous activities and dedicates herself to laying eggs. The young workers assume responsibility for the upkeep of the nest, obtaining food and looking after the larvae.

The number of workers increases so rapidly that, within a short time, there is not enough space for larvae and food supplies. The workers enlarge the nest by building new layers of cells. Toward the end of the summer, when the weather cools down, the queen starts to lay eggs that will develop into males and fertile females. Mating takes place, ensuring the continuation of the species but not of the community. The males die soon after they have mated, while the fertilized females disperse and find a place to hibernate. The nest gradually empties as the workers die. But in spring, those females that have survived the winter will give rise to new colonies and new individuals.

## The common wasp

The common wasp, *Vespula vulgaris*, can be distinguished from the hornet by its smaller size and

bright yellow and black color. It normally builds a nest underground, although it sometimes builds it in a tree. Resembling a hornet's nest, it consists of layers of cells joined together by supporting columns. The colony is organized along the same lines as that of a hornet; it consists of a fertile female or queen, a large number of sterile females that act as workers and a few males that appear at a certain stage in the season, purely for reproductive purposes.

## Velvet ants

The family Mutillidae in the suborder Apocrita contains about 4000 species of insects known as velvet ants. Despite their name, velvet ants are solitary wasps. They derive their name from their appearance: they have short, velvet-like bristles all over their bodies and antennae, often patterned in black, bright orange and scarlet; and the females lack wings and remain on the ground, where they run around, resembling ants. Male velvet ants are larger than the females and possess wings, enabling them to fly from tree to tree in search of food.

In temperate regions, velvet ants appear to mate in spring. A male seizes a female by her thorax and gripping her firmly with his strong forelegs, he flies off. Mating takes place in the air during this brief flight. After mating, the male lets go of the female and she falls to the ground. She runs about until she finds an established wasps' or bees' nest in which to lay her eggs.

The species *Mutilla europaea*, common in Europe and Britain, is about 0.6 in. in length and is an enemy of bumblebees. The mating season occurs in autumn. After mating, the fertilized female immediately digs herself a small hole in which she remains dormant throughout the winter. The male dies as soon as the weather starts to turn cold.

In the spring the female velvet ant wakes up and wanders about among the newly budding plants in search of a bumblebees' nest. Having found one, she digs a small tunnel, enabling her to reach the bumblebee's larvae. She paralyzes the larvae with her sting and lays her own eggs beside them. After a few days, the velvet ant larvae hatch and begin to feed on the bumblebee larvae. Once they are fully grown, the parasitic larvae build themselves small cocoons where they turn into pupae. They emerge as adult wasps at the height of summer.

ABOVE First-generation sterile female worker wasps of the species *Polistes gallicus* build the colony's nest and care for its larvae. The insects chew up pieces of dried vegetable matter in order to make the walls of the nest.

BELOW A common wasp gnaws small pieces of bark into a paste to make the walls of its nest (A). It builds the structure in horizontal layers, and surrounds them with an outer covering, shown by the lengthwise cross-section (B).

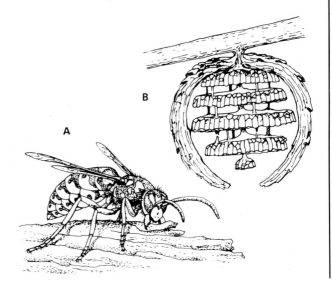

**ABOVE A small wasp of the species *Paravespula germanica* eats the flesh of berries and other fruit as well as preying on flies and butterflies. A little over 0.4 in. in length, it is found in all parts of the Northern Hemisphere. It makes a nest underground, often taking over abandoned mammals' dens. The nest may be as large as 12 in. in diameter, and at the onset of autumn it can contain up to 3000 wasps.**

## Hairy-flower wasps

The family Scoliidae contains the hairy-flower wasps. They are solitary wasps that are parasitic on beetle larvae. Scollid wasps, commonly referred to as just wasps, are distributed predominantly in tropical climates.

The species *Scolia flavifrons* is one of the largest European hymenopterans. It is black in color, with yellow spots on its head and abdomen. Mating takes place in June or July, and the fertilized female hairy-flower wasp immediately goes in search of a host on which to lay her eggs. Her favorite prey is the rhinoceros beetle, *Oryctes nasicornis*, which dwells hidden away in an underground nest. As soon as she locates a rhinoceros beetle nest, she settles on the ground directly above the nest and digs a tunnel. Once she has penetrated the beetle's hiding place, she paralyzes its larva by injecting a quantity of poison from her sting. After this, she lays a small egg on top of the beetle larva and then goes aboveground again in search of other victims.

After a short while, the hairy-flower wasp larva emerges from its egg and begins to feed on the tissues of the host. When fully grown, it weaves a small, silky cocoon outside the body of the beetle larva and transforms itself first into a pupa, then into an adult.

## Sphecoidea

The superfamily Sphecoidea contains about 29,600 species in 20 families and includes the thread-waisted wasps, the sand wasps, the bee-killing wasps and the spider-hunting wasps.

## Thread-waisted wasps

Members of the family Sphecidae, or the thread-waisted wasps, are extremely varied in their behavior patterns. They are predators and hunt arthropods of all kinds including spiders and insects. The males exist solely for reproductive purposes and disappear soon after mating. The fertilized females go on to build nests and lay their eggs. Before sealing the nest and leaving it, each female places some paralyzed insect or spider larvae inside, so that her offspring will have a supply of food.

A species of thread-waisted wasp, *Ammophila sabulosa*, is black in color with blue and red patterns on its abdomen. It is most active in the period from June to September, when it flies around, usually in sandy areas, looking for plants on which to feed. Mating also takes place at this time. The fertilized female builds a nest in the sand which usually consists of an oval, central chamber called the "incubation chamber" and a tunnel leading to the outside.

When she has completed the building work, the female thread-waisted wasp temporarily covers the entrance of her tunnel with a small stone and flies off in search of some suitable larvae, usually those of grasshoppers or butterflies, on which to feed her eggs. She paralyzes the grasshopper larvae with poison from her sting and carries them off to her nest, placing them inside the incubation chamber. She then lays an egg on top of the paralyzed larvae and leaves the nest, closing the entrance with great care, often disguising it with sand. When she has camouflaged the entrance to the tunnel, she goes away and repeats the operation. The egg hatches into a tiny, voracious larva, which immediately starts to eat the tissues of the victim.

It soon grows, transforms itself into an adult and leaves the nest.

## Feeding on grasshoppers or crickets

Another species of thread-waisted wasp, *Sphex rufocinctus*, tends to hunt grasshopper and cricket larvae. After fertilization, the female captures a suitable victim, paralyzes it and carries it off to a suitable spot where she builds a nest. The nest consists of an oblique tunnel leading into a central incubation chamber. She places her prey in the middle of the incubation chamber and then flies off to catch more victims. Once she has collected enough grasshopper and cricket larvae, she arranges them all on the floor of the nest and lays a small egg on the thorax of each one. Having laid all her eggs, she leaves the nest and seals the entrance, concealing it with earth. When the eggs hatch, the larvae feed on the tissues of the paralyzed larvae until they are fully grown. Then, around September, they weave small cocoons and enter into a state of dormancy until the following summer when they emerge as adults.

## Sand wasps

*Bembex rostrata*, a member of the family Nyssonidae, or sand wasps, preys mainly on flies. It builds two

**ABOVE The common wasp bears its sting, or aculeus, at or near the tip of its abdomen, in an organ that has evolved from the ovipositor. Although the sting of a common wasp can be painful, it is rarely dangerous. It is more likely to be troublesome to children and invalids, or if it affects delicate or perforated sections of blood capillaries. A few people are hypersensitive to wasp stings and may suffer shock.**

kinds of nest. First, it builds a "dormitory," where both males and females go to sleep; then it builds the nest that serves as an incubation chamber. The dormitory is simply an oblique tunnel dug in loose earth or sand that usually contains a small mound of earth at the entrance. Some species of sand wasps make short, blind passages at the bottom, which serve to mislead their predators. The incubatory nest usually consists of a large central chamber linked to the outside by a winding tunnel. The female wasp paralyzes suitable victims with her poison and carries them down into the central chamber where she lays her eggs on top of them. She then leaves the nest, closes the entrance and disguises it in various ways. She does not abandon her offspring but watches over the nest, day by day, until the eggs hatch. From then on, she keeps her young constantly supplied with fresh larvae.

A scoliid wasp (*Scolia procer*)

A bumblebee (*Bombus terrestris*)

A velvet ant (*Mutilla europaea*)

A ruby-tailed wasp
(*Euchroreus purpuratus*)
♂

A hornet (*Vespa crabro*)

A ruby-tailed wasp
(*Stilbum cyanurum*)

A tarantula-hawk wasp
(*Pepsis sp.*)

♀

A potter wasp
(*Eumenes coarcta*

A thread-waisted wasp (*Ammophila sabulosa*)

An ant (*Dinoponera gigantea*)

### Bee-killer wasps

The bee killer, *Philanthus triangulum*, a member of the Philanthidae family, poses a serious threat to beehives. Active only at the height of summer, it usually lives in close proximity to a hive. When in need of food, the bee killer wasp waylays worker bees as they fly along loaded with sweet nectar, which it forces them to regurgitate. When a fertilized female bee killer captures a worker bee, she paralyzes it and drags it down into her underground nest.

The bee-killer wasp builds a nest consisting of a long, oblique tunnel with a number of branches leading from the bottom end. Each of these secondary tunnels leads into an oval incubation chamber, and it is here that she places the paralyzed bees.

The female bee-killer wasp feeds her young with a different amount of food according to their sex. She places five bees in the incubation cell of each female, but only three in the cell of each male. She lays an egg in each cell, attaches it to a bee and then leaves the nest, sealing the entrance with care. The larvae hatch inside their individual cells and feed on the tissue of the worker bees. When fully grown, they each spin a small cocoon and undergo the metamorphosis into pupae and then into adults. The adults leave the nest, and the destruction of beehives continues.

### Favorite food

By contrast, *Larra anathema*, a species belonging to the family Larridae, is useful to agriculture, its favorite prey being the mole cricket. When a female of this species has been fertilized, she goes in search of a mole cricket's nest. Having found one, she reaches the prey inside by using the existing entrance or by digging a tunnel. Although the victim is considerably larger than she is, she manages to paralyze it by injecting poison from her sting. She then rolls it over on its back and lays an egg on its thorax. When the egg hatches, the larva feeds on the tissue of the live mole cricket, grows and transforms itself into a pupa, then into an adult.

Another species, *Tripoxylon figulus*, belongs to the Sphecoidea superfamily. Members of this species have a peculiar characteristic: they build their nests in tree trunks, inside the tunnels bored by wood-eating insects. They divide each tunnel into numerous cells by means of crosswise partitions, provide the cells with supplies of paralyzed prey and lay an egg inside each one. The

ABOVE **Members of the family Apidae have brushes on their legs enabling them to collect and transport pollen. In the most highly evolved species, such as the bumblebees, this apparatus takes the form of a basket called the corbiculum. Made of long interwoven bristles, it is situated on the tibia of the rear leg.**

wasp seals the mouth of the tunnel and flies off to repeat the process elsewhere. Meanwhile, the eggs hatch and the larvae feed upon the food that has been placed there. When fully grown, they pupate, mature into adults and fly away to begin their new lives.

### Spider-hunting wasps

Members of the family Pompilidae, or spider-hunting wasps, are large, active, long-legged creatures. The tarantula hawk-wasp of the southern United States and Central America measures up to 1.5 in. long and is possibly the largest hymenopteran in existence. Spider-hunting wasps occur all over the world, but are most common in tropical and subtropical areas. They feed only on spiders and will sometimes attack individuals much larger than themselves.

The species *Pompilus viaticus* of Italy is black and has red stripes on its abdomen. It is most active in March, when it flies above the fields and meadows in search of spiders. A spider-hunting wasp will fight with

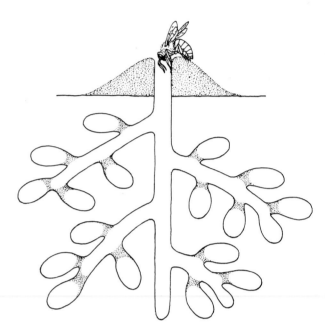

**ABOVE** The bee species *Dasypoda plumipes*, which belongs to the family Melittidae, makes its nest underground in spring. It digs a main tunnel plus a number of secondary ones, each ending in a small cell in which the female lays a single egg. The female has very large, hairy pollen baskets on her back legs that she uses to gather pollen. She then places the pollen in the cells where it provides food for the larvae.

**ABOVE RIGHT** A plan of the underground nest of the bee *Halictus malachurus*. Each tunnel ends in a cell where the female lays an egg. The larva will grow and develop, feeding on food provided by the female.

a spider, nearly always winning. It paralyzes its victim with an injection of poison from its long sting, then drags it down into a hole in the ground, lays an egg on top of it and leaves it there. The newly hatched larva immediately begins to eat the spider and has enough food to last until it reaches adulthood.

The species *Cryptocheiilus comparatus* feeds solely on tarantulas. Despite the fact that the prey is not only poisonous but also much larger than the female, she enters the tarantula's den paralyzing it with her sting. She then drags it along, sometimes for quite long distances, until she finds a suitable place to build a nest that consists of a tunnel dug in the ground. The wasp places the tarantula at the bottom of the tunnel and lays an egg on top of the spider so that the larva will have an abundant supply of food.

## Bees

Bees are hunting wasps of the superfamily Sphecoidea that have become vegetarians through the process of evolution. The change in diet probably occurred 135-65 million years ago, soon after the appearance of the first flowering plants. With their intricate colonies and ability to perform complex physical tasks, bees are the most highly developed of all hymenopterans. Their wings are well developed, their abdomens large and their bodies robust and often thickly covered with hairs. Females are equipped with stings. To aid pollen collection, all bees have small brushes on their legs, while some species carry additional brushes on their abdomens. In social bees, pollen brushes take the form of long, curved bristles arranged into a basket shape. Bees inhabit many parts of the world, although most species prefer warmer, drier areas.

Bees fall into either solitary or social categories, depending on their life-style—the majority are solitary species. Regardless of life-style, however, all bees share certain characteristics: they are strong, fast fliers that build complex nests. By day, they enter flowers to collect their food, which consists of pollen and nectar. Pollen supplies the bees with protein and vitamins, while they obtain essential sugars by transforming nectar into honey in their special "honey pouches."

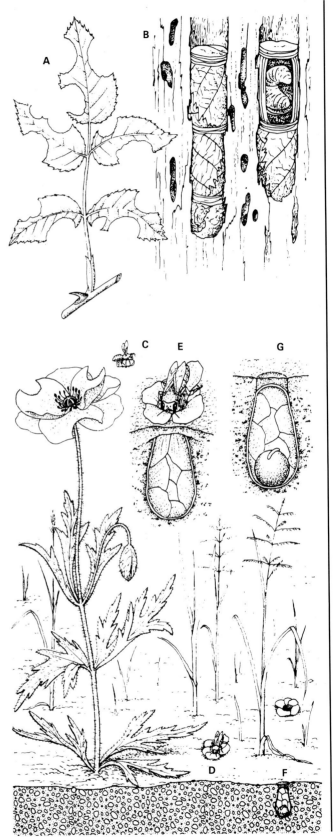

RIGHT **Leaf-cutting bees often build their nests in hollow trees. Females cut oval pieces from the leaves of rose bushes (A) and use them to line the cells of their nests (B). A female mason bee removes a piece of petal from a poppy (C) and takes it away to line its nest (D and inset E). After she has laid her eggs on a small ball of pollen and nectar, she covers the cell entrance with more poppy leaves (F and inset G).**

## Primitive species

The most primitive species of bee belong to the family Colletidae. Primitive bees are smaller than the more advanced species, and their coloring is often yellowish or brownish with dark stripes on the abdomen. Members of some genera, including *Hyaleus* and *Prosopis*, have no pollen-gathering apparatus at all, while members of the more advanced genus *Colletes* have pollen bristles on their legs.

Bees of the species *C. canicularis* (widespread in central Europe) appear at the beginning of spring, and hover above flowery meadows in search of nectar. Each fertilized female digs into the ground, building a nest that consists of a tunnel with a small vertical well at its bottom. When a female bee completes her nest, she fills the nest well with pollen and nectar, lays a single egg on top, and fills the well with earth. Since primitive female bees carry several eggs, they repeat the nest-digging and egg-laying process until they dispose of all their eggs; once they have achieved this, they die.

The family Melittidae contains a few species found only in parts of Europe and northern America. One of the best-known species is *Dasypoda plumipes*, an inhabitant of many parts of Europe. In spring, females build nests that consist of oblique central tunnels and a number of secondary tunnels with cells at the end. Like *C. canicularis*, the females lay single eggs inside each cell and gather supplies of nectar and pollen to feed the future larvae.

## The family Andrenidae

The bee family Andrenidae shows a higher level of evolution than the family Colletidae. All Andrenidae species—such as *Andrena cineraria* of central Europe—have pollen-gathering apparatus.

Female bees of the species *A. cineraria* build nests consisting of oblique tunnels that end in several small cells. If viewed from the side, the constructions

### Wasps, bees and ants (3)

The hymenopteran suborder Apocrita contains another major superfamily, the Sphecoidea. It contains about 29,600 species in 20 families—nine of hunting wasps and 11 of bees. The wasp families include the Sphecidae (thread-waisted wasps) containing the species *Ammophila sabulosa* and *Sphex rufocinctus*; the Nyssonidae (sand wasps), which includes the fly-hunting species *Bembix rostrata*; the Philanthidae (bee killers, such as *Philanthus triangulum*); and the Pompilidae (spider-hunting wasps) containing the common species *Pompilus viaticus* and the tarantula-eating *Cryptocheiilus comparatus*.

The 11 families of bees contain about 22,000 species. They include the *Colletes canicularis* of central Europe; the 0.08-in.-long *Halictus malachurus*; mason bees of the genera *Osmia* and *Chalicodoma* (such as *Chalicodoma muraria* of central and southern Europe); the leaf-cutting bee, *Megachile centuncularis*; and the solitary species *Xylocopa violacea* that grows up to 1.2 in. long. The family Apidae contains the best-known bees: the genus *Bombus* (bumblebees) containing such species as *B. terrestris* and *B. pratorum*; the "domestic" honeybee, *Apis mellifera*; the Indian bee, *Apis cerana*; the dwarf bee, *Apis florea*; and the South American stingless bees of the subfamily Meliponinae.

**ABOVE** Carpenter bees of the family Megachilidae build their nests in existing cavities, often in dead wood, rather than digging them in the soil. Instead of using glandular secretions to construct their nests, Megachilids collect various materials such as mud, leaves and animal hairs.

resemble bunches of grapes. Inside each cell, a fertilized female places a quantity of honey, upon which she lays an egg. When the female has disposed of all her eggs, she covers the nest entrance carefully to conceal it from possible predators and flies away. Upon hatching, the bee larvae feed on the honey stores. They leave their nests when they reach maturity.

### Parasitic bees

Several bee species of the genus *Nomada*, within the family Anthophoridae, are parasitic in the manner of cuckoos. *Nomada* bees enter the nests of other species while the occupants are out gathering honey and lay their eggs there. When a foreign larva hatches, it first attacks the legitimate occupant of the nest, then eats all the food supplies. It soon reaches maturity and becomes an adult ready to repeat the life cycle and violate a new nest.

### The smallest bees

The smallest known bees belong to the family Halictidae—some species are barely 0.08 in. in length. Halictidae bees build nests consisting of vertical tunnels that branch off into several egg cells. After filling a nest with pollen and nectar—a food supply for larvae—a fertilized female lays an egg in each cell and seals the entrance. In some species, the first larvae hatch out while the mother is digging cells in which to lay her last eggs. In such an instance, the offspring help their mother to gather food supplies or dig new cells.

Bees of the species *Halictus malachurus* practice a high degree of social behavior. The first generation of eggs laid by fertile females hatch into sterile females that take on the work of gathering food and enlarging the nest. From her second fertilization onward, the mother dedicates herself entirely to the task of laying

eggs. As winter draws near, her eggs produce a new generation of egg-laying females, which in turn produce males and fertile females. After mating has taken place between bees of the fertile generation, the colony begins to decline and its members die off in ever-increasing numbers. Only the fertilized females survive, reappearing in spring to produce new colonies.

## Leaf-cutting bees

Leaf-cutting bees, *Megachile centuncularis*, build their nests in hollow trees or in tunnels dug out of tree trunks by wood-eating insects. After mating, a female leaf-cutting bee flies off in search of a suitable nest site. Having found one, she flies to a rose bush and cuts oval pieces out of the leaves with her mandibles. The bee lines the walls of her nest with leaf pieces, at the same time building several egg cells. Before laying an egg in each cell, she fills them with pollen and nectar. The larvae grow peacefully inside their cells until they reach pupation age.

## Mason bees

Mason bees belong to the large family Megachilidae, which contains the most highly evolved species of solitary bees. The family Megachilidae contains two genera of mason bees, *Osmia* and *Chalicodoma*.

Members of the species *Chalicodoma muraria* inhabit many parts of central and southern Europe, where they build small, thimble-like nests by taking grains of sand and earth and mixing them with saliva. Each nest contains numerous small, elongated cells filled with honey and pollen. When a female bee has gathered sufficient food for her future larvae, she lays a tiny egg in each cell and seals the entrance. The larvae hatch out and spend the winter inside their cells. After undergoing metamorphosis, they emerge in spring as adults.

Females of one mason bee species build several bottle-shaped cells in sandy soil and line the walls with poppy petals. After laying eggs, they cover the cell entrances with more poppy petals. Before leaving their nests, the females conceal them carefully with coverings of sand.

The chosen nesting place of the species *Osmia bicolor* is the inside of an empty snail shell. An *O. bicolor* bee divides a shell into numerous cells and deposits an egg in each one, together with a supply of food for future larvae. In order to conceal the nest from potential

ABOVE A worker bumblebee collects pollen and nectar to take back to its nest where it will feed the developing larvae. Bumblebees have long tongues that enable them to reach the nectar from flowers too deep for honeybees.

BELOW Bumblebees live in small communities, in nests that are usually built underground. Their colonies last for only one year. The nest is composed of cells for storing honey (A), clusters of pupae (B) and clusters of eggs (C).

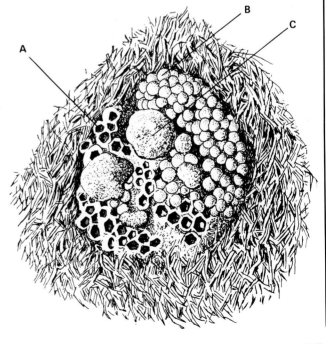

**ABOVE A worker honeybee gathers nectar and pollen from flowers. On returning to the hive, these foraging worker bees perform dances that indicate the location of their food supplies.**

**ABOVE RIGHT *Eucera longicornis*, a solitary bee, collects food so that it can provide each cell in its nest with a supply of pollen and nectar. It then lays its eggs in the cells and seals them.**

predators, the bee then covers the shell with a tent-like structure made out of pine needles, moss and blades of grass. A different mason bee species builds its nests inside small holes in tree trunks, dividing the holes into individual cells by making clay partitions.

## The family Apidae

The family Apidae contains the most highly developed species of Hymenoptera with the most complex behavioral patterns. Well-known Apidae species include the bumblebees and honeybees—social insects with the best organized communities in the insect world.

## Solitary Apidae

Apart from the well-known social bees, the family Apidae contains several relatively unknown solitary species, such as *Xylocopa violacea*, which is widespread throughout central and southern Europe. Its members are large individuals, some of which grow as long as 1.2 in. *X. violacea* bees usually appear in early spring when females fertilized the previous autumn emerge from hibernation. Upon emergence, the female bees immediately begin to build nests by digging tunnels inside rotting wood such as old tree trunks. The tunnels usually turn two 90-degree angles and reopen below the original entrance hole into the

outside air. Each bee fetches pollen and nectar to store inside its tunnel before laying an egg. It seals the entrance with a diaphragm-like structure and repeats the whole process several times until it has made seven or eight cells inside which the larvae can grow and develop undisturbed.

Another solitary member of the family Apidae is *Eucera longicornis*, which builds nests by digging tunnels in the ground. A typical *E. longicornis* nest consists of an oblique tunnel with many cells leading off its sides. The female bees provide each cell with a small heap of honey and pollen before laying one egg per cell. The bees work from one cell to the next, sealing the entrances as they go along.

## Bumblebees

Bumblebees (genus *Bombus*) are the most familiar social bees in the temperate countries—including Britain. The genus contains over 200 species only a few of which are tropical inhabitants. Bumblebees are squat, furry, black and yellow insects, their body bulk and fur allowing them to penetrate even the Arctic regions. They are important pollinators, since they have long tongues that can extract nectar from flowers too deep for honeybees.

Bumblebees usually build their colony nests in the ground—often in deserted mouse nests—although locations vary greatly between species. Bees of the species *Bombus terrestris*, for example, live in underground cavities, while the favorite environment of *B. pratorum* is moss and brushwood. *B. lapidarius* bees prefer preexisting holes under piles of stones, and colonies of *B. agrorum* can be found nesting on the ground in shallow cavities hidden by vegetation such as grass and moss.

## The laboring queen bee

Each bumblebee colony is founded in spring by a single queen—a female that was fertilized the previous autumn and spent the winter in hibernation. An emerging queen bee finds a natural cavity and brings moss, blades of grass, pieces of leaf and other material to line the walls. Upon completion of her building work, the queen bee blocks up the entrance, leaving only a tiny entrance hole. Next, she gathers pollen and nectar to form several small piles of food on the floor of her nest. She provides an additional food store for the developing young by constructing a wax "honey pot," which she fills with nectar. The queen lays eggs on top of each food pile, and covers everything over with a protective layer of wax secreted by special glands on her abdomen.

Once the queen bumblebee has protected her eggs with wax, the first phase of her work is complete. Since her efforts have brought her close to exhaustion, she rests while waiting for her eggs to hatch. After the larvae hatch, the queen devotes herself simultaneously to the tasks of gathering food, protecting and maintaining the nest and feeding her offspring. Since bumblebee larvae are incapable of obtaining food for themselves, their mother feeds them with a regurgitated substance similar to the royal jelly produced by honeybees.

Under their mother's care, the bumblebee larvae develop quickly, reaching adulthood after a short time. The first offspring are all sterile females that are slightly smaller than their mother. They immediately take on the role of workers within the developing community, attending to the tasks of gathering nectar and pollen, building new cells, enlarging the nest and feeding new generations of larvae as well as the queen herself. When the young worker bees take over responsibility for the colony, the queen devotes her energies to egg-laying.

## Industrious communities

As warm weather approaches, the first generation of bumblebee workers collects honey and pollen as new workers emerge from their cocoons. A colony grows rapidly, and by the end of summer it may consist of several hundred individuals. Bumblebees show the most primitive social organization of all social bees. Social castes are not clearly defined, since there is little physical difference between queens and workers. In many species, a queen asserts her dominance by aggression only.

With the coming of cold weather, fertile females and males hatch out in the nurseries of bumblebee nests. Once they reach adulthood, they mate, and from then on the colony falls into decline. In late autumn the queen bee, the sterile female workers and the males all die. Only the fertilized female bumblebees survive to leave the nest and fly off in search of a place to hibernate. Those that live through the winter emerge the following spring and form new colonies.

## Parasitic bumblebees

Although most bumblebees are hard-working social insects, a few species lead parasitic lives in the nests of other species. Queen parasitic bumblebees are unable to found their own colonies since they produce no worker caste. Instead, they lay their eggs in another species' colony, where unsuspecting host workers feed and protect the parasitic young.

## Bees without stings

The subfamily Meliponinae, of the family Apidae, contains stingless bees—most of which inhabit South America. Although the ancestors of the subfamily possessed effective stings, they lost the use of them through evolution. Meliponinae operate better developed communities than the bumblebees: their colonies survive for more than one year and strong physical distinctions exist between members of the different social castes. Meliponinae nests house large numbers of bees and usually consist of clusters of cells situated in holes in the ground or in trees.

A Meliponinae colony consists of a fertile female (the queen), many sterile females (the workers) and a few males that are driven out of the nest after they have fertilized the queen. When a colony becomes too large for its nest, the worker bees build several large cells known as royal cells. Since the larvae that hatch from eggs laid in royal cells feed solely on royal jelly, they develop into fertile queen bees. Each new queen helps to reduce the population by leading away a swarm of worker bees. A detached swarm flies to a suitable location and builds a new nest.

## Honeybees

Honeybees belong to the genus *Apis* of the family *Apidae*. The best-known species is *Apis mellifera—Apis*

ABOVE **Worker honeybees visit a great variety of plants when foraging for nectar and pollen to take back to the hive. Nectar is the bees' main source of carbohydrate and water,** **and pollen is their only source of protein. Honeybees eat the pollen and convert the nectar into honey on which they also feed. They store any excess honey in the hive.**

means "honey maker" while *mellifera* means "honey carrier." For centuries, honeybees have been prized by many nations for their honey and wax.

Social evolution has reached its highest peak in the genus *Apis*, since honeybees conduct the best organized communities in the insect world. In terms of behavior and structure, honeybees fall into three different social categories: fertile females (queens), sterile females (workers) and males (drones). A healthy honeybee colony contains one queen, about 200 drones and 40,000-80,000 workers.

### The queen bee

Queen honeybees have tapering bodies of about 0.8 in. in length. They live from three to six years, during which time each lays about 20 million eggs—an approximate average of 1,500 a day. Throughout her life, a queen stores sperm in her sperm receptacles, and it is highly likely that she controls the sperms' action, deciding whether or not to fertilize her eggs.

Since workers develop from fertilized eggs and drones from unfertilized ones, the queen can then decide the makeup of her colony's population. Her choice does not depend solely upon whim, however, but reflects the needs of the colony. Thus, males appear only in small numbers during mating periods, while workers are always produced in abundance. If the queen is killed or removed from her colony, the entire colony becomes disorientated and is unable to work properly.

The queen controls her subjects with a pheromone called queen substance, which is produced in glands near her mandibles and passed by mouth from worker to worker. Queen substance inhibits the development of the workers' ovaries—thereby making them sterile—as well as preventing them from building special queen cells for potential rivals. However, when she weakens with age or when the worker population is disproportionately large, the queen cannot provide enough queen substance to control her entire colony. Consequently, the first new queen to emerge expels the original queen and kills any subsequent new queens.

### Worker bees

Worker honeybees are smaller than their queen, and, unlike her, they have special wax-producing glands and a honey pouch, which transforms nectar and other sweet substances into honey. For collecting pollen and nectar, they have "pollen baskets"—hollows in the outer edges of their back legs that are partly covered by long bristles. Worker bees collect pollen and push it into their "baskets" with thick, brush-shaped tufts of bristles on their legs.

The life span of worker bees depends on the season in which they were born. During the busiest times of spring and summer, they live for four or five weeks only, but in winter, when they hibernate, their life span is considerably longer. Although worker bees are sterile, they hatch from fertilized eggs—like the queens. The differences between queens and workers begin to develop in the larval stage, due to variations in diet. The workers that take care of larvae have special glands near their mouths that produce a substance known as royal jelly. All larvae feed on royal jelly for the first three days of their lives, but from the fourth day onward only those destined to become

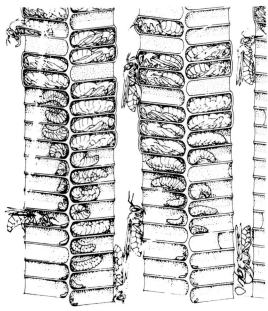

**TOP RIGHT The larval stage of worker honeybees lasts five or six days, after which the cell is sealed by workers and the larvae change into pupae (shown here).**
**RIGHT Honeybees use the nectar that they have collected from flowers to produce honey—enzymes act upon the nectar and water evaporates from it.**

**They store the honey in cells in their hive.**
**ABOVE The inside of a honeybees' nest may contain over 50,000 bees, including one queen and a variable number of drones. The bottom cells contain eggs, while those further up contain larvae that get larger toward the top. The pupae emerge from cells at the very top.**

queens receive it regularly. The rest eat "bee bread"—a type of paste made from pollen and honey.

Worker honeybees keep the hive functioning efficiently and make sure that their community is properly cared for. They fetch food, take care of the young, defend the nest and see that the hive temperature is properly regulated. Some workers produce wax to build combs (the inner hive walls), while others care for the larvae and remove waste matter from the larval cells. Many workers gather pollen, nectar and water, while some are responsible for storing these food supplies.

## Drones

Drones are squat-bodied, fertile males that have no pollen-gathering equipment or sting. They appear in late spring or summer to fertilize the potential new queens. The large presence of drones (200 or so) in a hive ensures that a queen is fertilized effectively.

Drones have a well-developed sense of smell and enormous composite eyes that provide them with exceptionally good eyesight. In combination, these two senses enable them to pick out the queen and reach her during a mating flight.

In a colony of bees, the queen and the drones make up the reproductive caste, which has the sole function of perpetuating the species. Both are treated with great consideration as long as they are useful to their colony. However, after drones have mated with the queen, they are merely tolerated by the worker bees, since they serve no useful purpose. When winter draws near and food supplies dwindle, drones become a burden on their community, and consequently they are denied access to the hive.

**ABOVE The cells of a honeycomb are hexagonal in shape, allowing the maximum number of cells to be built within a given area. Worker bees use secreted wax to build double-sided vertical combs of hexagonal cells.**

**Pollen and honey are stored in cells the same size as those used to rear worker larvae. Males (drones) are reared in larger cells and queens develop in large cells suspended from the comb.**

## The hive

Honeybees usually build their nests, or hives, in holes in tree trunks or in crevices between rock. The hive contains many vertical, parallel walls of wax known as combs—each comb consists of a series of double, horizontal rows of cells. Each cell is a hexagonal receptacle with a slightly domed base and an opening at its top. All the cells tilt slightly, to prevent their contents from spilling out. The size of the cells depends upon their intended use. The largest ones are cylindrical (rather than hexagonal) chambers —the royal cells for queen bee larvae. Cells intended for drones are slightly smaller, while those for workers are smaller still. Other cells contain pollen and honey.

A cell's location determines its function: all cells for rearing young are situated at the comb's center, while the small cells for honey storage are at the edges of the combs. Pollen fills a ring of hexagonal cells between the honey cells and the larval cells.

Narrow corridors separate the hive's many combs, leaving only a tiny space for bees to work and move about. Honeybees take care to ensure that their hives contain no empty spaces: they build combs in any space larger than a corridor and fill any space smaller with propolis, or bee glue. Propolis is a mixture of digestive waste matter and a resinous substance gathered from poplars and pines.

## Early work

Newly formed worker honeybees dedicate themselves entirely to the task of cleaning the cells and clearing waste matter from the hive. During their first two days, they are ill suited to the open air since they are unsteady on their legs. On their third and fourth days, worker bees feed the older larvae with pollen and honey. After their fourth day, their royal jelly glands are fully developed, and consequently they spend days 5-10 feeding the younger larvae. The workers expend much energy on feeding larvae, since every larva must eat about 10,000 times during its development—an average of 1300 times a day. At 10 days of age, worker bees change their duties and, for about a week, they receive food gathered by older workers and place it in storage cells. As the workers' royal jelly glands decline, their wax-producing glands begin to function, enabling them to build and repair comb.

## Guardians of the hive

Bees' tendency for aggression increases as they mature. From days 17-20, the workers guard the hive entrance, having developed effective poison glands. During this period, they run a serious risk of dying. If a bee stings an enemy with a tough elastic outer body covering, it cannot withdraw its sting. In trying to detach itself, it loses not only its sting but also part of its abdomen and internal organs. It dies in consequence.

## Nectar seekers

By their 20th day, worker bees become "field bees"—expert fliers dedicated to the task of seeking and gathering food. The younger and less expert bees gather nectar to make honey, while those with greater maturity and experience collect pollen. Bees settle on nectar-bearing flowers and suck nectar up through their digestive systems to their honey pouches. Inside the honey pouch, the action of various enzymes transforms the nectar into a honey-like substance. When its honey pouch is full, a worker returns to the hive and regurgitates its load into storage cells where it is fanned by younger bees until the excess water evaporates. The nectar-honey substance becomes pure honey once all its excess water is removed.

Some older field honeybees become scouts that fly far from the hive and search for pollen and nectar in unexplored territories. Upon their return to the hive, scouts report any findings to their community by performing coded "honey dances."

## Beneficial partnership

A symbiotic relationship exists between flowers and bees—bees use pollen as food and, in return, they ensure the fertilization of flowers. Flowers produce larger quantities of nutrient-rich pollen than are necessary for their fertilization. As the workers fly among flowers, they provide them with their only possible means of fertilization, transferring pollen with the long bristles and hairs that cover their abdomens.

## One queen per hive

The queen's enlarged abdomen distinguishes her physically from the worker bees. There is only one

**TOP** Honeybees will swarm in a cluster around the queen, while a few mature scout bees go in search of a suitable site to build a new nest. When they find one, the scouts dance to indicate the whereabouts of the new location.

**BELOW** The abdomen of the queen bee is longer than those of the workers. She lives up to six years and lays an average of 1500 eggs per day. For the first half of the year, the queen produces pheromones to prevent the birth of new queens. Then, when she is ready to leave the nest, she gives birth to fertile females or queens and leaves, taking some workers with her to establish a new nest.

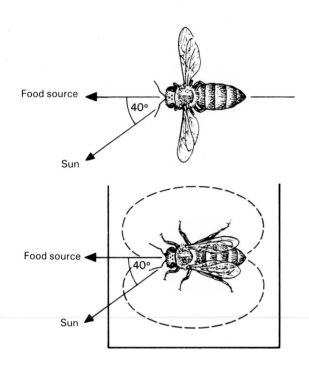

ABOVE Worker honeybees communicate information about food sources to their nest mates by dancing. If the food source is 40 degrees to the left of the sun (top), the bee indicates this to the other bees by performing a "tail-waggling" run across its figure-eight dance (bottom). The direction in which it flies indicates that the food is toward the sun, the 40 degree angle of its path indicates the angle of the food source to the sun, and the number of times the bee wags its body indicates the distance of the food source.

BELOW The dancer is attended by several followers who inspect her closely. The round dance (left) is used to indicate sources of food less than 80 ft. from the hive. The figure-eight dance (right) is used when the food supply is more than 80 ft. from the hive.

FAR RIGHT Hundreds of worker honeybees from a wild colony feed their young on protein-rich secretions and store food in special cells.

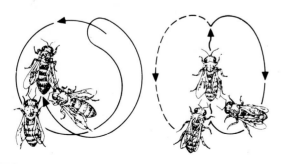

queen in the nest, and she prevents the development of rival queens by producing a secretion known as "queen's substance" from special mandibular glands on her abdomen.

The queen's substance contains pheromones, chemical messages that pass information through the colony and regulate its activities; it acts as a chemical control mechanism through the colony, preventing the workers from developing ovaries and suppressing their instinct to build potential queen cells. The workers that attend the queen take up the queen's substance and pass it through the colony during "mutual feeding." The mechanism of transferring food between individuals, known as trophallaxis, is an important method of passing information from one member of the colony to another.

From spring until the end of summer, the population of the colony expands until the hive is too small to accommodate the whole family. The resident queen, now old and failing, is no longer able to produce enough pheromonal substances to control the swelling community. In the absence of chemical direction, the workers believe that the hive has no queen and begin to rear new queens inside queen cells.

The old queen can hunt down her rivals in their cells and kill them with her sting. But normally the old queen, gathering together a swarm of workers and drones, abandons the nest and undertakes the "prime" swarm. Swarming occurs toward noon on a sunny day; the swarm gathers in a cluster on the ground, on the branch of a tree or in a hedge.

### New queen

In the original hive, the first newly hatched queen immediately stings her rivals to death while they are still inside their cells. The new queen flies up to mate with the drones. Only five or six of the hundreds of males in the colony reach the queen and fertilize her. After fertilization, the successful drones perish because their genitals remain attached to the queen. The workers in the hives repulse any drones that fail to mate because they are now a burden to the community. The fertilized queen then begins to lay her eggs.

### Color differentiation

During pollination, bees recognize the different colors and shapes of flowers. Although they cannot distinguish between red and green, they perceive

yellow, blue, purple and white. Bees are also able to recognize ultraviolet light, a faculty that they exploit to tell the difference between flowers that appear white in color to humans. Many flowers have developed colored markings to guide bees to the nectar.

## Passing information

Social communication is important in a highly organized society, such as that of the bees. There are two principal means of communication—pheromonal and social. Known as social hormones, pheromones coordinate and determine the physiological characteristics of the community. For example, the queen produces special substances to control the development of rivals and stimulate the workers to build combs.

When a scouting bee discovers a field of flowers, the other worker bees from the hive swarm into the field soon afterward. The scout does not always accompany the others back to the field, which may be over a mile away from the hive. Consequently, bees have learned to communicate through ritual dances, so that workers can pass on information about the new source of nectar—its quantity and its distance and direction from the hive. Because the dances take place in the darkness of the hive, the other bees follow the gyrations of the scout as it moves over the surface of the comb by touching it with their antennae.

## Round dance

The three reference points on which this remarkable signaling dance depends are the hive itself, the food source and the sun. Bees even know the position of the sun on cloudy days, because they can discern the ultraviolet radiation that it emits. If the source of food is less than 80 ft. from the hive, the scout performs a "round dance," circling alternately to the left and to the right until it excites the other workers so that they gather around.

The lingering smell of the flowers and the drops of nectar that the scout secretes from its honey pouch serve as a means of communicating the nature of the source of food. The intensity of the scout's dance increases according to the amount of food—the greater the amount of food, the more frantic the dance becomes.

If the food is more than 80 ft. away, the scout bee performs a second type of dance called the "waggle dance," or figure-eight. The scout runs along the vertical face of the comb in a straight line, then curves round in a semicircular movement back to its original starting point. It returns up the straight line, but curves around to the other side to form another semicircle and an overall figure-eight.

Throughout the dance ritual, the bee vibrates its abdomen with more and more intensity according to the abundance of the food source. The bee also wags its tail during the dance; the number of complete flicks of the tail gives a measure of the distance from the hive (each flick indicates an increase in distance of about 250 ft.). The whole maneuver occurs repeatedly until the message has been understood.

## Finding a new nest

Bees do not communicate with each other simply for the purpose of finding food. For example, during the swarming period from spring to summer, several worker-scouts disperse throughout the countryside to explore, then return to the swarm to inform their companions of the most suitable location for the new hive. In this case, the returning scouts perform the dance of the abdomen. The rhythm of the dance imparts the distance, the direction in which they form the straight line indicates the direction, and the degree of frenzy expresses the quality of the place.

As a result of the dance, other bees from the swarm become excited and fly away to explore the site in question. Afterward, they return and repeat the same dance. Sometimes, two scouts return with news of two sites of equal quality. Both start to dance, each indicating the direction of its newly discovered site and vying with the other to win over as many companions as possible. Once a majority has been established, the defeated group concedes.

## Open-air nests

The nests of the dwarf bees consist of a single, horizontal comb situated in the open. Obviously, they do not need to indicate the angle of the sun in relation to the source of nectar that they have discovered, so the direction of the straight line in the figure-eight dance tells them which way to go to find food. The nests of giant bees hang vertically, so the bees communicate the angle of the sun with a different dance. However, giant bees only dance on those parts of the comb from which the sky can be seen clearly.

## The temperature in the hive

Bees cannot regulate their own body temperature, but they can control the temperature of their surroundings. The temperature within the hive has to remain constant, regardless of the temperature outside. During the brooding period from spring to autumn, the temperature of the inner center of the nest, where larvae are reared, must remain at a constant 95.9°F. Any decline in the temperature causes the death of the larvae and, consequently, endangers the future of the whole colony. Worker bees in the nest collect above the larval cells and create heat by vibrating their muscles.

Bees ventilate the hive when the combs are in danger of melting from the heat, or when large quantities of collected nectar threaten to block the usual air currents. As soon as the temperature outside starts to rise, the bees employ two different methods of temperature control to keep the nest cool.

First, the workers crowd around the entrance to the colony and beat their wings rapidly to produce a current of fresh air that will ventilate the inside of the hive. If the temperatures rise steeply, the workers abandon their pollen and nectar gathering and bring back small drops of water to place at the entrance of the larval cells. Using their tongues, they stretch out each droplet until it becomes a fine film, thus producing a larger surface so that evaporation can take place more easily.

## Division of labor

There is a clear division of labor in the task of cooling the colony. The most experienced bees search for drops of water because they know the area well. Those workers that care for the larvae wait inside the hive and distribute the water where it is most needed. The evaporation of the water causes the temperature to drop.

Bees have many enemies and are vulnerable to numerous diseases. For example, they are prey to several large insects, the brown bear, the badger, the hedgehog and some birds, such as the honey-buzzard and the bee eater. If a predatory insect enters the hive, the guards usually kill it. As the body is often too large to be removed, it is then wrapped in propolis, a substance with strong antibacterial properties that prevents organic matter from decomposing inside the hive and spreading disease.

**ABOVE The cells of a comb reveal worker honeybees that are ready to emerge from their pupal stage. In the center, one is just emerging. Worker honeybees have an extremely short life span compared with queens.**

**Workers born in spring and summer, when activity in the hive is at its peak, live no longer than five weeks, but those born in autumn hibernate through the winter and sometimes live for seven or eight months.**

## Diseases

The principal bee diseases come from protozoa, bacteria and viruses. They can quickly destroy entire colonies, particularly in bee farms. The chemicals contained in propolis, or bee glue, have a strong antiseptic effect, and bees use this substance to fill up cracks and cover over the bodies of their enemies. They secrete it over any object or surface that could pose a threat to the colony.

## Ants

The 14,000 species of the family Formicidae, commonly known as ants, form the largest family of social insects. Ranging in size from 0.04 in. to 1.6 in. in length, ants originated in tropical zones. They now inhabit every continent of the world, except for Antarctica. Ants are gregarious creatures and have a high level of social organization.

# WEAVER ANTS
## — INSTINCT OR INTELLIGENCE? —

Weaver ants, Oecophylla smaragdina, *possess the remarkable ability to "glue" leaves together with silk produced by their larvae. The species inhabits southern Asia, Africa and Australia, where it constructs nests from the live foliage of any kind of tree or bush. Although weaver ant larvae produce silk, they do not spin cocoons, as do all other ant species.*

*The first stage in the construction of a weaver ant nest begins when a fertilized queen settles on a leaf and lays her eggs on its upper surface. When the larvae hatch, their mother grasps each one gently between her mandibles and, with great accuracy, seals the edges of leaves together with their silk. The queen "glues" several* leaves together, forming a shelter for subsequent batches of eggs. A completed weaver ant shelter resembles a large piece of cloth.

### Construction teams

After the birth of the first weaver ant workers, the queen devotes all her energies to the task of reproduction, allowing her offspring to hunt for insect prey.

As the queen weaver ant lays more and more eggs, the workers have to expand the nest to accommodate the growing colony. Rows of workers station themselves along a leaf border, grasping the leaf immediately above with their jaws. Together, they drag the upper leaf down until its edge is flush with the lower leaf. Each worker in a different "construction team" picks up a larva, squeezes it to stimulate its silk glands, and presses its mouth against the edge of a leaf. The worker ants position the larvae to deposit silk on one leaf's surface and anchor silk threads to the edge of the next leaf—they repeat the process many times until the two leaves are joined. Weaver ants always build their nests to a size just large enough to ensure that their colonies operate smoothly.

### Nature's tool users

Weaver ants are one of the few members of the insect world that use natural objects as "tools" to aid their survival. Other tool-using insects

include certain hymenopteran species that use small stones to beat the earth around the entrance to their nests. The use of tools occurs more often among higher animals: chimpanzees, for example, use branches to help them plunder ant and termite nests; razorbills mark out pathways with small pieces of bark; sea otters break open shells with stones, while striped mongooses and Egyptian vultures use stones to break eggs; Galapagos finches use thorns to pry larvae out of cracks in wood; and crows extract seeds with twigs.

## Instinctive behavior

The weaver ants' use of larval "glue guns" seems to suggest that they, and other tool-using animals, possess high intelligence. However, no tool-using creature has learned to continually develop tools in a systematic fashion—such behavior is limited to humans. Therefore, zoologists believe that the behavior of weaver ants is instinctive, and not rooted in intelligence. Tool use in animals is simply an adaptation to environmental conditions—a pattern of behavior rigidly fixed in a species' genetic code so that it is inherited by each new generation.

**ABOVE** Mature weaver ant larvae produce a thread-like substance from glands situated around their mouths. When building a nest, often in a tree, the worker weaver ants use the secretions like glue to seal the leaves together.

**ABOVE LEFT** As the colony increases in size, the workers have to expand the nest. Stretching themselves out to their maximum length, they take hold of a leaf and drag it toward a neighboring one in an effort to pull them together. They lean against the edges and use their strong legs and mandibles to hold the leaves together.

**FAR LEFT** A finished weaver ants' nest showing the leaves that have been fixed together with masses of the white, glue-like secretion produced by the larvae.

**NEAR LEFT** Initially the queen ant builds a small nest in which to shelter her first batch of eggs. Once they have hatched, the queen dedicates herself entirely to reproduction, and the workers take over the task of building and expanding the nest.

**ABOVE Carpenter ants of the species *Camponotus herculaneus* feed on the honeydew produced by aphids. In return for** providing the ants with honeydew, the aphids gain protection from the ants who often take them into their nests as guests.

Ants have large heads and curved antennae. Like aculeate wasps, they have thin, stalk-like petioles, or wasp waists, that separate their abdomens from the rest of their bodies. Several species of ants have small stings in their abdomens that connect to poison glands. All species of ants have several anal glands toward the rear of their abdomen; these sometimes secrete strong-smelling substances, such as formic acid or butyric acid. Ants also secrete pheromones, chemical messengers that control the development of colonies. The chemical composition of the pheromones differs among species, enabling ants to recognize members of different ant species.

## Caste system

Ant colonies number up to one million individuals; each member of the community actively participates in the colony and has a defined social position. There are usually three castes—fertile females (queens), sterile females (workers) and fertile males (kings). The female reproductives, or queens, are larger than the other members of the colony. They are fully winged at first and swarm out of their colony to mate and found new colonies.

Like all social members of the order Hymenoptera, queen ants have specialized internal sacs in which they store sperm from the males during mating. The reserve of sperm will last a lifetime, enabling them to fertilize eggs if necessary. Fertilized eggs produce females, while unfertilized eggs yield males. There is normally only one queen in each nest, but in some species several fertile females live together in harmony.

## Fertile males

The king ants are fully winged, fertile males. Smaller than the queen in size, they have shortened life cycles, only appearing at certain times of the year to fertilize the queens during the nuptial flight. After mating, the socially useless males perish.

The first-generation larvae of the new colony develop into workers; eventually, they will forage for themselves and supply the queen with food. The workers are always wingless, sterile females; they have large heads and well-developed jaws (mandibles). Since they are responsible for feeding the colony, worker ants have enlarged stomachs in which they store food. During feeding, the workers regurgitate the food in their stomachs and pass it from mouth to mouth to the others in the nest. Oral regurgitation, or trophallaxis, enables insects to communicate by passing pheromones to each other in their food.

## Leafcutter workers

The worker caste of each species adapts to its particular habitat and differs in structure and appearance. The leafcutter ants of the genus *Atta*, for example, have four types of workers, including large "soldiers" that guard the nest and smaller workers that gather food, attend to the queen and look after the nest. In parasitic species of ants, the workers are either small or have disappeared altogether.

The workers' social roles divide into three categories depending on their jobs within the colony. There is also a division of labor on the basis of age among worker ants. Immature workers see to the chores inside the nest, digging new tunnels, storing and carrying food supplies and looking after the queen and the larvae. The mature and more experienced workers go outside in search of food.

## Ants' nests

Ants' nests vary greatly in shape, size and location, depending on the species. Driver ants and army ants, for example, inhabit only temporary nests, from which they wander in large armies, consuming any insects in their path. Sometimes ant colonies occur underground, while other species build elaborate nests high up in the holes of rocks or trees. The parasol ants of the genus *Atta* construct special chambers within their nest, in which they cultivate fungus gardens. Underground ants' nests consist of several layers of tiny chambers, linked by a system of horizontal and vertical tunnels.

Parasitic species of ants, such as the jet black ants, are unable to build their own nests and occupy the nests of other species. The small queens of the species *Lasius umbratus* seek adoption into the nests of pioneer ants. Most of the invading queens are killed, but some integrate successfully in queenless nests; others kill the original queen and take her place. In either case, the workers of the other species will take care of her eggs and larvae.

## Cluster nests

The cluster nests of red ants are similar in structure to underground nests. The workers dig the base in the

ABOVE Leafcutter ants of the species *Atta cephalotta* cut out pieces of leaves and flower petals with their powerful jaws and carry them back to their nest. BELOW A diagram of the inside of a nest made by leafcutter ants of the species *Atta sexdens*. The ants gain access to their nest through the access tunnel (A). Leafcutter ants need a continuous food supply; they deposit leaves in a special chamber where they cultivate a fungus (B). The ants feed from the fungus, obtaining the nutrients released from the leaf material. Large numbers of ants live in the nest, and in order to breathe, they build air inlet tunnels (C).

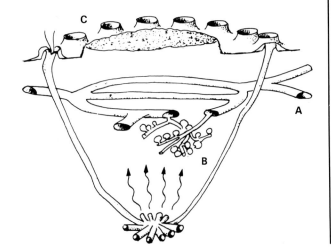

ABOVE A winged, female tree-dwelling ant of the species *Crematogaster scutellaris*. Only the reproductive members of the ant colony have wings, and swarm out of their colonies over a short period of time for their nuptial flight. The winged queens shed their wings once they have mated.

ground, or in a rotting log, and cover it with a mass of conifer leaves, broken twigs, grains of resin and debris. When viewed from above, the nest resembles an enormous dome. Inside the nest, there is an irregular labyrinth of tunnels and small chambers linked to the outside by air inlets.

Some ants dig their nests inside dead tree trunks. Because their mandibles are not strong enough to chew hard wood, the resulting structure consists of a network of deepened, concentric depressions that link up through horizontal tunnels dug out of the softest parts of the wood.

In tropical areas, some species of ants build their nests inside thorns or swellings on the leaves of certain plants (known as myrmecophilous plants). Some forms of acacia plant, for example, produce sweet substances especially to attract ants. The presence of ant colonies in the branches of plants is mutually beneficial—the plant profits because the ants clear away all parasitic insects.

## Papery paste
Certain species chew wood fibers, reducing them to a papery paste from which they build their nests. The nests of weaver ants are more elaborate in structure. Several weaver ants congregate and cling to leaves to weigh them down. As they perform this precarious act, other weaver ants take hold of their own larvae firmly and lay them along the edges of the trapped leaf.

The larvae then secrete a silky substance that binds the leaves together to form a small arcade (the whole nest is built using this method). Multiple nests also exist, in which two or more species of ant live side by side. Every ants' nest is equipped with an infrastructure of paths, emergency shelters and farming facilities.

## Queens
During their nuptial flight, the winged male deposits a store of sperm in the winged female. The young female then sheds her wings and shelters inside a nest that she builds herself. After laying her eggs, the female fertilizes them with stored sperm to produce the first generation of worker ants.

While brooding her first eggs, the queen remains inside the nest, feeding on the products of her own disintegrating wing muscles and stored food materials in her body. She lays plasma-rich eggs as an alternative source of food. The first-generation larvae of the new colony develop quickly and immediately set about building a new nest, helping the new queen to care for the second-generation larvae.

If there are several fertilized queens in one colony, they move to different shelters immediately after mating and start to lay eggs. When the larvae hatch, the queens cooperate in taking care of them. In many cases, only one queen survives within the new colony. The queenless workers become soldiers within the nest, living side by side with the surviving queen to form a mixed colony. In other species, the workers produced by the surviving queen take over completely and oust all unwanted queenless workers.

## Reproduction
All ants are social, forming communities that share a great many characteristics. However, differences do exist. For example, in most species the queen lays eggs continuously, but in a few species, such as those of the army ants, she produces them periodically. Among all communities, worker ants collect the newly laid eggs, take them to special brood chambers and regularly turn them until they hatch.

When the grub-like larvae hatch from the eggs, the worker ants carry them to another chamber in the nest. There, nurse worker ants feed, lick and generally look after them, assisting them in their molts until they pupate. Then they carry the pupae to a warm, dry part of the nest to complete their development.

Finally, again with the help of the worker ants, the adults emerge from the pupal case.

The queen lays both fertilized and unfertilized eggs. The fertilized ones develop into females, and the unfertilized ones become males. Most females develop into sterile worker ants, but during the breeding season, newly hatched females are fertile, potential young queens. Whether they become fertile or sterile depends on their diet. Larvae that are to become queens live on a liquid produced by glands on the head of the nurse workers, while larvae that are to become sterile workers only eat regurgitated food. Males are produced only during the breeding season, and their sole function is to mate with the young queens, thereby ensuring the survival of the species.

## Communication

Ants, like all social animals, need to communicate with one another to coordinate the colony's activities. They communicate by scent, by touch or—in rare cases—by sound. Scent plays a particularly vital role in the functioning of the colony. The larvae use sound to attract the attention of the nurse workers, to mark food trails, to identify intruders and as an alarm signal in times of danger.

Foraging ants use complex, mixed signals—both scent and touch—to recruit companions to help them collect food. When an ant finds food, it usually announces its discovery by dancing and waving its antennae. The dance excites its companions, and the ant leads them directly to the food. In some species, however, the ant marks a scent trail to the food for the rest of the colony to follow. To show what type of nourishment it has found, the ant regurgitates a little and offers it to its companions.

Worker ants use various alarm signals to warn the rest of the colony of danger. They make chemical signals with characteristic body odors, and they produce tactile signals by frantically dancing and waving their antennae. To make acoustic signals, some species hit their bodies against the walls of the nest; other species rub their abdomens against their thoraxes.

## Territorial behavior

Ants have developed clearly defined territorial behavior in response to competition for the available food resources. There is a certain area—or territory—surrounding every ants' nest that the colony energetically controls and defends. The territories controlled by different colonies can extend one inside the other or, if the ants belong to different species, they can even be on top of one another.

The behavior of ants inside their own territory differs greatly from their behavior outside it. If they are within their own territory, they will attack any predator that dares to invade the home area; if they are outside, they are far less aggressive.

**BELOW Army ants do not have a permanent nest. Instead, they lead a nomadic existence, marching through the forest in search of food. The workers carry the queen, developing larvae, and eggs (shown here). When the larvae pupate,** the colony temporarily stops marching. During this stationary phase, the queen lays thousands of eggs that hatch into ravenous larvae. After the pupae of the previous generation have turned into adults, the colony resume its march.

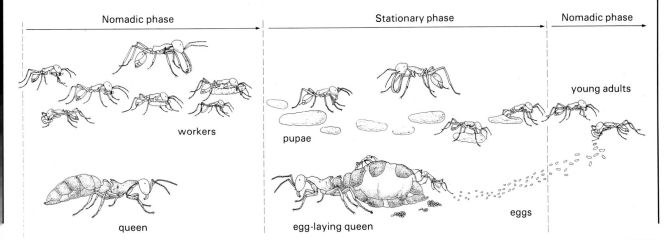

Nomadic phase — Stationary phase — Nomadic phase

workers

queen

pupae

egg-laying queen

eggs

young adults

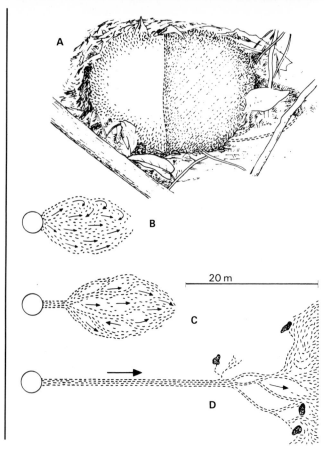

## Diet

Ants usually have a mixed diet, but some species, such as leafcutter ants, are exclusively vegetarian. Other species, such as the South American army ants, are exclusively carnivorous. Most species, however, have a preference for sweet foods. They frequently obtain sugary substances from nectar, sap and fruit. Many species, including the black garden ant, feed on the sugary secretions that sap-sucking insects produce.

Ants collect the sugary liquid—commonly called honeydew—by licking the droplets as they appear on an aphid's anus. In order to maintain their supply of honeydew, ants may "farm" the aphids, protecting them from predators, confining them to the most nutritious part of the plant, building shelters around them and even carrying them down into their nest to feed on plant roots.

## Army ants

The famous army ants of the South American genus *Eciton* are tropical, nomadic group hunters in the subfamily Dorylinae. They are large creatures, about an inch long, and they form huge colonies of up to 200,000 individuals with a single queen. The various castes within an army ant colony differ greatly in both size and appearance, depending on their role. For example, the huge-jawed soldier ants are twice the size of the workers and winged males.

All ant colonies have a nomadic life-style, and none of them have a permanent nest. They spend most of their lives marching through the forests in a vast column, flanked by the huge-jawed soldier ants. They devour any small animals in their path. "Scout" ants lead the column forward by laying a scent trail for the rest of

TOP LEFT A worker honeypot ant, bloated with honeydew from plants or aphids, hangs from the roof of its nest, unable to move. In this state, it serves as a living storage vessel, regurgitating the liquid for the colony during hard times.
LEFT South American army ants form temporary "living" nests above ground by interlocking their legs and jaws (A). The queen shelters in a cavity amid their bodies on one side of the nest (white area), while her brood occupy spaces on the other side (shaded area). At the start of a foraging raid for food, African driver ants swarm from their nest (B). As they move away from the nest, the ants form a system of branching trails (C). At the height of the raid, a massive column of ants follows behind the swarm, guided by scent trails from the scouts at the front (D).

the colony to follow. The center of the column consists of smaller workers, some carrying the queen and others carrying larvae and pupae, as well as large males.

During its nomadic phase, each ant colony rests in temporary, aboveground nests. To create a nest, a huge cluster of workers forms a mass of interlocking legs and jaws. The queen and her brood remain inside the "chambers" of the nest while raiding workers collect food.

## Fast breeders

The breeding cycle of the queen, which repeats every 30-40 days, determines the timing and duration of a colony's nomadic phase. A week or so before the queen is due to lay her eggs, the larvae of the previous generation of ants pupate. The colony stops marching and forms a nest. Workers leave the nest each day to forage for food, which they bring back for the rest of the colony.

During the stationary phases, the queen lays many thousands of eggs, and they hatch into new larvae. About a week later, the colony resumes marching, stimulated to do so by the emergence of new workers and males from the pupae of the previous generation. The growing larvae require so much food that the colony has to keep moving in order to find enough nourishment to sustain them.

With such a phenomenal reproductive ability, it is not surprising that army ant colonies are enormous. However, each colony regularly splits into two. When the young queens hatch, the males and workers surround them and carry off the two most vigorous queens in the colony—which may include the old queen—to form two new colonies. In addition, newly hatched males frequently fly off to join other colonies.

The African driver ants of the genus *Anomma* comprise another group of tropical hunters in the subfamily Dorylinae. They, too, form nomadic colonies, but they have no regular cycle of migrations and stationary phases because the queen does not lay eggs all the year round.

In the driver ants' stationary phase, the queen lays hundreds of thousands of eggs in semipermanent, underground nests. The eggs hatch into ravenous larvae. During the dry season, the queen only lays eggs that hatch into male ants. Once the males reach the adult stage, they mate with fertile females and then die. The fertilized females survive, and leave the

ABOVE The underground nests of harvester ants are often easy to identify, since the ants habitually discard seed husks around the openings so that they form ring-shaped mounds.
BELOW Harvester ants, such as this winged female, are widespread around the Mediterranean. They feed on the seeds of grasses and cereals that they carry back to their nests and store in large chambers. The ants store enough seeds to provide the colony with nourishment in times of drought.

# THE ANT COLONY
## — INTRUDERS IN THE NEST —

exists between ... ants ... certain sap-feeding insects, such as aphids, benefits both parties—the ants receive valuable honeydew, and the sap feeders obtain the ants' protection. The ants often take some of these sap feeders into their nest as "guests" and farm them. A range of uninvited invertebrates may also be found in the ants' nest and these are not usually beneficial to the ant colony. Such creatures—beetles, mites, wasps, cockroaches, crickets, other ants and even butterflies—have all evolved methods of tapping into the rich and nutritious supply of food that exists in the nest.

Since ants are quick to detect and attack intruders into their nest, any species wishing to infiltrate the colony must first develop a strategy to overcome this problem. The easiest way of preventing attack and eviction by their ant hosts is for the uninvited guests to simply avoid contact with the ants, but this is not always easy to do. Beetles and wood lice possess armored, ant-proof bodies that can ward off attacks from the ants. Many parasitic mites live on the ants themselves, clinging unnoticed to their hosts' bodies, feeding on their blood or even stealing the regurgitated liquid food with which ants feed one another.

### The art of mimicry

One common means of gaining access into an ant colony is through mimicry. Many species of beetles and wasps have evolved ant-like antennae and forelegs that deceive the ants in the dark tunnels of their nest. Other animals use behavioral mimicry to fool the ants: for example, the cricket Myrmecophila acervorum walks in the same manner as its ant hosts. Indeed, it can even alter its movements according to which species of ants' nest it has occupied. However, if the cricket is injured, and the ants discover the deception, they will immediately attack and kill the cricket.

Some invertebrates have evolved special glands for secreting substances that either repel or attract the ants. Many types of beetles and wasps use such secretions, but one of the most

*interesting examples is that of the caterpillars of the blue butterflies. These caterpillars have special glands on their bodies that secrete a sweet honeydew that ants find extremely attractive. When a foraging ant comes across one of these honeydew-secreting caterpillars, it carries it back to the nest where the ants periodically milk it. The caterpillar spends most of the year in the ants' nest, where it feeds on ant larvae—predatory behavior that the ants accept in return for the honeydew.*

*Ants themselves make up one of the largest groups of animals that parasitize other ant colonies. The phenomenon of ant parasitism is complicated, but basically it occurs when a newly fertilized parasitic queen enters the nest of another ant species and supplants the existing queen. The adopted colony accepts the new queen because of the attractive chemicals she emits.*

**ABOVE LEFT** Ant young are completely reliant on the workers for food and protection. The developing yellow and white pupae resemble adults, but they are immobile and highly vulnerable to being attacked by large and small predators, such as aardvarks, anteaters, beetles and other insects.
**LEFT** Harvester ants of the genus *Messor*, such as these two from neighboring nests in Kenya, do not tolerate any intruders into their territory and will engage them in battle — even if it happens to be another ant of the same species. The

harvester ants live in generally dry regions and so build their nests deep underground where they are not so affected by the hot climate. They usually emerge only to make brief trips to forage for seeds from grasses and grain crops which they store against periods of drought.
**ABOVE** Many ants feed on the sweet honeydew secretions of plant-sucking aphids (such as the small, blackish species seen here). The ants stimulate the release of the honeydew by gently stroking the aphids' abdomens with their antennae.

colony in search of somewhere safe to lay their eggs and start new colonies.

## Harvester ants

The harvester ants, members of the subfamily Myrmicinae, live in both temperate and tropical regions. They have highly evolved societies, with a pronounced caste system based on the division of labor. The ordinary workers are small, but there are also larger workers and huge soldier ants that have massive heads and powerful jaws.

Harvester ants usually live in desert, semidesert and Mediterranean regions. They make large, underground nests—sometimes reaching a depth of 6 ft. 6 in.—and feed primarily on grass and cereal seeds. They also eat small invertebrates and aphid honeydew. Harvester ants take their name from their habit of collecting huge quantities of seed and storing them inside special nest chambers to provide the colony with nourishment whenever there is a scarcity of food.

The smallest workers in a harvester ant colony have responsibility for gathering the seeds, and they forage for them in sizable groups. Inside the nest, the large workers remove the seed husks with their powerful jaws and throw them outside the nest. Then they chew the remaining grains to a sugary paste, which the smaller workers feed to the larvae.

Harvester ants keep their seed-storage chambers well drained to prevent the seeds from going moldy or germinating. If the seeds do become damp, the ants remove them from the nest and spread them out on the ground to dry in the sun. Occasionally, seeds germinate and take root outside the nest, forming a small accidental crop.

ABOVE Among harvester ants, it is the small workers that bring back the grass seeds for storing in the underground chambers, while the larger workers remove the husks with their strong jaws. Here, *Messor barbarus* of southern Africa take grass seeds into the nest and bring out empty husks. BELOW The Amazon ant is a species of slave-maker ant that depends for the full functioning of its colony on work done by enslaved wood ants of the species *Formica fusca*. Here, the Amazon ant workers (white) are seen raiding the nests of the wood ants, killing the adults and stealing their pupae and eggs in order to enslave the worker ants that will hatch from them.

**ABOVE** Wood ants are fierce predators, hunting insects—especially caterpillars—in groups, and carrying their victims back to the nest. They use their sharp jaws to give vicious bites and inject their victims with poisonous acid.

**ABOVE LEFT** The nests of wood ants are characterized by domed roofs built from twigs, pine needles and leaf stalks. Although there are galleries underground, the mound itself contains numerous tunnels, some of which open to the outside.

## Leafcutter ants

Leafcutter, or parasol, ants of the genus *Atta* comprise another group in the subfamily Myrmicinae. They are commonplace in the tropical regions of America, where they are serious pests of citrus and other crops. Like the harvester ants, leafcutter ants build enormous underground nests and have a pronounced caste system.

Some species of leafcutter ant have a habit of cutting the leaves from plants and carrying them to their nest—which is how the group derives its name. Inside the nest, the ants chew the leaves until they have formed a mulch. They use the mulch to cultivate special fungus gardens on which they feed. Some species of leafcutter ant collect dead leaves or caterpillar feces instead.

Leafcutter ants construct immense underground nests, consisting of a network of chambers and tunnels. On the outside of the nest, they build a hollow mound of earth and ring it with numerous craters. To regulate the circulation of air throughout the nest, the ants dig vertical shafts that emanate from the craters and converge at the base of the nest. To provide access to the nest, they dig a series of horizontal tunnels in the subsoil that open onto the outside some distance from the central mound. At their inner end, the horizontal tunnels lead into a large, circular gallery. Various sloping galleries leave the circular gallery and connect to the fungus gardens.

## Fungus garden food

Leafcutter worker ants vary in size from the tiny ants that tend the fungus gardens to the huge soldiers that patrol the pathways of the foraging ants. The leaf-gathering workers cut the leaves into manageable sized pieces, clasp them between their jaws and then transport them back to the nest—which may be many feet away. The worker ants hold their heads up high in order to carry the pieces of leaves above their bodies—hence their popular name, parasol ants.

In the nest, the smaller leafcutter worker ants chew up the leaves and cultivate the fungus gardens. They also care for the larvae, feeding them with the regurgitated fungus. In a leafcutter ant colony, the queen is large and lives for a long time, sometimes up to 20 years. Before a new queen leaves the nest for her nuptial flight, she stores a pellet of fungus in a small pocket in her mouth. After mating, she sheds her wings and constructs a small underground chamber. The queen deposits the fungus on the ground inside the chamber and tends it with the greatest of care, maintaining it with her own feces and crushed eggs. When the fungus is well established, the queen begins to lay her real eggs. She feeds crushed, sacrificial eggs and new fungus to the first larvae that hatch. When they mature, these first larvae form a new colony, thus assuring the continued development of the nest.

## Wood ants

The common wood ant, *Formica rufa*, is a member of the subfamily *Formicinae*. Widespread all over Europe, it lives in open woodlands and heaths, gathering in colonies that contain many thousands of individuals. It defends itself from potential predators by squirting them with formic acid from its abdomen and biting them with its sharp jaws.

Wood ants prey on invertebrates, and when they have caught a victim they carry the dead prey back to their nest. The workers eat it and regurgitate some to feed to the larvae. Like many other ants, common wood ants also feed avidly on aphid honeydew.

The members of a wood ant colony construct a large underground nest, usually around the base of an old, rotting tree stump. They cover the nest with an enormous mound of twigs, pine needles, leaves and other organic matter. Often over 6 ft. high, the mound contains many tunnels that open onto the surface and connect with the main part of the nest below the surface of the ground.

## Satellite colonies

The wood ant nest is a tiered labyrinth of intercommunicating tunnels and chambers. In the summer it is warmer inside the nest than it is outside, so the workers carry the eggs and larvae to the upper parts of the nest where it is coolest. In the winter, however, most of the colony moves down to the deepest parts of the nest to hibernate.

A wood ant colony contains several queens that inhabit the deepest part of the nest and lay eggs continually. Although both males and females have wings, they never mate in the air. Instead, they mate on the surface of the nest or on the ground. As soon as the female has been fertilized, she sheds her wings and prepares to lay her eggs.

If the female leaves the nest, she may take with her a group of workers from the family nest and search for a new nesting site. Alternatively, she may enter the nest of a large black ant, kill the existing queen and take over the colony. The black ants instinctively nurse the eggs that the wood ant queen has laid, so when the last of the black ants die, the colony that remains consists entirely of wood ants. Many wood ant colonies are situated close to one another, frequently as "satellite" colonies of a single parent colony and always competing for food.

## Honeypot ants

Within the subfamily Formicinae, there are several genera of honeypot ants living in the arid regions of America, Africa and Australia. Those of the genus *Myrmecocystus* occupy the southwestern deserts of the United States, where they feed on a wide variety of insects as well as aphid honeydew. They are called honeypot ants because of the unusual food-gorging habit of some of their members.

Some worker ants—approximately 300 in a colony —overindulge on liquid nourishment that the food-collecting workers have regurgitated. They take in so much liquid that their abdomens swell up to form huge, transparent, spherical storage bags. Unable to move about, the greedy ants become nest-bound and spend the rest of their lives hanging by their legs from the roof of the nest. When food resources outside are scarce, the bloated worker ants provide a living supply of food for the colony.

## Slave-maker ants

The Amazon, or slave-maker, ants of the genus *Polyergus* comprise another group in the subfamily Formicinae. Their colonies consist of fertile females, winged males and workers. The workers act as warriors and have the extraordinary habit of capturing ants from a colony of *Formica fusca* ants. They then set them to work as slaves in the Amazon ants' nest. The warriors rely on slave labor because they have developed outsize, pointed jaws that prevent them from carrying out their normal task of looking after the nest.

In a well-established Amazon ant colony, groups of warriors capture slaves by making raids on the nests of their intended victims. The warriors are interested only in collecting the eggs and larvae from the plundered nest, but they ruthlessly kill any resisting adults. They carry out their raids at regular intervals in order to replace slaves that die.

When the stolen larvae and pupae mature into adult workers, they accept the Amazon ant colony as their own and perform all the usual tasks of looking after it—carrying the eggs, nursing the larvae and pupae, searching for food and feeding the queen.

When a newly fertilized Amazon ant queen is ready to occupy her own colony, she takes over a nest of *Formica fusca* by killing the existing queen. The orphaned workers adopt her, and they care for her and for the eggs she lays. The Amazon workers that hatch from the new queen's eggs make slave raids to replace the *Formica* workers that die, thus creating a new slave-maker ant colony.

# BORN HUNTERS

The insects in this chapter cover a range of lesser known creatures whose larvae are either fierce, ground-dwelling or aquatic predators, or parasites. They include the lacewings, ant lions and tiny, parasitical strepsipterans

**ABOVE The female alder fly lays 200-3000 cylindrical eggs on foliage overhanging water. After about a fortnight, the larvae hatch and fall into the water below where they live in the mud, hunting worms and aquatic insects.**

**PAGE 2565 Adult owlflies often resemble butterflies, having hairy bodies and brightly colored wings. However, the wings are semi-transparent with a rich network of veins. Owlflies are carnivorous and catch prey on the wing.**

Alder flies, snake flies and lacewings are closely related to ants and represent the earliest known example of the pupal stage of development. They belong to three insect orders that first appeared during the Permian epoch 260-225 million years ago (the Megaloptera, the Raphidoptera and the Neuroptera). In the adult stage, alder flies, lacewings and snake flies have four large, richly veined wings that fold over their bodies when they are at rest. Adults are short-lived and usually do not feed. Their larvae have well-developed jaws and leg-like gills on their abdomens.

## Alder flies and dobson flies

The 260 species of the order Megaloptera divide into two families—the alder flies and the dobson flies. They mainly range through temperate regions of the world and are particularly common in Europe and North America. Deriving their scientific name from the Greek *mega* (giant) and *optera* (wings), they have two large pairs of wings. While the wingspan of many European species is only 1.2 in. wide, certain dobson flies in North America attain a wingspan of 6 in.

The order Megaloptera comprises the most primitive group of the higher insects. The adults measure 0.4-0.8 in. in length, with long antennae and dull, heavily veined wings. Although their larval stage of growth lasts for two years, they metamorphose from pupae to adults in a short burst of growth; the adult life cycle is short, rarely exceeding two weeks in duration. One member of the order Megaloptera is well known to anglers as one of the flies used in trout fishing, but the other species are generally not conspicuous to humans because of their smoke-colored bodies. The adults of European dobson flies flutter around the marsh grasses that grow at the edges of ponds and streams.

## Reproduction

Adult alder flies and dobson flies are short-lived. Megalopterans' sole purpose as adults is to reproduce and disperse the species. After fertilizing the female, the male soon falls prey to other animals. Similarly, the female provides no parental care for her young and perishes after laying her eggs. Breeding always takes place on the ground. It is usually preceded by a simple courtship ritual. In some species, the female produces a scent to attract a mate.

When male and female megalopterans meet each other, they communicate by vibrating their antennae, abdomens or wings on the ground, depending on the species. The female then walks away, followed by the male. When the female is receptive, the male places his head under her wings, grasps her with his front legs and mates with her by curving his abdomen forward.

Mating occurs in the spring. Soon afterward, the female lays 200-3000 brown, cigar-shaped eggs on the stems of plants or on stones near the water. The larvae hatch two weeks later, breaking through the eggshells by using a hard spike, or egg breaker, that they discard at their first molt. After hatching, they make their way to the water's edge and fall in. The larvae are active, underwater carnivores. They have powerful biting jaws and hunt for prey among the mud, pebbles and stones of the stream or lake bottoms.

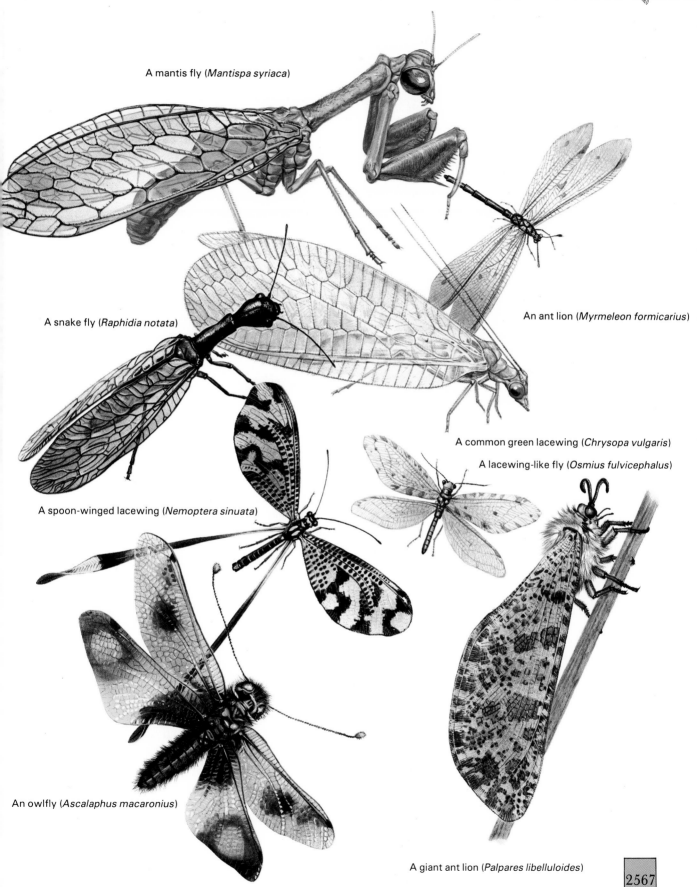

A mantis fly (*Mantispa syriaca*)

A snake fly (*Raphidia notata*)

An ant lion (*Myrmeleon formicarius*)

A common green lacewing (*Chrysopa vulgaris*)

A lacewing-like fly (*Osmius fulvicephalus*)

A spoon-winged lacewing (*Nemoptera sinuata*)

An owlfly (*Ascalaphus macaronius*)

A giant ant lion (*Palpares libelluloides*)

Snake flies, such as the species *Raphidia notata*, have long, mobile heads, and strike at their prey (such as aphids) in a snake-like manner. The females are ferocious, but their aggression lessens as their reproductive organs develop, so that by the time they are fully mature, they mate without attacking their partners.

The most striking feature of the alder fly and dobson fly larvae is the seven pairs of finger-like gills on their abdomens. The gills resemble small legs, each one being made up of a series of five joints clothed with bristles. A further gill occurs at the end of their bodies. The larvae protract and retract the gills, causing water to swish past them. When the oxygen content of the water is low, the larvae undulate their bodies while remaining stationary, increasing the flow of water over their gills. The bodies of the larvae end in a pair of legs bearing large claws that enable them to move about.

## Larval growth

The larval stage of the alder flies and dobson flies lasts for one to two years, largely spent in the mud at the bottom of the water. Growth is slow, but the larvae molt frequently. During winter, the larvae dig deep holes in which they spend the cold season. The following spring, they return to the surface of the mud.

Pupation usually occurs in damp soil near the water's edge. The larvae leave the water and dig an oval-shaped cell in mud or vegetable debris. Three weeks later, the larvae molt into pupae without spinning a cocoon. In many insect pupae, the legs and wings develop inside the pupal case. The wings of alder fly pupae are already free of the body but encased in special sheaths; they also have freely moving legs. While they are inside the pupal chamber, the young lie upside-down, supported by numerous spines that project from ridges on their abdomens. The pupal stage is very brief, and the adults emerge from their cells several days later. If a pupal chamber is open to the outside, the pupa molts into the adult inside the chamber, but if the pupal chamber is closed, the pupa digs its way out before molting.

## Snake flies

There are about 100 species in the family Raphidiidae of the order Raphidoptera. They range worldwide, except for Australia. Commonly known as snake flies, these land-dwelling insects are particularly common in Europe and North America. They measure 0.8 in. in length and have unusually long "necks," or prothoraxes (an extension of the first segment of the thorax). Their "necks" keep

their heads slightly raised in a snake-like fashion. Like alder flies and dobson flies, the snake flies have two pairs of heavily veined wings.

Fossilized remains of the snake flies suggest that they first appeared during the Carboniferous epoch 340 million years ago, and reached their evolutionary peak about 200 million years ago. Adult snake flies are predators with quick, sudden movements. They prefer plant lice, but also hunt insects, spiders and eggs, which they find under the bark of trees. When hunting, snake flies slowly stalk their victims and grasp them in their jaws. If the victims are large, the snake flies tear off their wings before eating the prey. When they have finished eating, the snake flies clean themselves scrupulously to get rid of any particles of food that remain on their feet, antennae or mouthparts.

As the female snake fly nears adulthood, she becomes an active hunter, sometimes preying on members of her own species—any male that approaches her at this time risks being eaten. After some weeks, the female's reproductive organs are completely formed and mature, and her hunger and aggression diminish. She then allows a male to approach her, even though the first encounter is aggressive.

Shortly after mating, the female seeks out a dead or decaying tree conifer in which she lays her eggs. The

**ABOVE** The common green lacewing is a nocturnal insect, instantly recognizable by its iridescent, membranous wings, green body and golden eyes. The wings contain specialized hearing organs inside the large veins that enable the lacewing to detect high-frequency sounds emitted by bats, one of their main enemies.

abdomen of the female is specially modified to form a long, slender, egg-laying tube, called an ovipositor. After finding a suitable tree, the female carefully examines each crevice in the bark with her ovipositor. Eventually, she finds a suitable crack and lays her eggs inside it in groups of 40-50. The larvae hatch out in July and feed initially on their own eggshells. They are long, agile creatures with biting mouthparts.

## Avoiding the cold

As winter arrives, the larvae congregate in sheltered places under the bark of trees, often in old tunnels vacated by wood-boring beetles. When the good weather returns, they resume their active life and molt once more. The larval stage lasts from one to two years, depending on the species and the climate.

After 10 or more molts, the larvae are ready to pupate. Each larva digs a hollow cavity in the bark of a tree, in which it molts into the first pupal stage

2569

## INSECTS CLASSIFICATION: 19

### Dobson flies and alder flies

The order Megaloptera contains about 260 species and is divided into two families inhabiting mainly temperate regions. The family Corydalidae (dobson flies) contains about 200 species; and the family Sialidae (alder flies) with 50-60 species in four genera.

### Snake flies

The snake flies belong to the order Raphidoptera. There are about 100 species found throughout the world, except Australia. They are particularly common in Europe and North America, and include the species *Raphidia notata*.

### Lacewings, mantis flies and ant lions

The order Neuroptera contains approximately 4500 species grouped into 16 families and three superfamilies. The family Coniopterygidae contains the smallest neuropterans, the dusty wings, of which there are more than 250 species worldwide. The superfamily Hemerobioidea has five families including the Sysyridae (spongilla flies) with 48 mostly tropical species; the Chrysopidae (green lacewings, such as the common green lacewing, *Chrysopa vulgaris*) containing over 1500 species in about 90 genera; the Mantispidae (mantis flies, such as *Mantispa syriaca*) of the tropics and subtropics; and the Osmylidae (lacewing-like insects, for example *Osmius fulvicephalus*) consisting of more than 100 species.

The superfamily Myrmeleontoidea includes the family Myrmeleontidae (ant lions, such as *Myrmeleon formicarius* and the giant ant lion, *Palpares libelluloides*) with more than 600 species in 300 genera found throughout hot and temperate regions; the family Ascalaphidae (owlflies) with some 400 species, mainly in temperate and warmer regions; and the family Nemopteridae containing about 130 species of spoon-winged lacewings (such as *Nemoptera sinuata*) and thread-winged lacewings from Africa, Asia and the Mediterranean.

without spinning a cocoon. Despite having limbs, the pupa lies motionless inside the pupal chamber. After 10 days, the pupa molts into a second, active pupa. The new pupa leaves its hiding place after a few days and runs nimbly over the bark before attaching itself to a tree trunk where it molts for the last time. Like the alder flies, adult snake flies only live for a short time.

### Deceptive mimicry

The 4500 species of the order Neuroptera group into 16 families, including the green lacewings, mantis flies and the spongilla flies. Ranging mainly through the tropics, the neuropterans differ widely in appearance, frequently mimicking other species of insect, such as butterflies, praying mantids or dragonflies. Neuropterans usually measure 0.2-2.8 in. in length and have a wingspan of 1-6 in. Their larvae are terrestrial predators, feeding with mouthparts that act as a sucking tube, taking in food by the action of a pump-like mechanism in the pharynx.

Adult neuropterans are almost all predacious in behavior and have chewing mouthparts. They are mainly active at dusk or during the night. The larvae not only differ widely from the adults in their appearance, but also in their habits—the newly hatched larvae of the spongilla flies, for example, are aquatic, while some mantis fly larvae live inside spider egg sacs, feeding on the developing eggs. The prominent differences in appearance between the larvae and the adults demonstrate that the members of the order Neuroptera are advanced in evolutionary terms. They usually undergo several molts from larva to adult. The adults have a relatively long life span and are not simply a reproductive stage.

### Dusty wings

The 250 species of the family Coniopterygidae include some of the smallest species of neuropterans. Ranging throughout the world, these 0.2-in.-long insects have a fine layer of white scales over their bodies and wings (their Greek classification name means "dusty wings"). Each microscopic scale is made of wax produced by glands all over the body.

Adult dusty wings are slow-moving creatures that feed on mites, red spiders, plant lice and the secretions of aphids. The larvae are fast-moving, also feeding on mites and aphids, and small insect eggs. Like the adults, the larvae have white, waxy scales on their bodies.

## Sponge eaters

The 48 species of the family Sysyridae, or spongilla flies, are the only neuropterans whose larvae are aquatic. The female spongilla fly lays her eggs in a silken net on branches overhanging water, so that the larvae fall into the water immediately after hatching. The larvae are green in color, growing to a length of about 0.2 in. They feed only on the body fluids of freshwater sponges, which they pierce with their slender sucking mouthparts.

When fully grown, the larvae have seven pairs of abdominal gills for breathing. They swim in a vertical position, using a snapping motion. Pupation occurs inside a double-walled, silken cocoon. Adult spongilla flies have black bodies and lacy, brown wings that rarely exceed 0.3 in. in length. They only take to the air at twilight, flying slowly through the aquatic foliage.

## Green lacewings

The 1500 species of green lacewings belong to the family Chrysopidae, meaning "golden eyes." They are delicate, green-bodied insects with four large, iridescent membranous wings supported by a network of blue-green veins. European lacewing species have a wingspan of 1.2 in. On other continents, the wings of lacewing species grow to twice that size.

Adult lacewings fly mainly at night and can be seen in the darkness because of their shining, gold-colored eyes. During the day, the lacewings remain hidden in the leaves of bushes. They are active predators, feeding on aphids, mites, small grubs and other small creatures. The long veins that pattern their wings contain hearing organs that can receive the short, high-frequency pips emitted by bats, thus allowing the insects to take evasive action.

## Human habitat

Green lacewings are sometimes attracted to houses by their electric lights, and may spend the winter inside, behind pictures or cupboards. Those individuals that winter indoors rarely eat and their greenish blue color is replaced by a reddish tint as their metabolism slows down, causing an increase in the number of red-pigmented cells. Species that live through the winter have an adult life cycle of up to eight months, while others only live for a month as adults.

Mating takes place at night, and the male dies shortly afterward. The female lives for another few weeks,

ABOVE Lacewings and their larvae are active predators of grubs, mites, aphids and other small creatures. The adults rest hidden in the foliage during the day and hunt at night.
BELOW The eggs of the green lacewing are laid in clusters on foliage where aphids feed. Each egg is attached to the plant by a thin thread that hardens rapidly on contact with the air. The function of this stalk is to hold the egg away from the surface of the leaf, thus protecting it from predation.

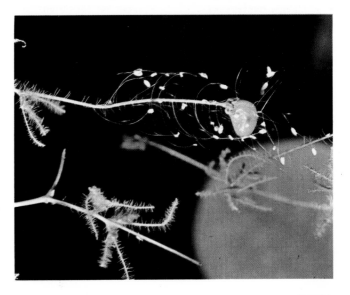

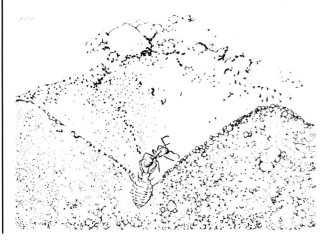

**ABOVE** The ant lion is inactive by day and vulnerable to predators, but its drab coloration provides good camouflage.
**BELOW** The ant lion larva leads a predatory life at the bottom of a conical, sandy pit. It digs the pit by moving backward in an ever-decreasing circle, flipping the sand out of the hole with quick movements of its head. The larva then buries most of its body in the sand, leaving only its large-jawed head protruding as it waits for passing insects or even large spiders to lose their grip on the pit walls and fall down into its clutches.

laying her eggs near colonies of aphids. She protects the eggs by attaching them to a leaf with a 0.2-in.-long thread. The female forms the thread by resting the tip of her abdomen on a leaf and squeezing out a sticky droplet of mucus. Then, she quickly raises the tip of her abdomen to draw the droplet out into a fine thread, to which she attaches her eggs. The thread hardens rapidly, forming a cluster of eggs that resembles a pincushion in appearance.

The larvae of green lacewings are predators of aphids. Using their sucking mouthparts, they feed on small insects and even practice cannibalism. Certain larval species camouflage themselves with hooked bristles on their backs, to which pieces of moss, lichen and grains of sand become attached. Those larvae that do not have spiny backs hide from predators under the empty skins of their prey. The larvae become adults after pupating in a silky cocoon.

The brown lacewings of the family Hemerobiidae have similar habits to those of the green lacewings. Like the green lacewings, their larvae feed on aphids and other plant suckers. In some species of brown lacewing, the adults' forewings resemble leaves in appearance. In times of danger, these insects fall to the ground and feign death. During the breeding season, the female lays up to 500 eggs, but, unlike those of the green lacewings, the eggs are laid singly on the underside of leaves or beneath the protective scale of scale insects.

## Mantis flies

Certain members of the order Neuroptera are famous for their resemblance to unrelated insects. The mantis flies, for example, resemble praying mantids. Measuring about 1.2 in. in length, they occur mainly in tropical regions of the world. Both praying mantids and mantis flies have large front legs that they fold toward their bodies like the closed blade of a clasp knife. Similarly, both hunt by ambushing their prey. Indeed, such is their close resemblance that only the long, membranous and thickly veined wings of the mantis flies distinguish them physically from their look-alikes.

After mating, the female lays up to 10,000 minute, oval-shaped eggs, each on its own tiny stalk. The larvae of the mantis flies bore into the egg sacs of spiders, where they molt into an immobile, maggot-like creature. The larvae remain within the egg sacs for several months, feeding on the developing spider eggs. Eventually, they spin themselves a cocoon inside the spider's empty egg sacs and molt into pupae. The pupae undergo a further molt into active second pupae, which break out of their cocoons and find a suitable place in which to metamorphose into adults.

## Lacewing-like insects

The 100 species of the family Osmylidae are similar to the lacewings in appearance; they differ in having three simple eyes at the front of their heads, as well as two large compound eyes. They cannot fly well and they live in the vegetation around running water.

The name Osmylidae comes from the Greek *osme* (odor) and refers to the fact that the males have two scent glands on their abdomen from which they release a smell to attract a female for mating. Following mating, the female lays small batches of cigar-shaped eggs on the side of vegetation near running water. The larvae are similar to those of the lacewings, but some are semiaquatic, feeding on the aquatic larvae of midges. When they pupate, the larvae break their long mouthparts in half.

## Ant lions

Ant lions are insects belonging to the family Myrmeleontidae within the order Neuroptera. Their name refers to their ferocious predatory behavior—ant lion larvae conceal themselves in pits where they lie in wait for small prey such as ants. They are short, fleshy creatures with large, spiny jaws. They prefer to live in soft, sandy soil—often at the foot of cliffs in places sheltered from the wind.

Adult ant lions bear a remarkable resemblance to dragonflies, but can be distinguished from them by their club-shaped antennae, closely veined wings and by the way they fold their wings when at rest. The weak-flying adults are only active after sunset, when they feed on fruit, small flies and the secretions of aphids.

## Death pits

The ant lion larva digs a funnel-shaped pit in soil with its back legs, throwing up the earth with violent, jerking movements of its body. The resulting hole is usually about 2 in. deep and 2-4 in. in diameter at its top. The ant lion lives at the bottom of its hole, hidden in the sand with only its long, powerful jaws protruding. When an ant or other small insect falls into the pit, the ant lion seizes it in its jaws. If the prey struggles a great deal, the ant lion hurls it against the wall of the pit, weakening it so that it puts up less resistance. If the prey attempts to climb back up the sides, the ant lion showers it with sand until it falls down onto the hole's bottom. The ant lion injects its captured prey first with a paralyzing poison—to immobilize it—and second with digestive fluid.

## Development and life cycle

From hatching until death at the end of adulthood, the ant lion lives for about three years. After mating, the female ant lion lays her eggs in loose clusters on sandy soil. The eggs are white and oval, with sticky surfaces that become encrusted with sand. Within a day of hatching, the young ant lion larvae dig pits for themselves. When the weather turns cold, they burrow into the subsoil. During their lengthy development, the larvae undergo three molts.

Ant lion larvae usually live through two winters. In the spring of the third year, they dig beneath the soil at the bottom of their pits and pupate inside spherical silk cocoons. The pupal stage lasts about a month, after which time the pupa cuts a hole in the cocoon with its jaws, and crawls partway out of the cocoon. The pupal skin splits and the emerging adult makes its way up to the surface of the soil.

## Owlflies

Owlflies comprise the 400 or so species of the family Ascalaphidae within the superfamily Myrmeleontoidea. Adult owlflies resemble butterflies since they have hairy bodies and large, brightly colored wings (usually black, with yellow or white markings). However, unlike butterflies, their wings are clearly veined and their mouthparts are adapted for a predatory life-style—butterflies are herbivores while owlflies are carnivorous. When hunting, owlflies hurl themselves at passing flying insects, grasp them tightly and kill them. When resting, owlflies fold their wings across the backs of their bodies.

After mating, the female owlfly lays a double row of 80-100 eggs on a blade of grass. The larvae resemble those of the ant lion, but are shorter and fatter with very short legs. Owlfly larvae have natural bristles on their backs: although the bristles sometimes function as decoration, the larvae more often use them to trap particles of soil for camouflage purposes.

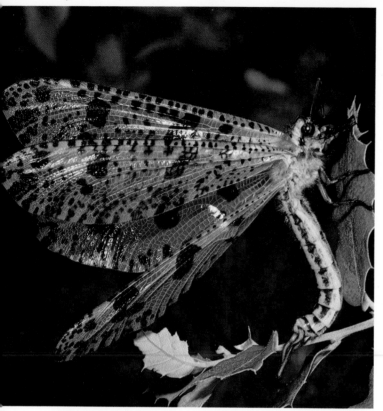

## Spoon-winged and thread-winged lacewings

Spoon-winged and thread-winged lacewings inhabit the hottest parts of Africa, Asia and the Mediterranean. About 130 species belong to the family Nemopteridae with the superfamily Myrmeleontoidea. Lacewings possess hugely elongated hind wings that resemble strands of wire or ribbons. The hind wings do not move during flight, but trail out behind the insects. Lacewings usually fly at twilight, although some emerge in dry cellars or caves during the day.

## True scorpion flies

Only males of the family Panorpidae (order Mecoptera) are true scorpion flies. The name "scorpion fly" refers to the upturned and enlarged tips of the males' abdomens, which are similar in appearance to scorpion tails. Scorpion flies have slender bodies with two pairs of long, membranous, patterned wings. Their heads extend into downward-pointing beaks with biting mouthparts at their tips. Scorpion flies usually live in vegetation at the edge of woods. Since they are poor fliers they seldom rise more than a few yards from the ground. They eat live insects, fresh insect corpses and rotting animal and vegetable matter.

Before mating, scorpion flies perform a courtship ritual in which a male approaches a female, placing a drop of sweet, sticky saliva before her. While the female feeds on the fluid, the male grasps her from the side and mates with her. Some species of scorpion flies mate for hours, the males continually depositing drops of saliva to subdue their mates. A few days after fertilization, the female lays her eggs in a damp and sheltered place. The larvae that hatch resemble bristly caterpillars. They burrow into loose soil, and, like their parents, eat dead animal and vegetable matter. Scorpion fly larvae molt between five and seven times before pupating just below the surface of the soil. After about three weeks, the pupae crawl up to the surface to allow adult scorpion flies to emerge from their skins.

**ABOVE LEFT** The giant ant lion has a wingspan of approximately 6 in., and the wings are decorated with dark brown flecks. The insect is active only at dusk or at night, feeding on fruit, small flies and aphid honeydew.

**LEFT** The butterfly-like owlflies are closely related to the ant lions, but in contrast to them, the owlflies are good fliers and are active during the day.

## Hanging scorpion flies

Hanging scorpion flies inhabit many regions of the world and resemble huge mosquitoes. The yellowish brown adults have elongated snouts with chewing mouthparts, long thread-like antennae and four pairs of membranous wings that fold across the back when at rest. Most species are nocturnal, living hidden in grass where they hang from vegetation with their forelegs and sway freely in the breeze—hence their name. While hanging, the scorpion flies seize small prey—such as flies and aphids—with their hind legs.

## Snow scorpion flies

Snow scorpion flies live in northern Europe and America. As their name suggests, they rest and move about on the surface of snow. They build their nests in moss and feed on dead or wounded insects. Adult snow scorpion flies are tiny, dark-colored insects that resemble larval grasshoppers, hopping about on their long hind legs. In both sexes, the wings are under-developed: females' wings form small, scale-like structures, while the males have finely spined wings.

## Twisted-winged parasites

Twisted-winged parasites inhabit all regions of the world except the Arctic, making up the 300 species of

**ABOVE** The scorpion fly (such as *Panorpa communis* seen here) is a carnivorous insect with primitive biting mouthparts located at the tip of a beak-like elongation of its head. It lives mainly in cool, damp woodlands, feeding on live and dead insects, as well as on rotting vegetation.

the order Strepsiptera. They vary in length from 0.04 to 0.2 in. The females of all species live parasitically, inside the bodies of insects.

Male and female strepsipterans differ greatly in both appearance and life-style. The males are biologically independent creatures with comb-shaped antennae and large eyes. Their hind wings are large, fan-like and membranous, while their forewings are reduced to short, stiff, club-shaped structures. During flight, male strepsipterans use their forewings as rudders to steer themselves through the air. When the males die, their forewings dry out and twist into spirals—hence the name "twisted-winged parasite." Adult male strepsipterans live for only 10 hours or so, spending most of their short lives darting through the air with their abdomens curled upward and the front parts of their bodies held vertically.

Female twisted-winged parasites are wingless, grub-like creatures that live as parasites within the bodies of insect hosts. Their respiratory, circulatory and

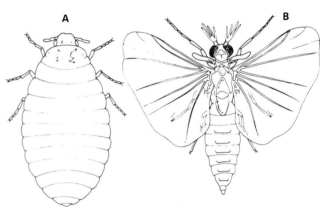

LEFT The male scorpion fly is easily distinguished from the female by the bulbous, glossy-brown clasping organs at the end of his body which he holds high over his abdomen.
ABOVE The female strepsipteran spends her entire life within an insect host and therefore has a wingless, grub-like body (A). The free-living male strepsipteran (B) has comb- or fan-shaped antennae with which he smells scent released by the female, and large membranous hind wings for flight.

---

## INSECTS CLASSIFICATION: 20

### Scorpion flies

The order Mecoptera contains about 400 species of scorpion flies, divided into eight families. These insects, which make up one of the most primitive orders, occur mostly in cool, moist regions of the world. The families include the Panorpidae (true scorpion flies); the Bittacidae (hanging scorpion flies); and the Boreidae (snow scorpion flies) of northern Europe and North America.

### Strepsipterans

The strepsipterans belong to the order Strepsiptera that contains about 300 species of tiny parasitic insects living all over the world, except in the Arctic regions. Their classification is continually being revised, but it is currently divided into seven families. One of them is the Stylopidae that parasitizes certain bees and wasps.

nervous systems are greatly reduced and many of their sensory organs are underdeveloped or missing— female strepsipterans have no eyes or mouth, for example. Females of the strepsipteran species *Stylopidae* attach themselves to the abdomens of bees or wasps. Although the insect host seldom dies, its appearance alters and it becomes sterile. The female strepsipteran burrows almost completely into the body of her host, protruding only slightly from between its abdominal plates.

As she is almost invisible, the female strepsipteran emits a special scent to attract males for mating. The male injects his sperm through a small hole between the female's thorax and abdomen; he dies shortly afterward. The fertilized eggs develop inside the female strepsipteran and, after a few days, between 1000 and 2000 larvae hatch out. The larvae are tiny (approximately 0.01 in. in length), with mouths, eyes and three pairs of legs that end in suckers. They leave their mother's body through an opening on her back, living on the host insect until it reaches a flower. The strepsipteran larvae then climb onto the flower and await the arrival of another bee, which carries them back to its nest. Once inside the nest, the strepsipterans parasitize the bee larvae and begin their parasitic life cycle once again.

# PORTABLE HOMES

Caddis flies are night-flying insects that haunt the areas around freshwater where they lay their eggs; their larvae live underwater and often build themselves mobile, protective cases made of shells, sand and silk

C addis flies first appeared some 280 million years ago and are among the oldest insect groups to undergo complete metamorphosis (developing from an egg, through a distinct larval and pupal stage, into an adult). Fossil evidence suggests that butterflies and moths evolved from them approximately 100 million years later.

There are over 7000 species of caddis flies, and they have changed very little in the last 280 million years. Although they are found almost everywhere in the world, there are only minor variations between adults of the different species. Adult caddis flies closely resemble small moths and are thought to be their early ancestors. The larvae are completely aquatic, living in silken tubes that they spin themselves—setting them apart from the other insect orders.

Like all other insects that mature by complete metamorphosis, caddis flies have an egg, larval, pupal and adult stage. Most caddis fly larvae spin silk tubes to protect themselves, decorating them with stones, plant

**ABOVE** The caddis fly larva of the genus *Limnophilus* builds its underwater case from the empty shells of various mollusks, bits of wood, plant stems and silk that it spins.
**FAR RIGHT** The adult caddis fly *Limnophilus rhombicus* is a moth-like nocturnal creature. Since its mouthparts are adapted for sucking, it can only feed on the sweet liquids that ooze from plants.
**PAGE 2577** Caddis flies form a vital part of the food chain—together with mosquitoes, dragonflies and other insects, they and their larvae provide food for birds and fishes.

matter or snail shells. Some species do not build protective cases, but construct nets in which to catch plankton or crustaceans.

Although the adult caddis flies of different species are similar in appearance, they vary greatly in size. Some "micro" species only reach 0.06 in. in length, while others can grow up to 2.4 in. They have two pairs of wings that are covered in small hairs, giving them the order name Trichoptera (from the Greek *trichos* meaning "hair" and *pteron* meaning "wing").

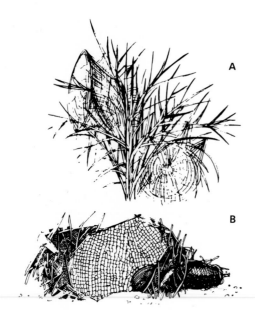

ABOVE Most caddis fly larvae feed on particles of organic matter that are carried along by the current of the river in which they live. In order to catch as much passing food as possible, the larvae have evolved various methods of trapping it. Some species, such as the net spinners, build circular webs (A) that not only catch more food, but — depending on the size of the web's mesh — only net particles of a specific size. Other larvae stretch nets between the cases in which they live and aquatic vegetation (B).

## INSECTS CLASSIFICATION: 21

### Caddis flies

Caddis flies form the medium-sized order Trichoptera with some 7000 species in 650 genera. The order is divided into three superfamilies, widespread throughout the world, except for the Antarctic region. The superfamily Rhyacophiloidea has 1600 species in four families. These include two primitive, free-living families that do not build purse cases: the Rhyacophilidae (with 450 species); and the Hydrobiosidae (with 150 species). The family Glossosomatidae (saddle-case makers) has 400 species around the world; and the Hydroptilidae (purse-case makers) has 600 species worldwide.

The other two caddis fly superfamilies are the Hydropsychoidea (net-spinning caddis flies, such as the great red sedge of Britain), which contains eight families; and the Limnephiloidea (tube-making caddis flies) with 27 families. These include the Limnephilidae, whose 1000 species are spread throughout the cooler areas of the world; and the Chathamiidae, whose four species live along the coasts of southeast Australia and New Zealand, the Chatham Islands (500 miles east of New Zealand) and the Kermadec Islands.

In some species, the hairs on the wings cause light to diffract, making the wings shimmer with iridescence. When the wings change their angle in relation to the light, they shine through a range of silky browns to black. Some species have yellow or orange markings, while others have silver streaks on their wings. Caddis flies are usually weak fliers and only fly if threatened or during the mating season. In some species, the females have become wingless or possess only rudimentary wings.

Caddis flies (particularly the males) have large, spherical, compound eyes on either side of their heads, usually with three simple eyes situated between them. They have long, thread-like antennae that they hold in front of their bodies when resting. Their mouthparts vary from species to species. In some species they do not function at all, while in others they are used for chewing or biting.

### A short adult life

Adult caddis flies have a short life span that may last for just a few days or a few weeks, depending on the species. During their adult lives, caddis flies have to struggle against considerable odds in order to stay alive. They are almost completely defenseless, relying on camouflage for safety, and their chosen habitat restricts their movements. Despite their wide geographical distribution, they are only found in large numbers in areas with streams, rivers or swamps that have banks covered in thick vegetation.

The adult caddis flies are most active at dusk and occasionally at dawn. When they fly, caddis flies hook their wings together, enabling both pairs of wings to move as one. Hooked plates attach onto horn-like spines arranged like the teeth of a comb so that the wings hold together even when caught by a sudden gust of wind.

ABOVE Caddis fly larvae camouflage themselves with a variety of natural materials. Some species build their "homes" from pieces of leaf material, others use twigs, snail shells and seed pods. Each family employs its own distinctive camouflage methods.

# PORTABLE HOMES

## A brief mating dance

During the reproductive period, which occurs shortly after the adults emerge, male caddis flies form small swarms and fly about, darting in and out of the vegetation. They search for the females, who wait among the foliage. Once found, the females join in the flight and perform an aerial dance during which they fly about erratically. The insects then mate, usually when the pair are safely settled on a plant stem. Very occasionally mating takes place during flight. Almost all caddis flies lay eggs (they are oviparous).

A few hours after mating, the female travels to a stem or stone jutting out above the water and, thrusting her abdomen into the water, lays her small, pale blue-green or whitish eggs. The eggs are sometimes encased in a long thread of jelly or they may be covered in a hard, cement-like substance that adheres firmly to the chosen substrate, usually a rock or the stem of an aquatic plant. In some species, the female's external skeleton is waterproof, enabling her to swim underwater. She uses her specially adapted middle legs to reach the bottom, and lays her eggs in the crevices between pebbles or between the roots of water plants.

## Distinctive cases

Caddis fly larvae are aquatic and usually build a silken case which they camouflage with sand, tiny pebbles, or pieces of plant debris. The shape of their cases, and the materials they choose for camouflage, are typical of the different species and help entomologists identify them.

Caddis flies overwinter as larvae and pupate in the spring. They usually emerge as adults in the early summer. Unlike the adults, which vary little in appearance from species to species, caddis fly larvae differ greatly in appearance, depending on the wide variety of ecological conditions in which they develop. Studies of the larvae have made it possible to divide the species into three clearly distinguishable super-families: the Rhyacophiloidea, or torrent lovers; the Hydropsychoidea, or net-spinning caddis flies; and the Limnephiloidea, or tube-case-making caddis flies.

The majority of species belonging to the superfamily Rhyacophiloidea (or torrent lovers as they are collectively, if slightly inaccurately, known) occur near running waters, although not all require it to complete their life cycle. The superfamily Rhyacophiloidea is divided into four families: the Rhyacophilidae and the Hydrobiosidae, both of which are free-living families that do not build purse cases; the Glossosomatidae, known as the saddle-case makers, and the Hydroptilidae, or purse-case makers. Each family has distinctive feeding and case-making habits. They are found throughout the world.

## Predatory torrent lovers

Of the 1600 species of the superfamily Rhyacophiloidea, 600 are free-living torrent lovers that build makeshift shelters immediately before they pupate. The 600 species belong to two families of predatory caddis flies, both of which feed on small water creatures. Most members of the two families do not exceed 0.3 in. in length.

## Saddle-case and purse-making caddis flies

The larvae of saddle-case caddis flies (family Glossosomatidae) develop inside dome-shaped silk cases. Small stones cover each larval case, providing the occupant with effective camouflage and armor. The bottom of each case is flat and contains two holes through which freshwater flows, allowing the larva to breathe and feed.

Purse-making caddis flies belong to the family Hydroptilidae and inhabit rivers, streams and still

2581

pools in most regions of the world. They are unique among caddis flies since their larvae undergo a process called heteromorphosis—creatures with heteromorphic development pass through two or more distinct larval forms. Purse-making caddis flies have two types of larvae: the first is a free-living animal that does not construct a silk tube around itself. The initial stage lasts from hatching through four larval molts, during which time the larva feeds on algae and minute single-cell organisms. In the final larval stage, the larva's body changes shape as its abdomen grows to a large size and becomes flattened. The enlarged larva builds a silk tube that resembles a purse, having a hinged opening at its front end. Most species drag their "purses" with them when they move about as protection from predators.

## Net-spinning caddis flies

The net-spinning caddis flies comprise the superfamily Hydropsychoidea—a major group within the order Trichoptera. They comprise some 2040 species that inhabit both fast-moving and still waters in all regions of the world. Unlike the mobile larvae of the purse-makers, net-spinning caddis fly larvae are stationary animals. They spend their larval lives in shelters that they construct from plant scraps, sand or bits of invertebrate shell, sealing them together with silk.

Net-spinning caddis fly larvae construct silk nets that channel food particles into their shelters. Diets vary

TOP A caddis fly larva pokes its head out of its protective case. Despite its cumbersome appearance, the case is lightweight and portable, allowing its occupant enough freedom to move about in search of food.
ABOVE Despite the fact that they seldom venture outside their protective cases, caddis fly larvae have developed several adaptations to life in fast-flowing water. The primitive, torrent-dwelling species of caddis fly larva shown here has tuft-like gills running down the sides of its thorax and abdomen. The larva anchors itself to the riverbed with a pair of prolegs that are located at the tip of its abdomen.

among species, since each species uses a different sized net and thereby controls the type of food entering its shelter. Some species of net-spinning caddis fly larvae spin narrow, silk-lined tunnels for food capture—one family constructs tunnels that stretch above the water line onto the damp soil of the stream's bank.

## The great red sedge

Britain's largest species of caddis fly is a net-spinner of the superfamily Hydropsychoidea. Fishermen have named the insect the great red sedge—"great," since it has a wingspan of over 0.2 in. The insect is a drab, smoky-brown color. Like most adult caddis flies, it sips fluids since it cannot bite or chew. The great red sedge is often attracted to moth traps at night.

The adult female great red sedge can lay as many as 700 eggs in one batch, twisting her abdomen so as to attach them to the underside of a floating leaf or other piece of vegetable material. The eggs are small, green and covered in a thick band of jelly-like substance. After about 10 days, the eggs hatch into great red sedge larvae that immediately swim to the bottom of the stream. On the streambed, each larva covers its soft body with a layer of silk, to which it sticks pieces of plant material and sometimes algae. The larvae take great care in selecting the building materials for their cases: usually, they choose pieces similar in size to each other and attach them to their silk coverings in a regular pattern. A typical larval case has a series of concentric circles running along its length.

A fully grown great red sedge larva measures about 1.4 in. in length. Immediately before pupation, the larva burrows below the surface of the streambed, sealing itself beneath the mud. Unlike most caddis fly pupae, the fully matured great red sedge pupa does not possess functioning jaws; thus it wriggles, rather than bites, its way out of its muddy burrow. Upon its emergence from the mud, the pupa swims to the water's surface and climbs onto a plant stem so that the adult caddis fly can emerge in the open air. Once it is secure on a suitable surface, the pupa splits along its back, enabling the adult caddis fly to crawl out and expand its wings.

## Tube-making caddis flies

The largest group of caddis flies belongs to the superfamily Limnephilidae—the tube-makers. Tube-making caddis flies occur throughout the world and comprise approximately 3360 species that are divided into 27 families. The Limnephilidae contains the largest of all caddis flies. Since the tube-making

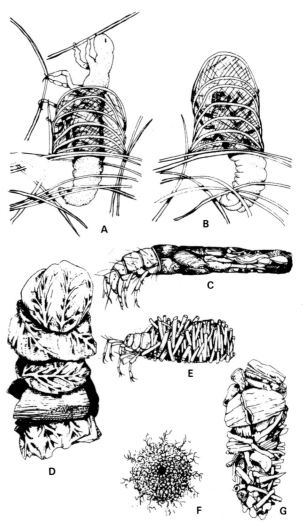

RIGHT Each species of caddis fly larva builds its own type of protective case; the design of a case depends upon the speed of water flow. Cases are constructed from small pieces of river debris and stones and are fastened together with a glue-like larval secretion. The drawings show two stages in the development of a larval case (A) and (B); the protective case of the species *Halesus digitatus* (C) and the leafy shelter of a *Nemotaulius punctatolineatus* larva (D). Drawings (E), (F) and (G) illustrate various protective cases of different *Limnophilus* species.

**ABOVE A caddis fly larva of the primitive species *Limnophilus rhombicus* in its protective case. The larva anchors itself inside the case with its prolegs—a pair of small legs at the tip of its abdomen. When it is disturbed the larva withdraws inside its case. ABOVE RIGHT Some species of caddis fly larvae form communities, gathering together in large numbers under stones and riverbanks. Although zoologists cannot explain the communal behavior of caddis fly larvae, they believe it is related to food availability. Members of the communal species shown here build their protective cases with tiny river stones. Since the case surfaces are very hard-wearing, the larvae have strong mouthparts to bite their way out after pupation.**

caddis flies are a very large group, its various species of larvae differ greatly in both form and life-style. Nevertheless, the larvae of most species construct silk tubes and cover them in a variety of animal, vegetable or mineral scraps.

## Mud-loving caddis flies

The mud-loving caddis flies are an important family, containing over 1000 species that are distributed throughout most countries, in a wide variety of habitats. Some species occur in habitats that are typical of other species of caddis flies, for example, streams and lakes, while others prefer temporary pools and a few species can even survive in brackish water. Mud-loving caddis fly larvae construct a variety of distinctive protective cases: some use spiral designs; others build with straight lengths of plant stems; and many use sand, pebbles and leaves in the construction of their cases.

## Saltwater caddis flies

The family Chathamiidae (named after the Chatham Islands in the South Pacific Ocean) contains four marine species of caddis fly that live along the coasts of southeast Australia and New Zealand. Since their eggs hatch in seawater starfishes, caddis flies of the family Chathamiidae have one of the most unusual life cycles of all the caddis flies, and possibly in the entire class Insecta.

Adult Chathamiidae caddis flies live and breed among marine plants that grow near to the intertidal zone. At low tide, the fertilized female flies out to rock pools and searches for a suitable starfish in which to deposit her eggs. The female injects her eggs into a starfish's body cavity through her specially adapted egg-laying tube or ovipositor. Soon after hatching, the young larvae leave their temporary host and develop as free-living creatures in rock pools, where they feed on calcereous marine algae.

# FLUTTERING JEWELS

Butterflies fly on shimmering wings from one nectar-rich flower to the next, attracting mates and even startling predators. Night-flying moths detect high-frequency sounds in order to escape their enemies

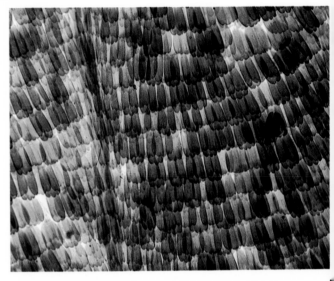

Butterflies and moths belong to the order Lepidoptera, the second-largest order in the animal kingdom, containing approximately 136,800 species. All lepidopterans have four wings covered in flat, powdery scales and mouthparts consisting of a sucking proboscis. However, it is difficult to classify butterflies and moths into distinct, consistent and accurate groups. The insects have many physical characteristics to take into account—for example, variations in wings, antennae, mouthparts, legs, reproductive organs and types of caterpillar—and entomologists disagree over the relative importance of the various features.

One of the oldest methods that has been used classifies the order into two groups: the day-flying butterflies and the night-flying moths. Unfortunately, the system is inaccurate because there are hundreds of species of day-flying moth. Another convenient but imprecise classification divides the insects into small moths (microlepidoptera) and large butterflies and moths (macrolepidoptera). However, with increased knowledge of the order, it is now possible to make a more detailed classification of the butterflies and moths, and at present the order Lepidoptera consists of five main groups, or suborders.

Butterflies and moths range throughout the world, but they are at their most numerous and most beautiful in the hot and humid tropical forests of South America and Southeast Asia. There is, however, no lack of butterflies and moths in the more temperate countries. Although they are smaller and less strikingly colored in cooler climates, they are still considered the "living jewels" of the countryside they inhabit. Some species even survive in cold climates, up to 20,000 ft. above sea level in the Himalayas.

**ABOVE LEFT** Unlike butterflies, moths have a variety of antennae shapes. The antennae of male gypsy moths extend into large, feather-shaped structures that detect a wide range of sound vibrations.

**ABOVE** The patterns of colors on the wings of butterflies and moths have two origins: color pigments in the scales on the wings transmit many colors, while other colors are caused by light refraction in special prism-like wing scales. The beautiful blue South American *Morpho* butterflies, for example, possess 35,000 refractive scales per square inch of wing—each scale measures approximately 0.00003 in. in diameter. In the 1980s, zoologists found evidence to suggest that *Morpho* butterfly scales are liquid, rather than solid crystals.

**PAGE 2585** A moth of the species *Parnassius apollo* hovers above a flowering plant. The species inhabits the mountainous regions of Europe and is common in Spain and Scandinavia.

## Form and function

Butterflies and moths vary considerably in size. Their body length can range between 0.4 and 4 in., and their wingspan can vary from 0.08 to 12 in. The area of their wings can differ greatly, too. In the smaller species, the wings can be as small as 0.05 sq. in., while in the huge tropical species, it can reach over 40 sq. in. The weight of butterflies and moths ranges up to about an ounce.

## Butterfly "dust"

All species of butterfly and moth have a dense covering of tiny, bristle-like hairs all over their bodies, giving them a velvety appearance. The hairs are flatter and shorter on the insects' wings—more like scales. They connect to the insect's wing by means of a thin

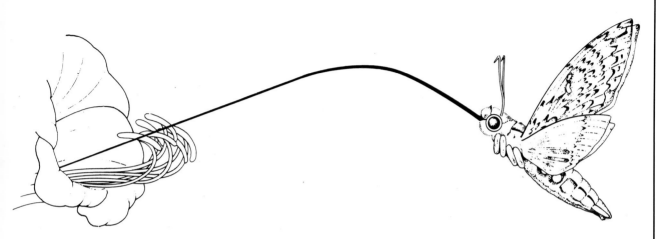

**ABOVE Most primitive species of moths suck food through feeding tubes. Some species, such as this Madagascan hawk moth, draw nectar through extremely long sucking tubes, or proboscises. Darwin predicted the existence of this type of moth before it was discovered, since only a creature of this kind could pollinate a particular variety of orchid.**

stalk that fits loosely into a socket on the wing. The scales are often brilliantly colored and are arranged in numerous patterns.

Butterflies and moths use their colorful scales for defense and as scent distributors for mating. If the wing is roughly handled, the minute scales come off. Some moths make use of this characteristic to escape from the webs of spiders. Instead of the moth's body sticking to the web, only its scales are trapped, leaving the insect free to fly away. Some males have tufts of hair on their wings, which they use to waft an attractive smell called a pheromone into the air where it will, hopefully, be picked up by a female.

Butterflies and moths have small heads that are usually well defined and separate from their thoraxes. On either side of their heads, they have two large, compound eyes. Some species may have as many as 6000 lenses in each eye. In addition to their compound eyes, some moths have a pair of ocelli, or simple eyes, situated midway between their compound eyes. The simple eyes may help regulate the sensitivity of the moth's compound eyes to varying light levels.

Although butterflies and moths are unable to focus on any object that is more than about an inch away from them, their eyes do have one advantage over the human eye. Humans cannot see ultraviolet light at the far blue end of the spectrum, whereas butterflies and moths can. With this ability, the insects can see patterns on the petals of flowers that remain hidden to humans. The patterns help the insects to identify the plants and guide them toward their nectar-producing parts.

### Homing scent detectors

Butterflies and moths have a pair of fairly long antennae in between and slightly above their compound eyes. They use their antennae—which can be thread-like, club-like, key-like or feather-like—to smell the air around them. In some species, the male's antennae are much larger than the female's, and they have comb-like fronds with which the insect detects small amounts of the female's sex pheromone. The antennae have highly sensitive nerve receptors all over them, and the males use them first to pick up the smell of the female and then to home in on her. Females, by contrast, use their antennae to locate suitable plants on which to lay their eggs, and to detect temperatures and tastes.

Only a few primitive moths have retained their chewing mouthparts, with which they feed on pollen. Among the rest of the lepidopterans, the mouthpart has evolved into a retractable, drinking-straw-like apparatus situated under the insect's head. Called a proboscis, the feeding tube is one of the most typical features of the butterflies and moths. It varies substantially in length, and when not in use the insect coils it up between its two protective mouthparts.

Most butterflies have long, thin proboscises that are designed for sucking the nectar out of flowers. Among moths, however, the proboscises have taken on a variety

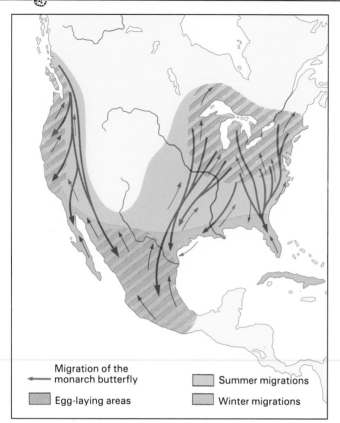

Migration of the monarch butterfly

Egg-laying areas

Summer migrations

Winter migrations

of forms. Certain hawk moths, for example, have short, robust proboscises for penetrating the wax walls of bees' combs in order to drink the honey. Some species have incredibly long proboscises—sometimes reaching a length of 8 in. Others have sharp ones for piercing the skin of prey animals in order to drink their blood. Members of the silk-moth family (as well as others) have fused mouthparts that can no longer be used for feeding.

In only a few species of butterfly and moth is the female wingless. Almost all species have two pairs of wings that are covered in scales and come in a variety of shapes and sizes. Some are simply lobe-shaped, while others are leaf-like, triangular, plumed or tailed. They are held together during flight by several different systems. In the more primitive species, a simple lobe on the forewing synchronizes the wings. In the more advanced species, a system of hooks and catches holds the wings together.

Most butterflies hold their wings tightly together and vertically to their bodies when they are at rest. Moths usually rest with their wings horizontal to their

ABOVE The map marks the migrations of the monarch butterfly. The purple areas indicate the regions where the butterflies lay their eggs and where the new generation develops. Monarchs spend the summer in the brown shaded area and winter in the green areas.
BELOW The migrations of many species of butterflies and moths are one-way journeys, since they are unable to cope with the extreme cold of the northern European winters.

The offspring of the painted lady species (red line) journey southward, while their parent generation perishes in the cold weather in the north. The silver "Y" moth (green line) migrates north and produces a second generation that usually dies before it can travel south. Both the clouded yellow butterfly (blue line) and the convolvulus hawk moth (purple line) make return migrations from more southerly regions.

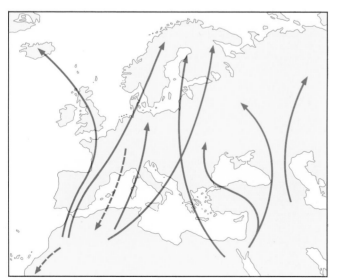

Painted lady

Convolvulus hawk moth

Clouded yellow butterfly

Silver "Y" moth

bodies and at a slight angle. Apart from their wings, butterflies and moths have three pairs of legs on their thoraxes. Most species have simple walking legs. Some have special tufts attached to their legs.

The final segment of an insect's body is called its abdomen. Among butterflies and moths, the abdomen consists of 10 similar segments. Unlike the thorax, it does not have wings or legs attached to it. The abdomen's main role is to house the digestive and reproductive organs. Different parts of the reproductive system are visible externally in different families of butterfly and moth—which makes these organs a useful means of identifying the families. In the males, a pair of claspers is often visible. The insects use them to hold on to the bodies of the females during mating. The females possess an extensible tube called an ovipositor, which they use to lay eggs within cracks in the bark of trees.

Butterflies and moths have an internal anatomy similar to that of other insects. However, their respiratory system is particularly well developed. Each insect usually has nine pairs of breathing outlets called

**RIGHT** All butterflies and moths pass through four distinct stages of development: the egg, caterpillar (the larval stage), pupa and adult; insects with a four-stage development undergo "complete" metamorphosis. Gypsy moths lay their eggs on plants, which provide food for the newly hatched caterpillar (top). A caterpillar's most important activity is eating—for this reason it has a soft, elastic skin that expands as the body fills with food (center). After several molts, the caterpillar pupates, having reached full growth (bottom). After some time, the adult insect, or imago, emerges from the pupa to begin a new life cycle.

**BELOW** The drawings illustrate the sequence of stages in the transformation of a caterpillar to a pupa (left to right).

# BUTTERFLIES AND MOTHS
## — MIGRATORS AND MARCHERS —

Many species of butterflies and moths undertake long migrations from one area to another. The distances covered can range from 100 miles to over 600 miles. The exact reasons for these great treks are still unclear, although climatic changes, such as those that occur during summer and winter, almost certainly play a major part.

Some of the most attractive butterflies and moths to occur in Britain are, in fact, migrants from continental Europe and North Africa. As the temperature rises in the south, and available food becomes more scarce, large numbers of insects move north to the cooler and more lush regions.

### The migrating monarch

The most famous migratory butterfly is probably the monarch of North America. It is a large butterfly whose bright orange wings with black and white markings warn predators of its poisonous nature.

Although it is native to North America, the monarch has become far more widespread as a result of its migratory habits. During the summer, monarch butterflies live and breed around the Hudson Bay area of northern Canada and in southern Canada. As autumn draws on, they start the long journey down to the warmer climate of Florida and Mexico, and the islands of the Caribbean, traveling up to 2000 miles or more. Here they

overwinter in huge numbers, usually resting on the same trees each season— their wings resembling bright orange leaves. So predictable is their migration pattern that hotels have been built near their roosting sites, and thousands of people flock to see them every year. At the end of winter, they start on the return journey north.

### Migrant hawk moths

Moths also migrate. However, they are not normally seen doing so, since the event either takes place at night or they migrate individually. The hawk moths are among the most successful of these migrants, equipped with strong muscles for flying and a streamlined shape. One of them—the hummingbird

*hawk moth—is a frequent visitor to the British Isles. It begins its migration from southern Europe and North Africa at the beginning of spring each year, and arrives in Britain in the early summer.*

*Several other species of moths have gregarious caterpillars, such as the camp-forming larvae of the tussock and eggar moths. The larvae of some butterflies are also gregarious in the early stages of their development.*

### The African army worm

*The caterpillars of some species gather together in such large numbers that they represent a major threat to crops. The most important of these is the common or African army worm— the caterpillar of the night-flying moth,* Pseudaletia unipuncta. *These caterpillars march in columns up to 13 ft. long and 3 in. wide, and appear in such numbers that they rival locusts in the amount of damage they do to crops.*

FAR LEFT **Like other members of its family, the convolvulus hawk moth is a strong flier. Every year it flies from North Africa to Scandinavia—a distance of some 2000 miles Zoologists do not understand the reasons for migration, but it is possible that convolvulus hawk moths migrate to find the best feeding grounds and to distribute their population.**

NEAR LEFT **Although it is fragile in appearance, the hummingbird hawk moth survives the rigors of a long migration, traveling from North Africa to northern Europe for the summer.**

TOP **The beautiful red admiral butterfly arrives in Europe in spring and produces a second generation before the end of summer. Unfortunately, as with most migrant species, red admiral butterflies cannot survive the cold European winters.**

RIGHT **Caterpillars of the pine processionary moths live in small, silk-covered communities. Many caterpillar species group together in large flocks capable of destroying entire crop fields.**

spiracles, with two pairs located on its thorax and the rest on its abdomen. Minute tubes that spread throughout the insect's body connect the holes and diffuse oxygen and carbon dioxide from the blood.

The reproductive and circulatory systems of butterflies and moths are essentially the same as in other insects, although some species of moth are thought to reproduce parthenogenetically (without mating).

## The caterpillar stage

A caterpillar is the name usually given to the larval stage of a lepidopteran. Caterpillars have simple bodies, since their main task in life is to eat as much as they can before pupating. Like the adults, they have bodies that are divided into three regions: the head, the three thoracic segments and the 10 abdominal segments.

The caterpillar's head is enclosed in a tough, hardened (sclerotized) shell that bears a number of sensory structures and appendages. Usually, it has a pair of powerful jaws for cutting, and in some species grinding, the food on which it lives. On either side of its mandibles, a caterpillar has short antennae. Behind them it has simple eyes, or celli. Most caterpillars have six eyes on either side of their heads.

Above and below its jaws, the caterpillar has lips that serve several functions. The upper lip, or labrum, is mainly a sensory organ. The lower lip, or labium, has taste-sensitive palps attached to it, and it carries the spinnerets from which caterpillars produce silk. Caterpillars that live in rolled-up leaves use the silk as a binding agent. Other species use it to build a platform from which to hang when they molt. Silkworms use the silk to build a cocoon. Others use it as an escape line in times of danger.

A caterpillar's body is roughly cylindrical in shape, with three pairs of legs on its thorax. Most caterpillars use their true legs for guiding food into their mouths. They use the five pairs of "prolegs" on their abdomens for walking. The prolegs are attached to their third, fourth, fifth, sixth and tenth abdominal segments. They are usually fleshy, with a series of hooks on their base. Caterpillars also use their prolegs for gripping, and they are capable of holding on with such force that it is almost impossible to pick them up

LEFT Caterpillars of the small tortoiseshell butterfly live and feed on nettles, forming communities of several dozen individuals. Stiff body hairs protect the caterpillars from predators.

without tearing them. The last two prolegs on the final segment of the caterpillar's abdomen are called anal claspers. The insect usually uses them to hold on to twigs or stems, but the claspers can be used as defense organs in some species, such as the whips found in the puss moth caterpillar.

## Offense, defense and bribery

Caterpillars are usually slow-moving animals, incapable of escaping from enemies by running for cover. To avoid being caught by one of their numerous predators, they have evolved many different defense mechanisms. Some of the caterpillar's simplest defense mechanisms merely involve playing dead or dropping suddenly to the ground from the plant on which it is feeding.

The caterpillar's most common tactic is to rely on camouflage. It is not a coincidence that the majority of leaf-eating caterpillars are green, while those that spend most of their time on bark are brown. Some larger species even change color as they mature. When they are young, they match the color of the plants on which they feed; as they become fatter and longer, they develop bands that break up the outline of their bodies.

Some species of caterpillar have bodies that are slightly lighter in color on the lower half than they are on the upper half. The tonal variations cancel out any shadows that could reveal their presence. Other species have hairs or lobes of skin running down the length of their bodies to enable them to merge in with their surroundings.

## Twig-like species

Certain species of caterpillar resemble small, inedible twigs in order to deter would-be predators. Members of the family Geometridae have become masters of this form of camouflage. To enhance their twig-like appearance, geometrid caterpillars typically have only two pairs of prolegs and lumps and bumps along their bodies.

Not all caterpillars attempt to look invisible. Some advertise their presence as much as possible with their bright colors. The most colorful caterpillars are usually highly distasteful, and their gaudy colors are a warning to predators. The larvae of the cinnabar moth, for example, have bright orange and black bands. They are particularly distasteful to birds, and with their conspicuous colors, birds are unlikely to

**ABOVE AND RIGHT** To deter predators when it is resting, the Indian leaf butterfly mimics a dry brown leaf, but if a predator is about to strike, it suddenly opens its wings to confuse its foe with its colorful inner wing surfaces.

**BELOW** The io moth frightens predators with its patterned wings. At rest, it resembles a yellowed leaf, but when threatened, it flashes a pair of deep blue eye markings on its underwings, which startle the would-be attacker.

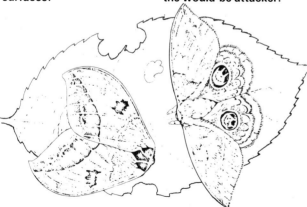

eat them accidentally. Burnet moth larvae and adults contain cyanide compounds, which they synthesize from the plant called the bird's-foot trefoil.

Other caterpillars protect themselves by combining camouflage with an offensive reaction. The puss moth, for example, is green and black at rest, blending in with its surroundings. However, if threatened, it rears up and displays a band of bright red marked with two false eyes. If its startling behavior does not deter the predator, the caterpillar resorts to a third offensive tactic. Swiftly, it raises two whip-like prolegs that produce two bright red filaments. The insect has yet a fourth line of action at its disposal if need be. From an area under its thorax, it squirts a jet of formic acid.

The caterpillars of the swallowtail butterflies use a chemical to ward off predators. When attacked, they rear up and extrude two tubes from behind their heads. From these, they spray a repellent liquid. A great many caterpillars use hair to make themselves appear larger than they really are, hoping to dissuade small birds from eating them. Their hairs often irritate the skin, eyes or tongue of vertebrate predators.

Both caterpillars and adult butterflies and moths commonly use eyespots to frighten off their enemies. Larvae of the elephant hawk moth are among the most life-like mimics of frightening creatures. When disturbed, the otherwise inconspicuous animal rears up and pulls its head into its thorax. Its thorax then swells, highlighting the two false eyes on the insect's sides similar to an animal between a snake and a shrew in size.

## Hairy defenders

Among caterpillars, the use of hair for defense takes several forms. Many species deter attacks from small predators with their hair coverings, which make them appear larger than they actually are. Hair defense effectively defends caterpillars against parasitic wasps and flies and small birds.

Caterpillars of some species protect themselves with irritant hairs on their bodies. Brown-tail moth caterpillars, for example, adopt a "safety in numbers" approach and form large, hairy colonies, often within cities, where their numbers may reach plague proportions at certain times of the year. The caterpillars continue to use their hairs during the pupal stage: when a larva prepares to pupate, it sheds its skin and hairs in such a way that the hairs become incorporated in the silk cocoon. If a female brown-tail moth hatches from the cocoon, she attaches a tuft of irritant hairs to her abdomen and saves it to cover her eggs with. Although brown-tails originally inhabited central and southern Europe and North Africa, they have been crop pests in North America since 1890.

## Ant bribes

Several species of blue butterfly, including the large blue (once common in Britain, but now extinct), gain food and protection from predators by living symbiotically in the nests of ants. When the blue butterfly caterpillar hatches, it feeds, like most other caterpillar species, on certain food plants. Between its second and third molt, however, the caterpillar wanders away from its food plants and searches for ants of a specific species—each caterpillar species will enter into symbiosis (a mutually beneficial relationship) with only one specific ant species. Ants detect the presence of the caterpillar when they smell its sugary "milk" secretion. Once the ants have found the caterpillar, they carry it to their nest, where they feed on its milk. Throughout its larval stage, the caterpillar feeds the ants, but at the same time, it eats the larvae and pupae of its hosts. The "blue" caterpillar pupates in the ants' nest, and the adult butterfly emerges in late spring.

## Mimicry and camouflage

Like the caterpillars, adult butterflies and moths use camouflage, startling coloration and repellent chemical secretions to deter predators. Camouflage is the most common method of protection among

---

## INSECTS CLASSIFICATION: 22

### *Moths and butterflies (1)*

The order Lepidoptera consists of 136 families of butterflies and moths grouped into 28 superfamilies and five suborders. The first suborder, the Zeugloptera, contains only one family—the Micropterigidae, a group of about 100 species of primitive moths with chewing mouthparts living in Europe, North America, Australia and New Zealand.

The suborder Dacnonypha consists of small moths with mottled wings. They comprise three superfamilies; one of them, the Agathiphagoidea, has only two species—the kauri moths of Australia and Fiji whose caterpillars feed on the seeds of the coniferous kauri tree.

The suborder Exoporia includes the superfamily Hepialoidea, which contains 510 species including the ghost and swift moths (family Hepialidae) of which the largest European member is the ghost moth, *Hepialus humuli*, with a 3-in. wingspan.

The suborder Monotrysia contains two superfamilies: the Incurvarioidea, which contains 440 species including the yucca moth, *Tegeticula yuccasella*, of the southern USA and Mexico; and the Nepticuloidea, which has three families and over 515 species of pygmy moths (such as the apple pygmy moth) spread throughout the world.

The final suborder, Ditrysia, is by far the largest in the order Lepidoptera. With 135,000 species, it is one of the most diverse groups known to entomologists. Within this suborder are found the more advanced moths and all the butterflies (see following classification boxes).

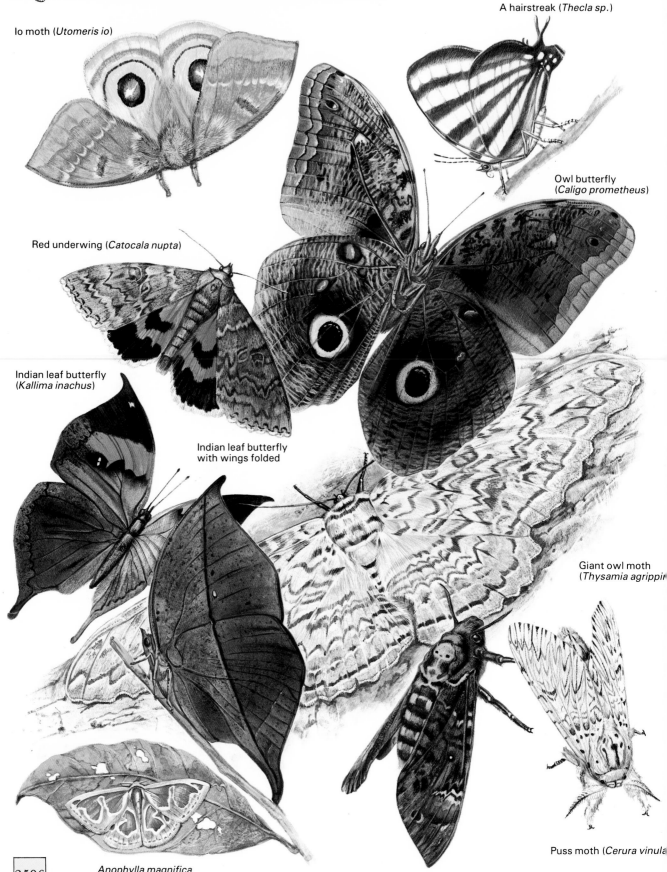

Io moth (*Utomeris io*)

A hairstreak (*Thecla sp.*)

Owl butterfly
(*Caligo prometheus*)

Red underwing (*Catocala nupta*)

Indian leaf butterfly
(*Kallima inachus*)

Indian leaf butterfly
with wings folded

Giant owl moth
(*Thysamia agrippir*)

Puss moth (*Cerura vinula*

*Anophylla magnifica*

Death's head hawk moth (*Acherontia atropos*)

adult lepidopterans. For example, the top surfaces of the forewings of most moths are usually colored brown and gray to blend in with the environment. The underwings of many butterfly species are drab in comparison with the multicolored upper surfaces; the different wing colorations enable butterflies to appear almost invisible when at rest. However, natural camouflage is only effective if the moth or butterfly remains perfectly still, as any movement would immediately betray its position to predators.

The dead-leaf butterfly is well known for its resemblance—when at rest—to a dead leaf. In flight, the dead-leaf butterfly is conspicuous with its bright blue and orange wings, but the instant it lands, it snaps its wings shut, leaving only its brown, leaf-like underwings exposed. The sudden change from gaudy butterfly to "dead brown leaf" confuses most predators.

Some moth species have evolved a secondary line of defense for use when natural camouflage fails. Predators are often startled by striking shapes, patterns and colors on the upper wing surfaces of moths; a common "startle pattern" takes the form of huge, staring eyes—one per wing. In addition to eyes, the owlet moth of Brazil has flanges on the edges of its wings: when held in a certain position, the flanges resemble an owl's beak. The atlas moth is one of the largest lepidopterans and an inhabitant of southern India and Southeast Asia. Its wavy, yellow wing borders deter almost any predator, since they bear a terrifying resemblance to striking cobras.

## Insect impersonators

The wasp and bee mimics are among the most realistic of the moth impersonators. The European hornet moth, for example, closely resembles a hornet, since it has clear wings and a black-and-yellow striped body. Although a newly hatched hornet moth has a fine layer of scales on its wings, it loses them during its first flight. Since real hornets are aggressive insects with powerful stings, predators stay clear of them. Hornet moths, therefore, capitalize on the reputation of the insects they impersonate.

The bright colors of some species of moths warn predators that their flesh is poisonous. Other non-poisonous moth species possess the bright warning colors of their inedible cousins and effectively deter potential predators.

## Fast fliers and slow gliders

Moths and butterflies are active fliers that use various methods of flight—some moths and butterflies are among the slowest insect fliers, while others can fly at speeds over 30 miles per hour. Although moths and butterflies differ greatly in their speed and agility through the air, they share a uniform wingbeat: the forewings and hind wings of most adult moths and butterflies link together so that they beat in unison. In butterflies (and some moths), the wings are held together by lobes on the hind wings that overlap the base of the forewings. Most moths have a number of bristles on the base of the hind wing that interlock with a catch-like flap on the forewings.

During flight, the wings of slow-flying butterflies beat up and down, producing lift and forward momentum. Usually, these butterflies have a lazy flight interspaced with periods of gliding. During bursts of flight, the wings of slow-flying butterflies beat as slowly as 10 strokes per second.

In more accomplished fliers, the wings move in a distorted figure-eight pattern through the air, giving the moths and butterflies greater forward momentum. Hawk moths, for example, reach speeds of over 33 mph using this method. The figure-eight wing movement enables the long, narrow wings of advanced fliers to achieve a high stroke rate per second. Many flower-visiting moths, and in particular the hummingbird hawk moths, fly backward by reversing the movement of their wings through the air. Some moths and butterflies confuse predators by mimicking the flying movements of poisonous or aggressive insects.

## Feeding—from fruit to feces

Moths and butterflies obtain liquid by sucking dew from flowers or water from damp earth. In tropical regions, hundreds of multicolored butterflies descend to drink from communal watering holes. The water provides them with minerals that have dissolved in the pool or stream.

Although certain primitive species of the superfamily Micropterigoidea retain chewing mouthparts and feed on pollen grains, most moths and butterflies eat liquid food. Adult moths and butterflies feed with a sucking proboscis or "tongue." When at rest, a moth or butterfly rolls its long, tube-like organ underneath its head, but when the insect feeds it extends its proboscis forward. A channel runs through the proboscis, so

that the organ functions like a flexible drinking straw, sucking up liquid (particularly nectar) from the bottoms of flowers.

Butterflies use their eyesight to spot a flower and use their sense of smell to detect whether it contains nectar. Most moths only use their sense of smell to detect nectar-rich flowers. Both moths and butterflies have distinct preferences for certain types of flowers.

Not all moths and butterflies drink from flowers. Certain species prefer overripe fruit to nectar and have short, robust proboscises with which they feed. Excrement, decomposing carrion and sweat are the chosen diets of some moths and butterflies. Several African members of the superfamily Noctuoidea feed in an unusual way: emerging at night, they cling to the eyes of sleeping cattle, often forming tightly packed groups, and suck out the tear fluid from the eye by inserting their proboscises under the eyelids. The moths remain feeding for up to a quarter of an hour, without any reaction from the cattle. It is thought that several diseases are transmitted by the feeding habits of these moths.

Some moths feed on carrion, but the vampire moth from Africa feeds on blood from sleeping mammals in a similar way to the tear-drinking moths. Like members of the superfamily Noctuoidea, it has been linked with the spread of certain diseases.

### Territorial defense

Butterflies, and some moths, are territorial and defend the boundaries of their domain from members of the same species and other insects (except in the breeding season). Males are most active in defending their territories, or habitual flight paths, from intruders, using various methods of defense.

**ABOVE AND ABOVE LEFT** Zoologists have studied the abnormal development of black coloration in the peppered moth. Two varieties of peppered moth inhabit northern Europe, and particularly the British Isles: one is light in color while the other is dark-colored. In industrial areas, the dark variety has a camouflage advantage over the light type, where previously white birch trees have become blackened by industrial waste.

Tropical butterflies of the family Nymphalidae from South America use brute force to defend their territories. Large and heavy in size, the nymphalids are rapid fliers. When an intruder lands on a flower within a nymphalid's territory, it swoops down and knocks the intruder off the flower. A nymphalid can dominate an entire forest clearing, even frightening off any hummingbirds that live there.

Some species of butterfly remain in one area while guarding their territory; the members of the family Papilionidae, for example, actively patrol the boundaries. The defender recognizes its own territory by using prominent landmarks such as bushes, streams, paths and rocks. Unlike insects such as dragonflies, aerial combat between opponents is usually brief—one of the rivals retreats before any serious damage is caused.

Originally, moths and butterflies (order Lepidoptera) were classified according to their size—small moths were known as microlepidopterans and larger species of moths and butterflies were called macrolepidopterans. Primitive moths are usually small, and more advanced species are generally larger. Taxonomists now divide the order Lepidoptera according to the arrangement of veins in the wings (wing venation), wing shape and genital openings.

Moths and butterflies group into five suborders—Zeugloptera, Dacnonypha, Exoporia, Monotrysia and Ditrysia. The suborder Zeugloptera contains only the family Micropterigidae—the most primitive family of moths. The adults are small and have well-developed mandibles; unlike other moths, their maxillae or jaw appendages do not form a sucking proboscis. The caterpillars of the family have eight legs, like the stone fly larvae, instead of six.

The micropterigidan moths' forewings and hind wings are similar in size and venation; a lobe-like device couples the forewings with the base of the hind wings, suggesting an evolutionary relationship with the caddis flies. The adult moths visit flower heads, feeding on pollen seeds and on marsh marigolds, which they grind with their chewing mouthparts. Indeed, the adults are a familiar sight in meadows during the spring as they fly from plant to plant in search of food. The larvae occur in leaf litter and feed on fungus and mosses in the early stages.

The small moths of the suborder Dacnonypha have not developed proboscises in the adult stage. They include the kauri moths of the family Agathiphagoidea, which occur in Australia and Fiji. Their caterpillars feed only on the seeds of the coniferous kauri tree. Like the pupae of the caddis flies, they can move their legs—they are not enclosed within the pupal case.

**ABOVE** The hornet moth is well known for its mimicry of hornets. Through evolution, the harmless species has assumed the appearance of another insect species that possesses devices for attack and defense. Predators steer clear of the hornet moth with its scaleless, transparent wings and yellow-and-black striped abdomen.

## Ghost moths

The suborder Exoporia contains the ghost moths and swift moths of the superfamily Hepialoidea. Among the largest species of lepidopterans, they are swift-flying insects that appear at dusk. Although five large species of ghost moths occur in Britain, the majority are found in Australia and South Africa, where they grow to a larger size and are often brightly colored. Like other advanced moths, their mandibles have become useless for chewing and no longer function.

During flight, male ghost moths emit a substance that contains pheromones. The pheromone acts like a chemical mating call and attracts females in the surrounding area. After fertilization, the females fly close to the ground where they deposit their eggs. The caterpillars that emerge burrow into the soil where they feed on the roots of grasses and the trunks of trees. Often called "otters" because of their burrowing habits, the caterpillars can be a serious pest on agricultural land if they occur in large numbers.

ABOVE The comma butterfly is named for the white, comma-shaped mark on the underside of its lower wing. At rest, its wings resemble pieces of flaking bark.
BELOW The broken color patterns of an adult puss moth allow it to rest against tree bark (A), unseen by predators; the puss moth larva (B) frightens enemies by its strange appearance and ability to squirt formic acid. Calpe moths suck tears from a cow's eye (C).
FAR RIGHT At the end of their southerly migration, thousands of monarch butterflies overwinter at a site in Mexico.

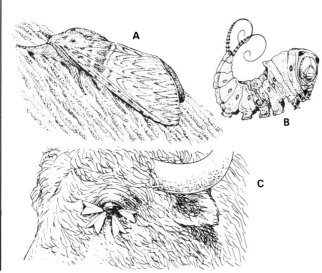

The caterpillars of the silver-spotted ghost moth, a species that occurs only in the coastal forests of the southern cape of South Africa, inhabits the trunk of the keurboom tree. Shortly before emergence, the pupa protrudes from the tree trunk.

## Minor miners

The suborder Monotrysia contains the superfamilies Incurvarioidea and Nepticuloidea. Unlike the more primitive families of moths, they have reduced wing venation, especially in the hind wings. The species in the family Incurvarioidae are leaf miners during the larval stage (they live between the two outer layers of leaves); sometimes they feed on the seeds inside fruit or tunnel in young shoots. Certain species later cut out flattened cases, which they use as portable shelters. The adults have long antennae, those of the male being longer than those of the female.

Included in the family are the yucca moths of North America and Mexico, which have developed a close relationship with the yucca plants. The females lay their eggs in the ovaries of the yucca flowers before applying pollen that they have previously collected. As a result of the pollination, the yucca produces seeds, some of which germinate and some of which feed their larvae after hatching.

Members of the family Nepticulidae are small to minute insects that include the smallest living lepidopterans, the pygmy moths *Johanssonia acetosea* of Great Britain and *Stigmella ridiculosa* of the Canary Islands, both of which have a wingspan of only 0.08 in. Leaf mining is characteristic of the pygmy moths. Their leaf-mining larvae tunnel into the tissue of the plant, forming a channel or blotch; some mine in the epidermis of stems or in buds. When the larvae reach maturity, they abandon their leaves and descend to the ground, where they pupate within minute silken cocoons. One of the main methods of distinguishing between species of pygmy moths is by the form of "mine" that their larvae build.

## Clothes moths

The suborder Ditrysia contains 21 superfamilies, 119 families and 135,000 species; all butterflies and many moth families belong to the Ditrysia. One of the best-known families of the suborder is the Tineidae (superfamily Tineoidea), which contains 3000 species of clothes moths. The inconspicuous wardrobe pest is

**ABOVE The spotted fritillary is commonly known as the "checkerspot" in North America because it has reddish yellow wings with black spots. It occurs in mountainous woodland and confines its feeding to a particular plant species or genus, where it feeds in localized colonies.**

a tiny, white, grub-like moth caterpillar with an appetite for materials such as wool and silk. Clothes moths have become less common in recent years, since clothes made from inedible man-made fibers have replaced many that were previously made from natural materials.

Not all ditrysian moths feed on clothes: many species eat through dried fruit, grain, antelope horns, feathers, furs or carpets, the grain eaters causing the most serious damage. Grain-eating moths appear suddenly during early summer and mate almost immediately. The fertilized females usually lay their eggs in grain storage buildings. Once the eggs hatch, the young caterpillars eat large quantities of grain throughout their short developmental stage. On reaching maturity, the caterpillars spin silk cocoons and pupate. After a short time, the adult moths emerge and begin a new life cycle. In favorable conditions, grain-eating moths can produce three generations a year.

## Bagworms

Bagworm moths comprise the family Psychidae within the superfamily Tineoidea. The family has one of the strangest life-styles in the suborder Ditrysia, since the two sexes have evolved into insects that appear to be completely unrelated to each other. The males are swift fliers with large, feathery antennae, while the females are typically wingless, legless, mouthless, and without antennae.

The bagworm caterpillar builds a silk case, which it camouflages with fragments of bark, pine needles, earth and leaves. The silk "saccule" resembles a bag and provides a nesting place for the caterpillar—hence the name "bagworm." The saccule expands to accommodate the growth and pupation of its occupant. If the adult emerging from pupation is a male moth, it breaks out of the saccule, waits for its wings to harden and flies off. However, if a female emerges from the pupa, it remains in the saccule and emits pheromones to attract males for mating. Most species of bagworm moths mate while the female is still in its saccule.

## Leaf-mining caterpillars

The family Lithocolletidae contains narrow-winged moths and leaf-mining caterpillars. Leaf miners bore into the thick parts of leaves or stalks, forming tunnels

and cavities on the insides, but leaving the outsides undamaged. The adult moths of the family are small, unremarkable insects that lay their eggs on the leaves of plants. The eggs produce flat, legless larvae that begin their lives by building silk cocoons in which they spend their entire larval stages. Newly hatched leaf-mining caterpillars have blade-like jaws with which they slash plant cells in order to suck out the sap. Toward the end of their larval development, the caterpillars undergo hypermetamorphosis—a form of metamorphosis that precedes pupation, producing a second larval form. After a short time, the new larval form pupates, developing into a fully mature adult.

## The small ermine moth

The distribution of the small ermine moth extends through most parts of Europe, reaching as far as the Iberian Peninsula and Asia Minor. The adults are conspicuous moths with white wings and black speckling, while the caterpillars are dull gray, with dark gray bands running down their backs and black spots on their flanks. The fertilized female ermine moth lays approximately 40 eggs on a food plant such as hawthorn and blackthorn. After hatching, the caterpillars live communally and construct a large, striking, protective web. The web expands in size as its occupants grow and mature. Large communities are capable of stripping their food plant of all its leaves. Upon reaching maturity, the caterpillars pupate in the communal web.

## Olive-bud moths

For centuries, the olive-bud moth has presented olive farmers with a pest problem, since it undergoes its entire life cycle on, or near, olive trees. The species usually produces three generations in a single year. Fertilized female moths lay the first generation of eggs on olive leaves. Although the emerging caterpillars feed on the leaf tissues, they do not cause severe damage. The caterpillars develop into adult moths that lay a second generation of eggs on the leaves on which the first generation developed. Caterpillars of the second generation weave complex, silk nests on the olive flowers and, like their parents, do not cause damage to the olive trees. However, when the third generation appears, it feeds on the flesh of the young olive fruits, causing irreparable damage to the crop.

**ABOVE Indonesia contains some of the most beautiful butterflies in the world, such as this species of swallowtail, *Papilio karna*, from the** **lowland forests of Java. Its brilliant green coloration serves as ideal camouflage as it flies among the thick vegetation.**

## Bell moths

When viewed from above, moths of the family Torticidae resemble bells, hence their name, "bell moths." Bell moths are small with parasitic habits.

For centuries, the vine bell moth has been a troublesome parasite of grape vines in the Northern Hemisphere. It appears in June, and, shortly after mating, the fertilized female moths lay groups of eggs on vine leaves. Immediately after hatching, the caterpillars disperse over the plant and hide in different places. They hibernate over winter in woven canopies of thin silk. When warm weather returns, the caterpillars reappear and attack and eat the young vine shoots. The affected leaves shrivel up and then either fall off the vine or become enveloped in the silk caterpillar threads. Toward the end of May, the caterpillars pupate and, after a few days, emerge as adults, ready to begin a new life cycle.

The green oak bell moth appears between June and August in oak woods. Its caterpillars live on the leaves of oak trees, and, if their numbers are large, they can completely strip a tree of its leaves. Once this has happened, the caterpillars drop to the forest floor on silk threads and begin eating the forest's undergrowth. To avoid detection by predators, the caterpillars fold leaves over on themselves and hide between the two surfaces.

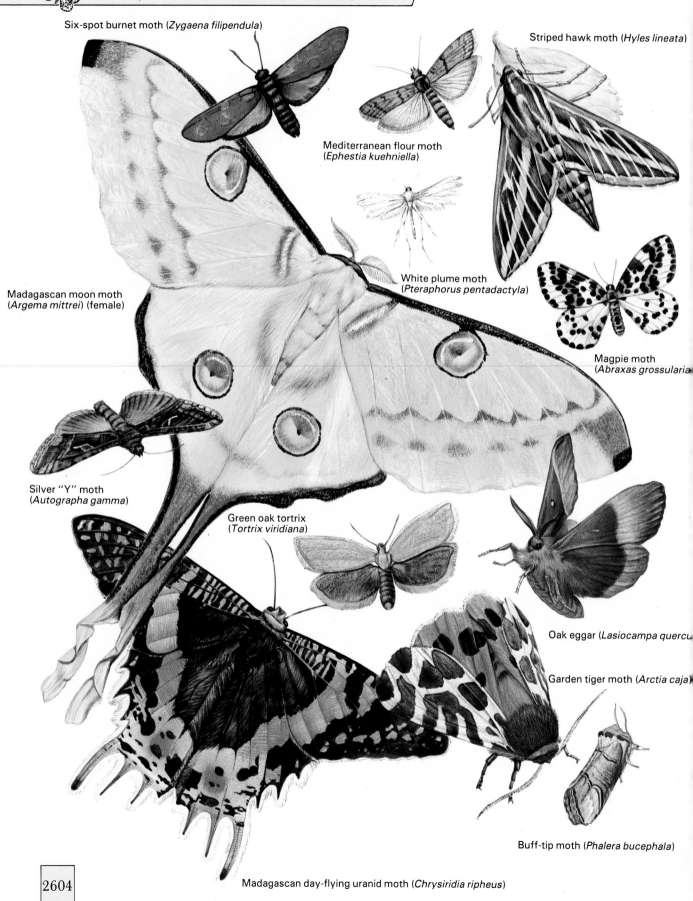

Six-spot burnet moth (*Zygaena filipendula*)

Striped hawk moth (*Hyles lineata*)

Mediterranean flour moth
(*Ephestia kuehniella*)

Madagascan moon moth
(*Argema mittrei*) (female)

White plume moth
(*Pteraphorus pentadactyla*)

Magpie moth
(*Abraxas grossularia*)

Silver "Y" moth
(*Autographa gamma*)

Green oak tortrix
(*Tortrix viridiana*)

Oak eggar (*Lasiocampa quercu*)

Garden tiger moth (*Arctia caja*)

Buff-tip moth (*Phalera bucephala*)

Madagascan day-flying uranid moth (*Chrysiridia ripheus*)

2604

Immediately before pupation, each caterpillar moves to the margin of a leaf, bends the edge over, and constructs a shelter by wrapping the leaf around with silk threads. Inside their leaf shelters, the caterpillars spin cocoons and undergo metamorphosis.

## Goat moths

The goat or carpenter moths belong to the superfamily Cossoidea. They are generally large and powerful moths whose caterpillars eat wood and make tunnels in the trunks of trees and the pith of reeds. The goat moth is a typical representative of the family Cossidae. It used to be quite common in Britain, and was often found in old orchards that had fallen into decay. But it has become rarer as its habitat has disappeared. These moths are slow fliers and look clumsy on the wing.

After mating, the female goat moth lays her eggs in the crevices of the bark of such trees as poplar, lime, elm and ash. The small caterpillars hatch from the eggs after a short incubation period. Keeping together, they immediately tunnel into the trunk, where they spend the winter resting. When spring arrives, each caterpillar starts building a new tunnel, penetrating more deeply into the trunk. Because wood is low in nutritional value and the larvae feed only on wood, it can take three or four years for the caterpillar to reach adulthood. When mature, the goat moth caterpillars may measure 4 in. in length. They smell strongly of goat—a characteristic that gives the family its common name. In Europe, the caterpillars are commonly called "red wood-eaters" partly because of their bright red backs and red pupae.

During the goat moth caterpillars' final year as larvae, they overwinter in a semimotionless state. At the beginning of the following spring, they begin to make the final tunnels along which they will travel to the outside world. Before this, however, they undergo the final stage of their larval life—the transformation that will complete their metamorphosis. On their journey to the outside, the large caterpillars stop near the tunnels' exit holes, block them up and pupate. Sometimes they crawl out of the tree trunk and pupate in the soil at the base of the tree. By the beginning of June, the goat moths are fully formed in their pupal cases and are ready to emerge as adults. Once they break free into the open air, they are ready to begin their new life cycles.

ABOVE As soon as the larvae of the bagworm moths hatch, they make portable cases or "bags" in which they live until reaching adulthood. The larvae construct the cases by cementing silk, twigs and leaves together to form a camouflaged exterior that protects them from predators.

BELOW The larvae of the bagworm (A) feed voraciously before entering their cases to pupate (B). In the pupal stage, the bodies of the larvae develop differently according to their sex. Male bagworm moths develop wings (C); the females are wingless and remain in the bag.

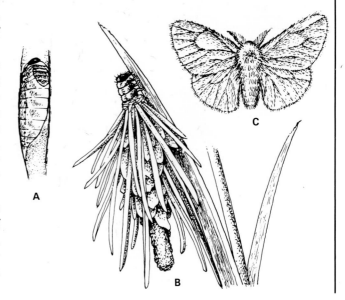

# BUTTERFLIES AND MOTHS
## — ATTRACTIVE SCENTS —

Butterflies and moths are not usually gregarious animals and rarely exhibit social behavior. They do not, therefore, need complicated methods of communication, as they need only communicate with members of the opposite sex when they mate.

Butterflies and moths emit certain signals to attract potential mates. The most highly developed of these methods relies on chemical stimulation, in the form of pheromones. The French entomologist Jean-Henri Fabre observed that the female great peacock moth emitted a special scent that attracted and stimulated the males. The moth had emerged one spring morning in Fabre's laboratory and he isolated it under a wire mesh bell. The naturalist was most surprised to see his house invaded that evening by male great peacock moths.

### Strong-smelling pheromones

Fabre observed that the attractive power of the female's scent was not masked even by substances that smelled strongly to humans. After placing a number of containers full of petroleum, naphthalene, lavender and tobacco around the female, he discovered that, even though the atmosphere in the room had become unbearable for humans, the male great peacock moths were unaffected and arrived at the same rate.

Such behavior is not unique to the great peacock moth. Female Indian meal moths, for example, also attract males of the same species by emitting a scented substance that remains in the air for a long time. The female Chinese silk moth releases a substance called bombykol that is effective even at a considerable distance—males respond to the scent signal of a female up to 5 miles away, provided the wind carries the scent in the right direction.

### Sensitive receptors

The males detect the chemical stimuli using the sensitive receptors on their feathered antennae. These organs are only found in the males. Once the male has located the female, he then courts her to persuade her to mate. He emits a less powerful scent that can only be

detected at a short range, sometimes only an inch away. These scents can even be perceived by humans, and they cover an extremely wide range. Depending on the species, they may smell of musk, geraniums, violets, primroses, sandalwood, orange blossom, and even chocolate or chloroform.

### Brown butterflies

Males of the brown butterflies have scent-secreting glands on their forewings; they actively fly around the females, using their wings like a fan to diffuse the air perfumed by their scent. Other male butterflies and moths have a special scent-producing gland on the enlarged tibia (fourth joint) of their third pair of legs. These glands secrete a substance that smells of ripe pineapples. During their rather distinctive, unsteady flight, male brown butterflies continuously shake their scent-emitting tibia in the direction of their partners.

Some butterflies have evolved special adaptations to enable them to communicate more easily. Male tiger butterflies of the genus Danaus, for example, have special glands in their wings and abdomens that secrete their chemical stimulants. These insects dip their brush-like structures, located at the end of their abdomens, into two pouches on the wings, and then open the hairs of the brushes into a radiating pattern to release the scented liquid into the air to persuade the females to mate.

### Visual communication

Generally, however, butterflies and moths rely on visual communication during courtship. The insects have brightly colored patterns on their wings, and it is thought that these colors may act as a signal to members of the opposite sex. Usually the males display their coloring, either by resting on a twig and agitating their wings, or by

taking off and performing energetic maneuvers. In many cases, they may transmit clicking sounds that they produce with special stridulating, or scraping, organs on their wings, suggesting that they use audible communication methods. The females, excited by the patterns and by the movements of the colored wings, approach the males and, by raising their abdomens, invite them to mate.

**ABOVE** Like other members of the genus *Danaus*, the monarch butterfly is poisonous to birds and other insectivores. It communicates its danger with warning coloration—it has distinctive white, yellow and black stripes on the upper and underside of its wings, so that predators quickly learn to recognize and avoid it.
**FAR LEFT** Although the peacock butterfly is not dangerous, it has large "peacock eye" marks on its wings that startle and deter some of its potential predators from attacking.

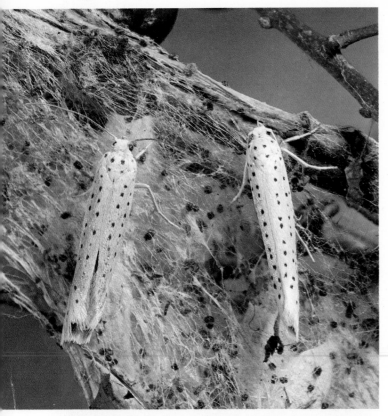

**TOP** Ermine moths spend their larval stage inside a silk "tent" that they build to protect them from parasitic wasps and flies. As the larvae grow, the tent expands, allowing them to pupate in the safety of their silk nursery.

**ABOVE** The members of the bell moth family are similar in appearance. Although they are small in size, bell moths cause great damage to stored goods and crops. The vine bell moth feeds on vines. Its caterpillars feed on the tender spring buds and young leaves.

## Moth mimics

The clearwings are moths that have long, thin wings with few or no scales and are therefore transparent. The combination of this feature, together with the black, yellow and red striped coloring of their abdomens, makes them visually similar to the bees and wasps. Their caterpillars bore tunnels in vegetable tissue, causing severe damage to certain crops. The largest clearwing species is the hornet moth whose behavior is such that it may be mistaken quite easily for a hornet. The moths emerge from their hiding places toward the end of the evening and fly off rapidly in search of food. They also fly during the daytime, and one may often encounter them in woodlands throughout Europe, especially on summer mornings.

After they have been fertilized, the female hornet moths lay their eggs either in the cracks of tree trunks or directly on the ground. In the former case, the emerging caterpillars begin to tunnel into the bark; those on the ground must first find a tree. They stay inside the tree for at least two or three years, and then move toward the bark at the beginning of spring, where they pupate. When they are ready, the closed pupae force their way out of the tree trunk. The cases then break, releasing the adult hornet moths, which fly away.

## Destructive grain moths

The gelechids constitute a superfamily (the Gelechioidea) that is made up of moths with dark, inconspicuous coloring. Their caterpillars are mainly plant eaters, feeding on a wide variety of plant species. However, a few species have caterpillars that are parasitic on other arthropods, feeding on the eggs of spiders and scale insects.

The Angoumois grain moth (named after the French region of Angoumois) is a notorious gelechid species, attacking cereal crops and often causing considerable damage. On spring evenings, they move into cultivated fields and mate. The fertilized females lay their eggs on the young ears of wheat, and the caterpillars that hatch from the eggs immediately bore into the grains. The females also lay their eggs in warehouses or granaries, and it is here that the grain moth does the most damage. Once the eggs have been laid, the hatchling caterpillars emerge and burrow into the grain. They will only be seen again once they have

RIGHT The goat moth is a large, stout insect with brown, intricately mottled wings. It flies at night and is sometimes attracted by the lights of houses. By day, the goat moth rests on the trunks and branches of trees, where its color and markings provide effective camouflage. Its larvae burrow in living wood, especially willows and poplars, and take several years to reach adulthood. They take their name from the "goaty" smell that they produce.

---

## INSECTS CLASSIFICATION: 23

### Moths and butterflies (2)

The suborder Ditrysia in the order Lepidoptera contains 21 superfamilies, 119 families and 135,000 species of moths. The superfamilies include the Tineoidea, which contains the family Tineidae (whose 3000 or so species include the clothes moths, such as genus *Tinea*) and the family Psychidae, the bagworms; the superfamily Yponomeutoidea containing some 1600 species, including the small ermine moth (genus *Yponomeuta* in the family Yponomeutidae) of Europe and Asia Minor; the Tortricoidea, with the green oak tortrix, *Tortrix viridiana*, of the family Tortricidae; the Cossoidea, the goat or carpenter moths, with over 1150 species, including the goat moth, *Cossus cossus*, of Europe and North Africa; and the Sesioidea containing the clearwings (family Sesiidae), including the hornet moth, *Sesia apiformis*, of Europe.

Further superfamilies include the Zygaenoidea, which has 1600 species in nine families—these include such species as the six-spot burnet moth, *Zygaena filipendula*, of Britain and mainland Europe; the Pterophoroidea, with the large white plume moth, *Pteraphorus pentadactyla*; the Pyraloidea, with over 20,700 species, many of which are destructive, such as the greater wax moth, *Galleria mellonella*, whose larvae feeds on the wax inside beehives, and the European corn borer moth, *Ostrinia nubilalis*; and the Geometroidea, containing the measuring worm moths whose larvae are called "inchworms." Geometrids include the magpie moth, *Abraxas grossulariata*, and the peppered moth, *Biston betularia*, which has a black or *carbonaria* form in sooty, industrial regions of central and northern Europe.

pupated and turned into adults. Each female can lay up to 200 eggs. In addition, the moth's life cycle is so short that inside a granary, where the environmental conditions are favorable, the grain moth may produce up to five generations within a single year. The number of caterpillars that develop thus becomes enormous, and explains their destructive power.

Some species of gelechid moths are pests of pine trees, potatoes, tomatoes and fruit trees. One of the greatest threats to cotton production comes from the cotton bollworm, the caterpillar of a species of gelechid moth that attacks the bolls or seed pods of cotton plants.

### Protected by cyanide

The burnet moths of the superfamily Zygaenoidea— like other members of the superfamily—are garishly colored. They secrete an oily liquid containing poisonous cyanide that makes them highly unpalatable; as a result, insect-eating birds hardly ever attack them. Their caterpillars are very bulky, their bodies covered with hairs and warts. Their bright green and yellow colors warn predators that they are poisonous if eaten. They live and feed on the leaves of various plants, such as sorrel, vetch and trefoil. On reaching maturity, the caterpillars pupate inside small cocoons and then emerge as adults.

**LEFT** Unlike most adult moths, the six-spot burnet moth has brightly spotted forewings, which serve as a warning coloration to potential predators. The caterpillars of the six-spot burnet moth feed on bird's-foot trefoil, a plant that contains cyanide. Stores of cyanide remain in their bodies after they reach adulthood, making them highly dangerous to eat. They contain enough cyanide to make small children seriously ill if eaten.

**ABOVE** The scaleless wings and yellow stripes of the clearwing moths (for example, the *Aegeria vespiformis* shown here) are intended to mimic wasps. Although these moths do not sting, their resemblance to stinging insects probably deters potential predators.

The six-spot burnet, a typical member of the superfamily, is very common in Britain and in the rest of Europe. It is a small, brightly colored moth that flutters around meadows during the daytime in search of nectar. After fertilization, the females lay their eggs on the leaves of the bird's-foot trefoil and die soon afterward. The caterpillars feed on the host plants. On reaching maturity, they weave small, papery cocoons and then pupate. After completing their development, the caterpillars break the fragile, protective case and emerge into the open.

The characteristic feature of the plume moths is their unusual wings, which are divided by deep, longitudinal slits, giving them the appearance of plumes. One of the most common species is the large white plume moth. Each of its wings is divided into five feather-like sections. When it is resting, the moth holds its wings stretched outward and folds its legs against its body. In this position it looks like a white "T." There are a number of glands under the wings that secrete a scented liquid to attract females.

The plume moths are quite frequently seen in early spring as they fly over meadows, wastelands and gardens, seeking food or a suitable place in which to lay their eggs. After the caterpillars have hatched, they feed on the leaves of convolvulus and bindweed. They then pupate and soon become adults. A second generation may begin to develop before the end of the year, although in this generation the pupae do not complete their development. Instead, they spend the winter in a resting state and then undergo the final metamorphosis in the following spring.

## A family of pests

The pyralids are a superfamily (Pyraloidea) comprising approximately 20,700 species of fairly small moths with inconspicuous coloring. They are all active in the evening or at night, and often cause severe damage to crops. One of the species, the greater wax moth,

**ABOVE The white plume moth's wings have lost the triangular shape and rounded edges of other butterflies. They extend in lobes or threads, commonly known as "tails," and the borders are** perforated or "torn," into ribbons. Even though the surface area of their wings is reduced, the white plume moth is a surprisingly good flier. When at rest, its body forms a distinct T-shape.

lives in the vicinity of beehives and is the scourge of beekeepers. After the female has been fertilized, she enters a hive to lay her eggs, despite the fierce and furious defensive action of the bees, which usually kill female greater wax moths.

The caterpillars of the greater wax moth hatch from their eggs and make minute tunnels inside the wax comb. Here, they feed on the wax itself, or preferably on the wax and other residual substances from the bees' digestive systems. In both cases, their activities result in the general devastation of the hive—the cells deteriorate, the bee larvae waste away and die, and refuse accumulates inside the comb. The situation becomes more dramatic at the time of pupation, when the caterpillars weave small silk cocoons and group themselves together. In many cases, they form a carpet of cocoons, completely covering the comb. The hive cannot survive under these conditions, and the bees are forced to leave it and build a new one.

Another pyralid that is harmful to farming is the European corn borer moth, which relentlessly attacks corn crops. It normally appears in large numbers in early spring. After mating, the females fly off to lay their eggs on corn plants. The newly hatched caterpillars immediately burrow into the plant, eating everything in their path as they head for the nutrients stored in the individual kernels of the cob. Young shoots are often the target of their attacks; the caterpillars completely destroy the immature cobs. By gorging themselves in this way, the caterpillars quickly increase in size. When they reach maturity, they move toward the outside of the plant, where they build themselves small cells in which they turn into pupae. In a short time they complete their development, and on becoming adults they emerge ready to attack the corn again.

Before the end of the year, a second generation of European corn borer larvae appear, but their pupation lasts throughout the winter and they only emerge as adults during the following spring.

The small, grayish green caterpillars of the garden pebble moth cause much devastation to crops of cabbage, cauliflower, horseradish and related plants —attacking the pods of the plants and devouring them completely. After finishing one pod, each caterpillar moves on to the next and so on, thus destroying a considerable number. If the pods are too small, the caterpillar secretes a silk thread with which it wraps them up to form a small, protective nest for itself.

## Aquatic moths

The pyralids include many species of moths whose development is in some way connected with a watery environment. One of these is the ringed china-mark moth, whose smooth caterpillars actually live in the water. The caterpillars are well adapted to life underwater, since their breathing tubes stick out from the sides of their bodies and serve as gills.

One particular feature of the ringed china-mark moth is the presence of two forms of females: the scarce, winged females that live on dry land, and the more common wingless females that lead purely aquatic lives. The latter only rise to the surface in the breeding season to meet males and mate with them. When the females have been fertilized, they go back into the water and lay groups of eggs on submerged objects. The aquatic caterpillars that emerge from these eggs penetrate the tissues of water plants and remain there, feeding on the plants. At this early stage in their development, they do not have gills but take in oxygen from the water directly through their skin. In due course they develop gills, growing more gills each time they shed their skins. On reaching maturity, the moth larvae rise toward the surface and attach themselves to submerged stems. Here, they build themselves shelters by binding together small pieces of leaves. The caterpillars pupate inside these shelters, undergoing the final transformation into adult insects.

## Geometrids

The superfamily Geometroidea contains about 20,000 species. They include dull-colored moths although some are adorned with particularly complex patterns. The caterpillars are markedly different from those of other superfamilies, since they have two pairs of false legs (called prolegs), rather than the four pairs common to most other species. Because these prolegs are situated only at the front and rear of their bodies, they move by "looping" their bodies, arching them into a loop to bring the two ends together, and then stretching themselves out by throwing their front ends forward. The whole movement makes it appear as if they are measuring the ground or the twig along which they are moving, giving rise to the scientific name of the superfamily—Geometroidea—from the Greek *geo* "earth," and *metres* "measurer." It is for this same reason that they are commonly called inchworms.

Geometrid caterpillars are superb mime artists, and can be mistaken for dry twigs when they remain still. A typical representative of the superfamily is the magpie moth. Its caterpillar is a pest to gardeners because it likes to attack currant, gooseberry and hawthorn bushes. The adults usually mate in the first months of summer, after which the females proceed to lay eggs on currant, hawthorn, and other bushes. Toward September, the eggs break open, releasing small caterpillars that attack the leaves of the host plants.

When the cold season arrives, the magpie moth caterpillars descend to the ground to look for hiding places in which to overwinter. When spring arrives, they emerge from their shelters and climb back into the trees to gorge themselves on the tender shoots, after which they pupate. The final transformation from pupa to adult moth takes place inside a woven, protective canopy. As soon as they have emerged, the adults are ready to begin a new life cycle.

## Black pepper, white pepper

The peppered moth is distributed in large numbers throughout the central and northern regions of Europe, and is another member of the geometrids. It is a medium-sized moth with a whitish coloring dappled with black markings that give it a peppered

ABOVE Wax moth larvae are pests that cause a significant amount of damage to beehives. The adult wax moth is dull in color but easily recognizable because of its peculiarly shaped forewings. Like their larvae, they are pests, causing serious damage to grain and cereal stores. Nowadays, wax moths are often used in laboratory experiments because they are easy to rear.

appearance. The moth became famous when a dark or melanistic form was found living in the industrial areas of England. The melanistic form, *carbonaria*, has been shown to stand a better chance of remaining invisible while resting against the soot-blackened trunks of trees than the more pale-colored form. The peppered moth has proved invaluable in experiments designed to find out more about the phenomenon of industrial melanism, shedding light on the process of evolution.

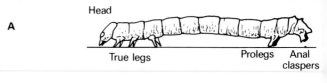

A

Head

True legs

Prolegs    Anal claspers

B

C

D

ABOVE The caterpillars of the geometrid moths are often called "inchworms" because they move along a surface with a "looping" action as if they were measuring it inch by inch.
ABOVE RIGHT The caterpillar and adult of the magpie moth are unwelcome visitors to garden plots. They feed on black-currant and gooseberry leaves and can cause extensive damage.
RIGHT The "inchworm" caterpillar only has one pair of false legs (prolegs) rather than the four or five pairs that are common to most other caterpillars. To move along, it fixes its prolegs and anal claspers to the surface and pushes its body forward (A). It then holds onto the ground it has attained with the three pairs of true legs at the front and pulls its long abdomen forward (B), so that it forms a steep arch or loop (C). The caterpillar then pushes the front of its body forward again (D) and repeats the process.

Toward the end of spring, the adult female peppered moths lay their eggs on various species of birch and other deciduous trees. The caterpillars are either moss-green or a grayish-brown in color and have a distinctly notched head. They also have wart-like structures that run the entire length of their bodies, closely resembling small buds or twig joints. On reaching their maximum size, the caterpillars leave the plant and burrow into the soil where they pupate. The pupae spend the winter in a state of hibernation and then reappear in the spring to complete their development and recommence their life cycle.

Another species that is important because of its harmful behavior is the mottled umber moth, whose caterpillars can completely denude a tree of its leaves. In this species, the males have wings while the females lack them. Consequently, the behavior of the two sexes is different; the males fly around the foliage of trees and the females clamber along the trunks.

Mottled umber moths mate toward the end of autumn, after which the males soon die. The females lay their eggs on the twigs of the host plant and, when they have finished, also die. The eggs spend the winter in a resting state until they break open in the spring, releasing small caterpillars. These grow by feeding on the leaf tissues of the invaded plants. On reaching maturity, around July or August, they move down to the ground by lowering themselves on silken threads, produced from special glands on their heads. Having reached the ground, they pupate and undergo the final change into adults. The adult insects emerge in the autumn.

## Noctuid moths

The noctuids, or owlet moths, are the largest superfamily within the order Lepidoptera, numbering some 37,270 species. Noctuid moths inhabit all areas of the world, including the polar regions and the tropics. Although body size varies between species, most noctuids have long, bristly antennae and stout, hairy bodies with inconspicuous coloration. However, the family also contains many species with brightly colored hind wings (hind wings fold under the forewings when a moth rests): such species usually become visible only during flight, when they spread their wings, displaying their colored markings. Noctuid moths are generally nocturnal feeders; their caterpillars eat a wide variety of foods and damage crops by feeding on the leaves and shoots. At certain times of the year, adult noctuids collect in very large groups and undertake extremely long migrations.

## Prominent moths

The family Notodontidae contains the prominent moths—medium and large-sized moths, with stout bodies and dull coloration that blends in easily with the environment. When threatened, the distinctive caterpillars extend and retract abdominal organs that resemble double whips. On such occasions, they also secrete an irritant liquid that effectively repels their enemies.

## Puss moths

Puss moths are large prominents with hair-covered bodies and decorative coloration. They are nocturnal animals, remaining hidden among foliage during the day to evade their predators. Puss moths emerge in the early evening and fly in circles among the trees, searching for food and—during the mating period—

**ABOVE** The caterpillar of the puss moth often occurs on the stony or clay banks of rivers, particularly among willow bushes. When on guard, it raises the forequarters of its body, revealing three pairs of thoracic legs and several pairs of legs on its abdomen. It breathes by drawing in air through small, white openings along the side of its body. In some other species, these openings can form part of their defensive markings.

partners. The fertilized females usually lay their eggs on poplars and willows; the caterpillars that hatch from the eggs gain energy for growth by feeding on the leaves and buds of the trees.

The puss moth caterpillar has a bright green body and a dark red head. Its abdomen terminates in two thread-like, extendible appendages that it can wave to frighten off predators. Once it is fully grown, the caterpillar leaves the foliage of its tree and climbs down the trunk to find a hole or a projection on the bark that provides shelter. When it finds a suitable place, the caterpillar weaves a small, rigid, silk cocoon, combining it with sawdust and bark glued together with saliva. Inside the protective cocoon, it turns into a pupa and hibernates. With the arrival of the first warm weather in spring, the pupa completes its development to become an adult moth, ready to begin a new life cycle.

ABOVE The female vaporer moth lays masses of smooth, spherical eggs on the surfaces of leaves and twigs of wild plum, rose or sloe. The eggs remain on the leaves all winter before hatching at the end of May. During metamorphosis, the caterpillars spin a loose cocoon around themselves and turn into brown, glossy pupae with exceptionally long hairs on their backs.
PAGES 2618-2619 The vivid markings of these scarlet tiger moths warn predators of their unpleasant taste, and break up the moths' shapes, making them harder for enemies to find.

## Buff-tip moths

The buff-tip moth is a prominent with coloration that accurately mimics natural foliage—it is almost impossible to see a buff-tip while it remains hidden during the day. At sunset, however, they become active, flying around among plants in search of food. In spring, during the mating season, the females emit scent signals to attract the males for mating. Once they have been fertilized, female buff-tips fly to the leaves of plants and lay many eggs in close contact with each other, so that they form a type of crust. The females cover their eggs with detachable, irritant hairs from their abdomens. When the caterpillars hatch, they stay close to each other, forming large groups. Buff-tip caterpillars feed on the tissues of the leaves, which they completely eat away. On reaching maturity, they descend to the ground and pupate, hibernating in silk cocoons. The pupae hibernate throughout the winter, emerging in the spring as fully developed adult moths.

## Tussock moths

The family Lymantriidae contains some of the most destructive of the lepidopteran pests—the tussock moths. Of the 2500 species, several are of economic importance since, when feeding in large groups, they can destroy large areas of vegetation. Most species are medium-sized moths with drab-colored bodies and small heads. Both the caterpillars and adult tussock moths are equipped with irritant hairs that deter predators.

## The gypsy and vaporer moths

The destructive gypsy moth—a lymantriid species—is indigenous to northern Europe, where it is a serious pest of deciduous trees. Unfortunately, the pest now inhabits America, since it escaped captivity there in the 1860s and established a new population of its species. There is a marked difference between male and female gypsy moths. Vaporer moths are lymantriids that share many characteristics with the gypsy moths.

The adult male moths of both species appear between June and late October. The females, being wingless, cannot fly; prior to their emergence from the pupal case, they release pheromones that attract males for mating. The two sexes mate as soon as they meet—no special courtship rituals are involved.

If a female lays eggs at the end of summer, they lie dormant over winter and hatch in the spring. The caterpillars of the vaporer moth are striking in appearance, with three tufts of yellow hair sticking out of their backs, resembling a toothbrush. Several species of tussock moth possess similar hair tufts.

## Farmer's nightmare

The caterpillars of the turnip moth—a noctuid of Europe, Africa and Asia—wreak widespread damage on many types of horticultural crops. Adult turnip moths usually appear in late May, and shortly afterward the fertilized females lay their eggs on vegetation. Immediately after hatching, the caterpillars begin to devour any edible substance that they find. If their numbers are large, turnip moth caterpillars may damage considerable portions of agricultural crops. Since they are nocturnal feeders like their parents, the caterpillars leave the vegetation before daybreak and hide in the soil, where they remain concealed until sunset. They reach maturity toward the end of summer and pupate in the soil, undergoing their final metamorphosis into adult moths—the second generation of adults appears around the middle of October. After mating, females of the second generation lay a new batch of eggs. The caterpillars that hatch from the eggs live in the same way as their predecessors, and pupate before the onset of winter. Throughout winter, they hibernate in cavities in the soil, awaking in spring to continue their life cycle.

## Tiger moths

Approximately 5000 species of tiger moths comprise the family Arctiidae. Adult tiger moths are brightly colored medium to large insects, while their caterpillars are agile and covered with hairs. The long hairs of the caterpillars provide effective protection against predators such as insect-eating birds and parasitic wasps. Adult tiger moths repel their enemies by secreting foul-tasting chemicals: if swallowed, the secretions cause nausea, thereby discouraging future attacks.

Garden tiger moths—inhabitants of the mountains and steppelands of Europe and Asia—are typical members of the family Arctiidae. The adults, which appear around July and August, are brightly colored:

their forewings are white with black markings, while their red hind wings have five roundish black spots. The caterpillars are dark reddish brown, with long hairs that completely cover their bodies. They normally live on field and meadow plants, such as dock and dandelion, feeding on the leaves but not causing significant damage. Full-grown caterpillars pupate, weaving small cocoons from which the adult garden tiger moths emerge.

The scarlet tiger moth—a less common species than the garden tiger moth—lives in damp areas of woodland in the Far East. The adults emerge from their cocoons in midsummer and often fly during the daytime in search of food, even though they are primarily nocturnal creatures. The name "scarlet tiger" is misleading, since the species has metallic blue-green coloration with whitish markings; the hind wings are purple in color with black spots. Scarlet tiger moth caterpillars feed and live on meadow plants.

## Spotted wings

Noctuid moths of the genus *Catocala* are entirely harmless. Although they have brightly colored hind wings, they are inconspicuous as long as they remain stationary on the trunks of trees. If a predator comes too close, the moth surprises its enemy by suddenly unfolding its colorfully spotted wings and flying into the air. Before the predator has a chance to reorient itself and attack, the moth has more than enough time to hide.

In Britain, one of the most common species of moth in the genus *Catocala* is the red underwing. Fertilized females lay their eggs on the leaves of poplars and willows. The eggs overwinter before hatching, and the caterpillars then feed on the host tree. They grow steadily, and when they reach maturity the caterpillars enclose themselves in small, silky cocoons. They turn first into pupae and then—during the summer—into adults. The rosy underwing is similar in appearance to the red underwing, but it is becoming increasingly rare and does not occur in Britain.

## Fast-flying hawk moths

Members of the family Sphingidae are commonly known as hawk moths or sphinx moths. The vast majority have sturdy, hairy bodies and plain wings, although a few species are strikingly colored. Some

**ABOVE The bold black and white markings of the cream-spot tiger moth break up its outline when it settles on a shaded hedgebank, making it almost invisible against its surroundings.**

**BELOW Although moths can fall prey to bats, which are also nocturnal, they have sensory organs that enable them to detect the bats' high frequency locating radar and take avoiding action.**

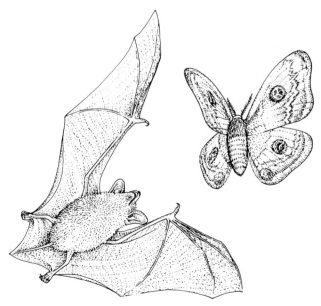

grow to a considerable size, and several of the tropical species have wingspans up to 8 in. wide. The hawk moth's triangular-shaped silhouette is excellent from an aerodynamic point of view, which partly explains why the insects are such good fliers. Some species have been known to reach speeds of over 30 miles an hour.

Hawk moths have characteristically long proboscises, which enable them to suck nectar while they hover in the air above flowers. Hawk moths are the sole pollinators of many nocturnal flowers such as jasmine, fuchsia, convolvulus and orchids, since they are the only insects with sucking organs long enough to reach their nectaries.

Hawk moth caterpillars have a characteristic horn-shaped spike at the tips of their abdomens. They are usually brightly colored, but with camouflage markings that make them inconspicuous at a distance so they can browse freely among the vegetation. Close up, their stripes probably serve to warn enemies of their poisonous nature.

### The honey-stealing hawk moth

One of the most impressive species of moth in the British Isles is the death's-head hawk moth, a large moth with a wingspan of 5 in. It has acquired its name from the variable whitish marks on its back, which can look remarkably like a skull. The species is extremely common in the warmer parts of Europe, Africa and southwest Asia, but is only a summer visitor farther north.

During the summer months, at dusk, the adult death's-head hawk moth flits about among vegetation in search of food. It has a hard, pointed proboscis that enables it to pierce the skins of various kinds of fruit and suck out the sweet juices. It often invades beehives and makes its way into the combs, ignoring the angry reaction of the bees. For this reason, it used to be called the bee tiger hawk moth. In most cases, the bees succeed in killing the moth. They cover its large body with wax and propolis, and leave it inside the hive. Later on, beekeepers often uncover its mummified remains. Occasionally, however, the death's-head hawk moth succeeds in plundering the bees' honey and pollen and escapes from the hive more or less unharmed.

### Vocal and fearless

The death's-head hawk moth is one of the most vocal of all moths, both as a caterpillar and as an adult.

In the caterpillar stage, it grinds its tough mandibles together to produce a series of unexpectedly loud clicks. While making the noise, it throws its brightly colored body from side to side. As an adult, the moth is able to make a squeaky, rasping noise, probably achieved by forcing air down its toughened proboscis.

In the warmer parts of its range, the adult death's-head hawk moth usually appears in the spring, when it mates. As soon as a female has been fertilized, she lays her eggs on a wide variety of poisonous leaves such as woody nightshade, thorn apple, deadly nightshade or potato. When the caterpillars hatch from the eggs, they are bright yellow with blue and purple wedges of color running down their backs. The bright coloration warns predators that they are poisonous.

When fully grown, the death's-head hawk moth caterpillars hide away in cracks in the ground and pupate. Those that have fed on potato crops are often plowed up at the end of the year and are eaten by predators. The survivors remain in their pupal form throughout the winter and complete their development into adults the following spring. In early summer, the adults migrate. The majority of them go no further than northern Europe, but some cover extremely long distances and have been found within the Arctic Circle.

**ABOVE** When feeding, the silver "Y" moth drinks nectar by inserting its long, tube-like mouthparts into a flower. Like humans, moths (and butterflies) have color vision and are attracted by bright flowers (except red ones, which are beyond their vision). Moths and butterflies can also see the ultraviolet end of the color spectrum, and are able to detect patterns of ultraviolet colors on flowers that are invisible to human eyes, but which can be revealed by photography.

## Nocturnal beauty

The oleander hawk moth is so named because, during the caterpillar stage, it feeds on oleander leaves, as well as on grapevines and periwinkle. The caterpillars have large, bright green bodies with two blue spots toward the front. The adult is also large, with a wingspan of up to 5 in. It is extremely brightly colored, with intricate patterns on its wings. When newly emerged, its colors are so vivid that it is considered one of the most beautiful moths in Europe.

The oleander hawk moth is a typical nocturnal species, spending the daylight hours completely immobile among the vegetation. As with the tiger moths, its striking colors blend in with its surroundings, making it almost invisible. When the sun sets, it wakes up and darts about from flower to flower, sucking nectar. The oleander hawk moth is widespread

caterpillar stage, when they feed on many types of plants, and sometimes cause serious damage. Their bodies are covered with numerous warts, protuberances and long, irritating hairs that they use to deter predators.

Processionary moths are members of the family Thaumetopoeidae that weave silky nests around the branches of trees. They remain inside their nests during the day, and emerge at night to feed greedily on the leaves and buds of the trees. They have a characteristic way of proceeding in single file, follow-the-leader fashion, each caterpillar touching the one in front with its head. The leader spins a thread that each successive caterpillar reinforces. Together, they create a long, silken rope that guides them back to their communal nest. There are no British representatives of this family.

### Close-knit silk spinners

The pine processionary moth, which feeds on all types of pine tree, is the most representative species in the family. The tiny adult emerges sometime around July and mates during the night. The fertilized females then fly to one of a number of types of pine tree—such as Scotch pine, cluster pine, mountain pine or white pine—and they lay their eggs at the base of the needles.

The eggs of the pine processionary moth hatch into caterpillars about a month later, in mid-August. The caterpillars are tiny, hump-backed creatures covered in tufts of orange hair. They stay on the pine tree in a close-knit group, and tuft-by-tuft, they begin to chew the tree's needles. At the same time, they also spin a silken web around the whole of that part of the tree. The resulting nest looks like a small, silken bag, the inside of which is divided into a number of cells. Toward the onset of winter, the caterpillars take shelter inside the nest and hibernate.

As soon as the warmer weather comes the following spring, the caterpillars of the pine processionary moth wake up. Finding their tree almost completely bare of pine needles, they crawl down the trunk in a long procession. When they reach the ground, they proceed in single file to another pine tree nearby and climb up it. When they reach the foliage, they separate and start eating the young needles. After they have satisfied their hunger, they form a column once again and retrace their steps, following the thread they left behind on the way.

**ABOVE** The forewings of the Clifden nonpareil moth mimic tree bark while its hind wings are marked with bright bands. In the resting position, the first pair of wings completely covers the hind wings, and the moth is inconspicuous on tree bark. If an enemy approaches, however, the insect rapidly uncovers the second pair of wings to startle the predator, enabling it to escape.

throughout the Mediterranean area, and sometimes collects in large numbers and migrates from the north African coast to central and northern Europe.

Many other types of hawk moth are capable of migrating considerable distances. The convolvulus hawk moth, for example, journeys to central and northern Europe at the beginning of the summer. Once there, it reproduces, and members of the second generation return to the place of origin. Another species with an enormous capacity for migration is the hummingbird hawk moth. Each year, in May or June, members of the species cross the Alps from southern Europe and fly into central and northern Europe.

### Communal caterpillars

Moths that belong to the family Thaumetopoeidae are small and plain. They are better known in the

Back in their nest, the caterpillars hide until it is time for their next foray. They continue the foraging behavior until the end of May, at which point they leave the nest permanently and take shelter in individual holes in the ground. There, each one spins a small, silken cocoon and pupates. The adult moth emerges from its pupa at the beginning of July.

## Tiny nuisances

The pine processionary moth is a menace, partly because of its ability to strip entire pine plantations bare and partly because of its irritating hairs. If its hairs penetrate the skin, the damage they cause may amount to no more than acute itching and swelling, but if they come into contact with the eyes or mucous membranes of the nose, they can cause serious inflammation. Consequently, it is most important not to touch a nest with bare hands.

The oak processionary moth, another species in the family Thaumetopoeidae, feeds on oak trees. The caterpillars are hairy and build large, bag-shaped silken nests on the trunks and branches of the trees. They take refuge in their nests during daylight hours but, unlike the pine processionary moth caterpillars, they do not hibernate. When winter draws on, they turn into pupae and then into adults. The adult moths

**ABOVE** Hawk moths are some of the best fliers of the lepidopterans. With their powerful thoracic muscles, streamlined shapes and tough build, they achieve speeds of over 30 miles an hour. The oleander hawk moth has delta-shaped wings with a span of 5 in. Its coloration acts as camouflage, rather than as a warning to predators.

appear toward the end of August. They mate and start laying their eggs on the branches of oak trees. The eggs lie dormant inside a protective covering throughout the winter and hatch in the spring.

The oak processionary moth has its own peculiar way of moving from tree to tree in search of food. One caterpillar assumes the role of leader. Immediately behind it come two caterpillars side-by-side, then three in a row, and so on until there are about 20 caterpillars in a row. Subsequent rows have progressively fewer caterpillars, with a single caterpillar taking up the rear. Like other species of processionary moth, they each create a long, silken rope that leads them back to the communal nest.

## The giant silk-making moths

Members of the family Saturniidae are commonly known as silk moths. They are unusually large, and some tropical species, such as the Asian atlas moth,

## INSECTS CLASSIFICATION: 24

### *Moths and butterflies (3)*

The Noctuoidea is the largest of the superfamilies in the suborder Ditrysia, order Lepidoptera. It has nearly 40,000 species of largely night-flying moths in 14 families that occur throughout the world. These families include the Noctuidae (noctuid or owlet moths) with more than 37,000 species, including the turnip moth, *Agrotis segetis*, of Europe, Africa and Asia, the giant owl moth, *Thysania agrippina*, of tropical America, the red underwing, *Catocala nupta*, and the silver "Y" moth, *Autographa gamma*; the Notodontidae (prominents) with such species as the puss moth, *Cerura vinula*, and buff-tip moth, *Phalera bucephala*; the Lymantriidae (tussock moths) whose 2500 species include such pests as the gypsy moth, *Lymantria dispar*, of northern Europe, and the vaporer moth, *Orgyia antiqua*, of Europe; the Arctiidae (tiger moths), which include the garden tiger moth, *Arctia caja*, common throughout Europe and temperate Asia to Japan, and the scarlet tiger moth, *Panaxia dominula*, of the Far East; and the Thaumetopoeidae (processionary moths).

The superfamily Sphingoidea has less than a thousand species and only one family, the Sphingidae (hawk moths). These fast-flying moths occur throughout the world, but are at their most plentiful in the tropics. They include the death's-head hawk moth, *Acherontia atropos*; the oleander hawk moth, *Daphnis nerii*, of Europe; the convolvulus hawk moth, *Herse convolvuli*, of tropical Africa and Asia; and the hummingbird hawk moths (genus *Macroglossum*).

The superfamily Bombycoidea has 12 families and some 3400 species of moths. These include the atlas and emperor moths of the family Saturniidae (such as the Asian atlas moth, *Attacus atlas*, one of the world's largest lepidopterans, with a wingspan of 10 in.; and the lesser emperor moth, *Saturnia pavonia*, of temperate Europe and Asia); the silkworm moth, *Bombyx mori*, of the family Bombycidae, whose cocoons are used for the commercial production of silk; and the lackey moth, *Malacosoma neustria*, of Eurasia, and lappet moth, *Gastropacha quercifolia*, which ranges from Europe to China and Japan (both of the family Lasiocampidae).

have wingspans of up to 10 in. Their bodies are short and squat, and they rarely have a proboscis. In general, their wings are not strikingly colored but they usually have large eyespots on them to scare off potential predators. Silk moth caterpillars are large and colorful, and their bodies often have a protective covering of protuberances, spines and clumps of stinging hairs. Many types are specially reared to produce "wild" silk and, in some parts of Asia, they are eaten by humans.

The tree-of-heaven, or ailanthus, silk moth of the family Saturniidae, is a large moth with a wingspan of over 5 in. Originally from Asia, it has been introduced into both Europe and North America. In southern Europe, this nocturnal moth is commonly found in gardens and hedgerows.

Adult silk moths appear in the spring. They mate immediately, and the females lay their eggs as soon as they have been fertilized. Although the females place their eggs in a variety of trees, their favorite is the ailanthus. Soon after the caterpillars hatch, they begin to devour the leaves. They grow rapidly, and quickly reach maturity. Then each caterpillar folds up a leaf and wraps it in a silken web, forming a shelter in which to spin a small cocoon. The caterpillars undergo their final transformation within their cocoons, and emerge as adults the following spring.

### Lethargic females

The southern European great peacock silk moth is the largest species of butterfly or moth in the south of Europe, with a wingspan of over 6 in. Its wings are reddish in color, and each has a large eyespot in the middle. At dusk, the males dart about among woodland trees and grassy fields in search of the females, who are extremely lethargic by comparison and rarely leave the plant upon which they were reared.

The females do not take off and fly to trees, such as pear and ash, until they have been fertilized. Once in a tree, they lay a number of eggs that hatch into yellowish caterpillars. The caterpillars are voracious eaters and immediately attack the leaves and new buds of the tree, chewing away at them continuously. They grow quickly, sometimes reaching a length of over 4 in. As they grow, their color changes from yellow to bright green. They also develop many clubbed hairs and a large number of bright blue tubercles that resemble a crown of thorns.

When the silk moth caterpillars are fully grown, they stop eating and head for a sheltered place where they can spin their large silky cocoons and turn into pupae. They spend the winter in hibernation and wake up the following spring to complete their development, finally emerging as adults.

The only species of silk moth found in the British Isles is the emperor moth. It is widely distributed and, in certain areas, is quite common. With a wingspan of only 2.4 in. it is considered a small species of silk moth. There is a marked difference in size and color between the males and females. The males are smaller and more brightly colored.

Adult silk moths emerge from their cocoons as spring approaches, and the males fly about during the day in search of receptive females. The females usually take to the wing only at night. After mating, each fertilized female flies to a suitable food plant, such as bramble, heather, loosestrife or sallow, where she lays a long string of eggs. The caterpillars that hatch from the eggs are blackish in color and feed on the leaves of the host plant. As they mature, the caterpillars turn bright green and develop 12 bands of yellow lumps with a black patch at their base and a ring of spines at the top. When they reach their full size, they each spin a cocoon and wrap it in a silken web. Like the majority of silk moths, the emperor moth hibernates during the pupal stage and completes its development the following spring.

### The silkworm moth

The family Bombycidae consists of smallish, drably colored moths that occur in eastern Asia and Africa and includes the silkworm moth *Bombyx mori*. It is a light-colored moth of Chinese origin. The only completely domesticated insect, it is unable to feed itself or exist in the wild. Silkworm moths are ideal insects to keep in captivity because, through cross-breeding and artificial selection, they have become docile with no instinct to wander or hide themselves. As a result of the excessive crossbreeding, silkworm moths have genetically altered over the past 3500 years of domesticity. There remain no wild populations, and if released into the wild, they would soon die. Selective breeding has encouraged the silkworms to produce larger cocoons and higher quality silk.

The silkworm moth has been used for the production of silk since the reign of the Chinese

TOP **A caterpillar of the tawny prominent moth raises its strangely shaped abdomen in self-defense. When attacked, the caterpillar defends itself with the purple, thorn-like appendages on its back and lashes out with its fork-shaped** abdomen. In addition, it sprays poisonous liquid from holes underneath its neck.
ABOVE **An adult pine processionary moth rests during the daylight hours, relying on its natural color camouflage to protect it from predators.**

which passes the winter as eggs. Silkworm moths lay their eggs (seed) at night on the leaves of mulberry trees. The eggs hatch after about 20 days into tiny larvae (silkworms). The silkworms are helpless and need to have their food of mulberry leaves brought to them by the adult moths. They grow rapidly, shedding their skins four times. Each skin change involves 24 hours of inactivity when they do not feed.

Silkworms reach their full size within a month, when they stop feeding altogether and begin to make side-to-side weaving movements with their heads. Commercial silk growers supply the silkworms with branches on which to spin their cocoons—known as the "ascent into the woods." Inside their cocoons, those that are kept for breeding the next generation undergo the final transformation into pupae and then into adults, finally emerging ready to begin a new life.

## Unraveling the silk

The silkworms spin their cocoons from silk. They fuse two strands of silk together so that if cut across (in cross-section) they resemble a figure-eight. For commercial purposes it is important to remove the silk before the pupa matures. If left to mature, the emerging moth will cut its way out of the cocoon at one end, severing the continuous thread of silk. Once severed by the moth, the silk is useless to the silk producers.

The silk growers dry out the cocoon required for silk production, killing the pupating moths. The cocoon is then immersed in hot water, which dissolves the outer layer of silk glue or sericin, and releases the ends of the threads. By gently pulling a few strands of silk at a time away from the edges of the cocoon, the continuous thread of silk (made of fibroin) is unraveled and wound onto a spool.

## Eggars or Lasiocampidae

Members of the family Lasiocampidae, or eggars, occur throughout the world. They have rounded, squat, shaggy bodies and short, rounded wings with bland coloration that blends in with the vegetation in which they live. Some species, such as the oak moth, are camouflaged, making them difficult to detect when they are resting on the oak trees which they inhabit. Vividly colored species, with elongated, narrow bodies, they occur only in the tropics. The females lay large numbers of eggs in the branches of trees. The

**ABOVE** The silk moth family contains some of the largest of all insects—the adults of some species have a wingspan of over 12 in., while their larvae may reach lengths of 4 in. and widths of 0.8 in. However, not all the silk moths are giants: this British male emperor moth, for example, has a wingspan of about 2 in. It is one of Britain's largest moths.

**FAR RIGHT** The warmer parts of Europe provide a home for some of the larger silk moths, such as this ailanthus moth. Like all butterflies and moths, it requires time to expand and harden its wings after emerging from its pupal case. A newly emerged adult moth is exposed to many dangers since it is unable to fly or use its startling eyespots to deter predators. If the silk moth falls from its twig, it risks irreparable damage to its wings. With damaged wings, the moth cannot fly and, if it is a male, it is unlikely that it will be able to mate.

Empress Si-Lang-Chi some 2000 years ago. The silk trade developed slowly throughout Asia and India, but the secrets of its production remained a mystery to the rest of the world until AD 555, when two monks smuggled some silkworm moths' eggs out of China inside their bamboo staffs. The theft led to the establishment of the silk trade in Europe.

Silkworm moths are squat, hairy insects that cannot fly. They produce one generation of offspring a year,

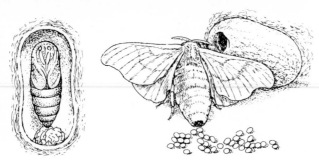

during July and August, and spend the summer evenings fluttering about among the foliage looking for a mate.

## A bracelet of eggs

Fertilized female lackey moths lay their eggs on the branch of a tree, arranging them in a ring so that they surround an entire twig like a bracelet. The eggs remain dormant throughout the winter and hatch the following spring, producing tiny, gregarious caterpillars. The caterpillars chew the leaves and buds of the host tree. At the same time, they bind the leaves together with a silken web, forming a kind of communal nest. Like many pest species, the lackey moth caterpillars are polyphagous feeders—they will eat many different types of plants and trees, including hawthorn, oak, willow and most fruit trees.

When the lackey moth caterpillars have reached a more advanced stage of development, they lose their gregarious instincts and disperse among the foliage, although their appetite does not diminish and they continue to eat the leaves. They reach full size in June, when they spin silk cocoons and pupate.

## Autumn-leaf camouflage

The lappet moth inhabits areas stretching from the eastern shores of the Atlantic as far east as China and Japan. It has a bulky body and is one of Europe's largest lepidopterans. It has copper-reddish wings with notched edges and, when at rest, its hind wings jut out slightly from under the forewings. In this position, the moth resembles a dead leaf. The lappet moth inhabits hawthorn, sallow and apple trees and causes little damage. Although common in some parts of Europe, it has become rarer elsewhere because of the use of pesticides in orchards.

The adult female lappet moth only lays a small number of eggs, and although the caterpillars devour large quantities of foliage, there are too few of them to pose a serious threat. They are typical nocturnal moths that appear at the height of summer and flutter about among the trees at night in search of food and a mate. A fertilized female lays her eggs on the branch of a tree. The eggs hatch in September, and the caterpillars feed during the night. By winter, they have grown up to a length of 0.8 to 1.2 in.

When the weather turns cold in autumn, the caterpillars hide in the cracks and crannies of tree

TOP A silkworm (family Bombycidae) climbs a plant-stem in search of a suitable spot for pupation. The larva's silk—valued by humans for over 2000 years—is the unraveled, continuous thread with which it spins its cocoon; a single cocoon yields between 2600 and 3300 feet of silk thread. Despite this high yield, 50,000 silk worms are required to make 2.2 lbs. of raw silk. In 1980 the world's silk industry destroyed nearly 1,524,215 million silkworms in its production of 30,000 tons of silk.

ABOVE LEFT After spinning its tough, protective cocoon, a silkworm sheds its skin and becomes a pupa.

ABOVE RIGHT Since humans keep great numbers of silk moths in captivity, the ability to fly has been bred out of the original silk-producing species. In consequence, female silk moths have become little more than egg-laying machines.

eggs hatch into hairy caterpillars that feed on the leaves until they reach maturity. Once mature, they spin silken cocoons where they transform into pupae.

The lackey moth, one of the most common species of lasiocampids in the British Isles, often collects in large numbers and can cause severe damage to vegetation and crops. A squat, furry moth with yellowish wings, it occurs throughout Europe. The newly formed adult moths emerge from their cocoons

trunks, and lie dormant throughout the winter. The lappet moth caterpillars are flat underneath, enabling them to press themselves against the branch of a tree or a bush where, if they are unable to find a more sheltered resting place, they can survive hard frost, sleet and icy winds. The caterpillars are gray in color and when resting on bark, they are difficult to find. They remain dormant until the following spring. On waking, they resume feeding and pupate in July inside silken cocoons. The moths emerge from the cocoons after two weeks.

## Butterflies

The superfamily Hesperioidae, the first of the butterfly groupings, contains two families including the family Hesperiidae, or skippers. Although classified as butterflies, skippers are moth-like in appearance and habits and differ from all the other butterflies. Skippers comprise a large family with hundreds of different species distributed throughout the world. Most species have clubbed antennae with a slender, hooked extension; wide heads with large protruding eyes; robust thoraxes with short, powerful, veined wings; and strong, conical, hairy bodies. They are usually small in size, although some tropical species that inhabit the American tropics and

**ABOVE Many species of moths and butterflies have evolved colors and shapes that closely resemble natural foliage. Apart from having the coloration of dead leaves, lappet moths have developed stem-like protuberances at the base of their heads; the species has developed its camouflage to such an extent that its shape has altered. When resting, it pushes its hind wings down, increasing its resemblance to a leaf.**

**PAGES 2630-2631 The lesser emperor moth inhabits the woodlands of Asia and central and northern Europe. Two round, brightly colored eyespots, known as "peacock's eyes," decorate the moth's wings; the striking markings often discourage predators, since they resemble the eyes of a larger creature. Unlike other species of emperor moths, the lesser emperor moth is most active during daylight hours.**

subtropics, and other species that occur in eastern Asia and India, have wingspans of approximately 3 in.

Skippers are usually brown and tawny-yellow, but some of the tropical species have bright metallic blue and green colors on their wings. Skippers are unusual in that they fly both by day and night and, like moths, are sometimes attracted to artificial light. They fly in short, sharp, rapid movements, darting about from flower to flower.

## The blues and azures

The family Lycaenidae belongs to the superfamily Papilionoidea, and consists of small, sometimes brilliantly colored butterflies that occur all over the world. The family includes a group of butterflies known as the blues. The blues' caterpillars are usually flattened on the underside and convex on the back, with short hairs, short feet and retractable heads. They often live in the company of ants, some even eat them. They have special organs that secrete substances to attract the ants. However, most lycaenid caterpillars live in trees where they feed on the foliage. The pupae are short, roundish, immobile and often hairy. They either lie on the ground under leaves or moss, or are tied with a girdle to branches of trees, head upward.

## Milked by ants

The large blue butterfly lays its eggs on the herb called thyme. The newly hatched caterpillars feed on the flower heads until they reach their third larval stage when they change their diet completely. The caterpillars wander off, producing a sugary secretion from special glands on their backs. Ants pick up their trail and carry the caterpillars back to their nest. Once inside the nest, the ants "milk" the caterpillars of their sweet secretions, while the large blue butterfly

ABOVE At first glance, butterflies of the skipper family resemble typical moths. Skippers are intermediate lepidopterans, occupying a position somewhere between butterflies and moths, since they display traits from both groups. During daylight hours, the strong-flying large skipper butterfly "skips" or flits restlessly from one flower to the next. The skipper shown here has lost most of its wing scales.

caterpillars eat the ant larvae. The caterpillars pupate the following spring and emerge three weeks later, hurriedly escaping from the ant nest.

## Paying for protection

Belonging to the same family as the blues, the azure butterflies of Papua New Guinea and northern Australia have a mutually beneficial relationship with ants. However, unlike the blues, they do not eat the ants' larvae or eggs; instead they bribe the ants to protect them.

The Genevieve azure butterfly occurs in southeast Australia. The adult male has vivid violet wings, and the females are greenish blue with a pale yellow pattern on their forewings. They are medium-sized butterflies with a wingspan of about 2 in.

Female Genevieve azure butterflies lay their eggs on the parasitic mistletoe that infests many trees, such

## INSECTS CLASSIFICATION: 25

### Moths and butterflies (4)

The first of the butterfly groupings, the super-family Hesperioidea (skippers) in the suborder Ditrysia, contains two families and over 3100 species. The family Hesperiidae contains most of the skippers, such as the dingy skipper, *Erynnis tages*, of Britain and southern and central Europe.

The vast majority of butterflies belong to the superfamily Papilionoidea (true butterflies). It is a large group with over 15,000 species divided into 13 families. These include the Lycaenidae, a diverse family that includes such species as the large blue, *Maculinea arion*, occurring across Europe to Siberia and Japan, the azure butterflies of Papua New Guinea and northern Australia and the moth butter-fly, which ranges from India to northern Australia; and the Papilionidae (swallowtails), which includes the European swallowtail, *Papilio machaon*.

The family Pieridae (whites and yellows) contains the cabbage-white or large white, *Pieris brassicae*; the small white, *Artogeia rapae*, of North Africa and Europe; the clouded yellow, *Colias crocea*, of southern Europe and North Africa; and the pale clouded yellow, *Colias hyale*, of central and eastern Europe.

The family Nymphalidae (brush-footed butterflies) is the largest of the butterfly families, with over 200 genera and more than 4000 species in several subfamilies. These include the Nymphalinae, which contains such famous species as the Camberwell beauty, *Nymphalis antiopa*, of Europe and North America, the red admiral, *Vanessa atalanta*, the painted lady, *Cynthia cardui*, the small tortoiseshell, *Aglais urticae*, the peacock butterfly, *Inachis io*, and the comma butterfly, *Polygonia c-album*; the Heliconiinae, which contains the small postman, *Heliconius erato*, and postman butterfly, *Heliconius melpomene*, of South America; and the Charaxiinae, which contains the two-tailed pasha, *Charaxes jasius*, found along the Mediterranean coast, Ethiopia and Central Africa.

Other families include the Morphidae with the tropical South American genus *Morpho*; and the Satyridae (browns) with more than 3000 species, containing the marbled white, *Melanargia galathea*, of North Africa and Europe (including southern England) to the Baltic coast.

ABOVE A green underside butterfly of the "blue" family feeds on plants such as vetch and broom. Most species of blue butterflies have complicated life cycles: some live in ants' nests, where they provide sugary secretions in return for shelter; others secretly feed on the eggs and larvae of their ant hosts.

as eucalyptus and oak. The caterpillars produce sweet-tasting secretions from "honey glands" that attract ants of the genus *Camponotus*. The ants carry the Genevieve azure caterpillars back to their nest, which may be up to 100 ft. away. Both the ants and the caterpillars are nocturnal, and at nightfall the ants escort the caterpillars up the tree to the mistletoe where the caterpillars feed. While they are feeding, the ants keep a lookout for any predators, and if any approach they will fight to protect their valuable charge. In return, the ants lick not only the sugary secretions but also proteins and important amino acids from other glands along the caterpillars' bodies. At dawn the ants guide the caterpillars back to their nest.

### A caterpillar with armor

The caterpillar of the moth butterfly occurs in the nests of weaver ants in the forests of India through to northern Australia. It has a large, oval, leathery shell

Pale sapphire (male)
(*Iolaus lalos*)

Peruvian blue
(*Morpho didius*)

Purple emperor
(*Apatura iris*)

Small tortoiseshell
(*Aglais urticae*)

Bhutan papilio
(*Bhutanitis lidderdalei*)

Sulawesi swordtail (male)
(*Graphium androcles*)

South American
jumping metalmark
(*Mesosemia sp.*)

South American nymphalid
(*Agrias claudia*)

2634

Javan nawab
(*Papilio dehaani*)

Guianas cattle heart
(*Papilio childrenae*)

Blue mountain butterfly
(*Papilio ulysses*)

with a rounded base and a sharp ridge running around its top, covering its back edge. The caterpillar enters the nest of weaver ants, pushing itself along, keeping its carapace close to the ground so that the ants cannot crawl underneath. The ants defend their territory by biting the caterpillar's armor, squirting it with acid and adopting threatening postures. The caterpillar shrugs off these attacks and continues into the heart of the nest until it reaches the nursery, where it feeds on the ant larvae. Ants keep their young in sticky bundles, enabling the caterpillar to take nine or ten larvae at once.

When the moth butterfly caterpillar has finished feeding and is ready to pupate, it attaches itself to a leaf and pupates inside its protective carapace. As the metamorphosis takes place, the flat armor inflates. The adult butterfly emerges into a nest of angry ants. As it clambers out of its old pupal case, the ants converge and attack. Grabbing its hair in their jaws, they try to pull the butterfly to the ground, usually failing. Some ants try to grab the butterfly's legs, but covered in slippery scales, the legs are difficult to hold. Slowly, the butterfly's wings expand and harden and it makes its exit from the nest and flies away.

At present it is not known whether the caterpillar of the moth butterfly uses chemicals to mislead the ants, but its close relative from Africa, *Euliphyra*, is thought to fool the ants into believing that it is an ant larva by secreting a special chemical.

## Swallowtails

Members of the family Papilionidae are typical daytime butterflies. Known as swallowtails, they are usually large, brightly colored butterflies that occur throughout the world. Many species display a high degree of sexual dimorphism (marked differences between males and females). In some species of swallowtail, the females of a single species occur in various color forms, whereas the males all look the same. Generally though, swallowtails have large, compacted, rounded wings, small bodies and small heads. They have long, thin legs with two claws on their feet, and their front legs, in both the males and females, are well developed.

Swallowtail caterpillars vary from hairless to spiny or even hairy, and they all have a forked organ called the osmeterium just behind their heads. Conspicuous in color, it exudes a pungent smell, and when disturbed,

ABOVE **The small copper is an aggressive butterfly with strong territorial instincts. It protects its air space with such determination that even birds stay clear.**
BELOW **The drawing depicts the life cycle of the typical blue butterfly—a parasite of ants' nests. Blue butterflies and their** caterpillars enjoy a symbiotic relationship with their hosts: the ants provide the caterpillars with care and protection, in return for their valued sweet secretions. Although the ants carry the caterpillars to flowers to feed, the gluttonous "guests" respond by eating the ant larvae.

the butterfly shoots it out, waving it in the air. Most swallowtail caterpillars do not spin cocoons before pupating. Instead they hang from branches, head downward, camouflaged as leaves or twigs.

The common swallowtail, *Papilio machaon*, occurs throughout Europe and North Africa. In Britain it occurs in the low-lying marshy or flooded areas of Cambridge, Suffolk and Norfolk. Different from the European species, the British common swallowtail, *Machaon britannicus*, is smaller in size and a darker yellow in color, and does not fly as well as its continental relative.

Female swallowtails lay their eggs on fennel, wild carrot and milk parsley. The eggs hatch into pale green caterpillars marked with bands of black and orange. British subspecies produce only one generation a year, whereas the continental forms produce two—the second generation have much lighter yellow wings, and their brown markings are powdered with yellow. The caterpillars that pupate at the end of spring have green pupae, and those that overwinter as pupae are brown.

## The whites and yellows

Butterflies of the family Pieridae have clubbed antennae and white or yellow wings decorated with

**ABOVE** The family Papilionidae contains some of the largest and most beautiful butterflies in the order Lepidoptera. One member of the family—the beautiful European swallowtail—inhabits the British Isles. The wingspan of the giant Queen Alexandra's birdwing of Indo-Australasia measures up to 11 in.—the first specimen of the massive species was brought down by gunshot.
**RIGHT** The clouded yellow butterfly (family Pieridae) inhabits most regions of the world. In some countries, the populations of certain species have grown to such an extent that clouded yellows present farmers with a serious pest problem. Parasitic wasps and flies are the natural predators of clouded yellow butterflies.

darker markings. They are known as whites or yellows. Almost all of them display marked differences between the sexes. The males are usually lighter in color with a black mark at the tips of their wings, and the darker females are often yellow or pale orange. Pierids occur in most countries around the world. Some species are great travelers, seen occasionally in large numbers flying over the sea.

## The familiar cabbage-white

The cabbage white, or large white, butterfly occurs in North Africa, western Europe, Asia, Siberia and even in the Himalaya mountains. It produces three

ABOVE A red admiral butterfly rests on sumach leaves. It inhabits Europe, western Asia, northern Africa and North America. In summer, the red admiral travels long distances, pausing often during its journey to feed on fallen pears. If left undisturbed, it remains near its food source for several days.

or four generations a year (although in Britain, cabbage whites are immigrants from Europe and only produce two generations). The caterpillars are small and feed upon cabbages and other members of the cabbage family. The adult cabbage-white butterflies are a common sight in gardens and vegetable patches. They hover above flowers in search of nectar and a mate. From time to time, cabbage-whites from southern Europe and North Africa congregate in large swarms which may fly over the Alps, even reaching Scandinavia.

## Gregarious cabbage eaters

Fertilized females lay their eggs on many types of vegetable, mainly those of the cabbage family, depositing them on the undersides of leaves. The eggs hatch into gregarious caterpillars that stay together in groups, greedily devouring the leaves. Because they often occur in large numbers, they do severe damage to vegetable crops. When fully grown, they lose their gregarious tendencies and go off separately to hide in cracks in the walls, rocks or the bark of trees, where they

pupate. The pupae of caterpillars born in the autumn halt their metamorphosis and lie dormant throughout the winter, ready to complete their development as soon as the weather warms up in the spring.

## Killed by the cold

Members of the genus *Colias* are common throughout the Northern Hemisphere. One of the most common species is the clouded yellow. Migrating to Britain and other parts of northern Europe in the summer, it is active between April and September. It produces two generations during the summer, but clouded yellow butterflies cannot survive the cold winters of northern Europe, and the second generation of butterflies will perish in the first cold days of winter.

Like many other yellows, the caterpillars of clouded yellow butterflies are grass-green in color with a white and orange streak running down their sides. They feed on clover, lucerne and vetch. When fully grown, they attach themselves to the stems of plants and pupate. After about 20 days, the adult butterflies emerge.

## The butter-colored fly

The origin of the name "butterfly" is uncertain, but some entomologists believe it refers to the common butterfly called the brimstone. The male of this species has pale yellow wings that are similar in color to butter, hence butter-colored fly, shortened to "butterfly."

## Brush-footed butterflies

The family Nymphalidae, or brush-footed butterflies, includes among its members both the smallest and the largest of all butterfly species. Many of the large species have brightly colored wings; the uppersides are often colored with red and yellow while the undersides are dull and have "cryptic" patterns—they protect the butterflies by concealing them in their habitats. Although they are brightly colored, nymphalids are not poisonous and are eaten by birds and lizards. They can be distinguished from other butterflies by their small front legs, which lack claws and are useless for walking or perching. Tufts of scales cover most nymphalids' legs, from which they derive their common name "brush-footed." Male nymphalids have scent scales, or androconia, on their wings that produce perfumed substances called pheromones. The pheromones serve to excite females, encouraging them to mate. A large number of brush-footed

butterflies have distinct differences between the sexes (a phenomenon called sexual dimorphism), and many species practice mimicry. The caterpillars usually have a covering of spines and tubercles arranged in longitudinal rows.

### An Indian tropical

The Indian leaf butterfly of the subfamily Nymphalinae occurs in the tropical forests of India, Burma and south China. The undersides of its wings and the arrangement of its veins resemble a leaf, and when at rest the butterfly is well camouflaged. However, when disturbed, it opens its wings to display the brightly colored upper surfaces. The caterpillar of the Indian leaf butterfly feeds on various tropical nettleworts.

### Poisonous prey

Members of the subfamily Heliconiinae occur mainly in the forests of South America. They generally contain foul-tasting poisons, and are unpopular to most predators. As a result, many other species of

**ABOVE** Although the black-veined white butterfly was once common throughout northern Europe, it has become scarce in recent years. Black-veined whites sometimes damage fruit trees, but their small numbers ensure that they do not present a serious menace to orchards. The last British black-veined white was spotted in 1925.

butterflies and moths mimic them. Although similar in color and size, the mimicking butterflies rarely contain the poison, but the outer resemblance is sufficient to ward off predators.

The tropical American passionflower butterfly or small postman, *Heliconius erato*, occurs in a wide variety of forms and colors. Unlike most other butterflies and moths, its ears, which take the form of air sacs, are situated at the base of its hind wings.

The closely related postman, *Heliconius melpomene*, matches nearly all the color forms of the small postman and occurs in the same areas.

Nearly all heliconid butterflies lay their eggs on the leaves and stems of various species of passionflower. The caterpillars that hatch from these eggs are usually

**ABOVE Butterflies of the "brown" family avoid predators by using avoiding tactics in flight. While other butterfly families rely on camouflage, bright warning colors or eyespots for their protection, brown butterflies fly in an erratic, fluttering fashion, making it difficult for flying predators to seize them.**

brown or white and covered in long, barbed spikes. Voracious feeders, they will strip and kill a passionflower if a female butterfly lays too many eggs on it. To prevent this from happening, the passionflower has evolved its own defense strategy. At the base of each leaf, a prime site for egg-laying, the passionflower produces a number of tiny, egg-shaped, nectar-producing growths. The female butterfly only lays a certain number of eggs on a particular leaf, and it is thought that the egg-mimicking growths on the plant discourage the butterfly from laying more than one or two on a particular leaf.

## Rajahs and pashas

The genus *Charaxes* contains species that are sometimes called charaxes, rajahs or pashas. They are all colorful and have bold markings on their wings. They occur in Africa, India, Pakistan and Burma. There are no British species, but the two-tailed pasha, *Charaxes jasius*, occurs as far north as the Mediterranean coast, especially in Italy. It has brown wings with a light yellow-red border; its hind wings are decorated with a row of blue spots, and it has two spurs on the trailing edge of each hind wing. The undersides of its wings are brighter in color and richer in design. The caterpillar has a green head with four red horns. It has a green body with a yellow stripe down each side, and two vivid blue spots on its back.

The caterpillars of the two-tailed pasha feed on the strawberry tree.

## Iridescent Amazonian beauties

Members of the genus *Morpho* occur in forests from Mexico to northern Argentina, and they are most abundant in the Amazon Basin. Known as morphos, they are large butterflies, noted for their beautiful iridescent coloring. The males have brightly colored wings with a metallic sheen, particularly of blue, but also of red, brown or yellow. These colors are not produced by pigments in the wing of the butterfly, but by some other process that is at present unknown. For a long time it was thought that light refraction within the minute scales on their wings formed the pure colors, but if this were true the colors would change when viewed from different angles. However, the wings remain a constant color regardless of the angle from which they are viewed. A recent theory suggests that the scales are liquid crystals.

## The browns

The family Satyridae comprises over 3000 species that occur in the tropics and in both polar regions. Usually called browns, their wings are brown or buff and marked with eyespots on one or both sides. They have small front legs that lack claws. The slender caterpillars lack long hairs or spines and feed on grasses or similar plants. The caterpillars hibernate in winter among grass stems. The pupae usually hang suspended by the tail, although some lie free on the ground or among grass stems, which they may spin lightly together to provide extra shelter.

The marbled white, *Melanargia galathea*, has a wide distribution and occurs in North Africa, Europe and the Baltic coast. In Britain it occurs in the greatest numbers in southern England.

The upper surfaces of the adult marbled whites are marbled black and white, while the undersides of the males are gray and white and those of the female are orangey-brown. They are on the wing from June to July. Female marbled whites lay their eggs on various species of grass, including cock's foot and cat's-tail. The caterpillars have light brown heads and either a light green body with a pale green stripe, or a pale brown body with a yellowish stripe. Overwintering while still small, the caterpillars complete their development the following year.

# SHOWPIECE AERIALISTS

House flies, mosquitoes and midges are noted for their matchless maneuverability in the air. Although minute and flightless, fleas can also reach for the sky, achieving jumps of over 13 in. in height

ABOVE **Flies rely on their compound eyes to spot prey and avoid predators. A phenomenon called "flicker vision"—the almost simultaneous perception of dozens of individual light stimuli—enables a fly** to interpret, and act upon, incredibly fast movement in its environment.
PAGE 2641 **A crane fly, or "daddy-longlegs," of the species *Tipula oleracea* hangs between blades of grass.**

The order Diptera, the fourth-largest order in the class Insecta, consists of two-winged flies—commonly known as true flies. With over 90,000 species in three suborders and 114 families, flies are one of the most diverse of all animal groups. They occur in great numbers in every conceivable habitat from the deserts of Australia and Africa and rain forests all over the world to the edges of the polar regions and the sea. One species of fly, *Heleomyia petrolei*, has even managed to make its home in pools of petroleum. Hardly a single habitat has escaped the attention of flies.

Not only do flies occur almost everywhere, but they have also adapted to many different life-styles. Many people think of them as either bloodsuckers or the eaters of excrement and decomposing flesh. However, many flies play an important role as pollinators and predators that curb the populations of pest species. If they did not feed on rotting organic matter and return valuable nutrients back to the soil, the world would soon be overwhelmed by putrefying wastes.

Despite their benefits to the environment, flies have been responsible for widespread damage to both humans and their crops. They transmit malaria, sleeping sickness, typhoid and yellow fever, and other lesser-known protozoal infections that account for the deaths of millions of children every year.

Flies cause devastating damage to the health of livestock by laying their eggs in the mucous membranes of an animal's eyes and nose or directly inside any open wounds that it has. As soon as the larvae hatch, they burrow into the animal's flesh and feed on it. The wounds caused by the feeding maggots often become infected by other organisms, too. Humans can also become hosts to the flesh-eating maggots laid by flies.

Among the species of fly that damage crops, fruit flies are particularly devastating. By laying their eggs inside the maturing fruit, fruit flies can destroy complete orchards. They have a short life cycle, so they multiply rapidly and quickly overwhelm crops.

## Two wings

Flies are unique among insects in their physical appearance. While most insects have either no wings at all, two pairs of wings or a pair of wings and a tough wing cover, flies have only one pair of wings. Their second pair has become reduced to two club-like organs that are used as stabilizing devices or minute gyroscopes. The head of a fly bears two compound eyes that are usually quite large and often brightly colored. Between its eyes, a fly has two antennae that are generally short but vary in shape and size.

The mouthparts of bloodsucking flies consist of two sections—one to pierce the skin of a victim and the other to suck its blood. After settling on its prey, the fly first stabs the skin with its dagger-like mouthparts. To stop the blood from coagulating before it has finished sucking, the fly injects some of its own saliva—which contains an anticoagulant—into the victim's bloodstream.

Flies that obtain their food without biting their prey have mouthparts adapted to form a trumpet-like proboscis, or feeding tube, for lapping or sucking. The feeding tube is sensitive to touch, and the flies use it to feel the ground as they move along in search of food. Flies that lack biting mouthparts can only ingest food in liquid form.

## Fly courtship

Like many other groups of insect, flies have various ways of attracting members of the opposite sex. Probably the most studied courtship behavior is that of the fruit fly. When a male and female meet, they turn head-on to each other. The male approaches close to the female and sticks out his tongue. The pair then perform a "dance" that consists of a series of sideways steps. During this phase of the courtship the male slowly opens his wings, and eventually the female stands still. After circling around her, the male hops onto her back and mates with her.

Mosquitoes attract their mates by making a high-pitched whining noise with their wings. It is the female that makes the enticing noise, and each species has its own particular signature tune. Gnats and midges use wing noise in their courtship behavior, but it is not the only facet of their display. They also gather in large numbers and hover over a suitable object, such as a rock or bush, that serves as a landmark for them. While they are in the air, the gnats and midges perform a nuptial dance and finally home in on the female's wing noise.

## The lure of dung

Some flies rely on dung to feed their larvae. The males use the highly attractive scent of fresh droppings to entice the females to them. There may be from 10 to 20 males in the area, and once the females have arrived on the scene, the males immediately swarm all over them in an attempt to mate. As with other species of insect, the last male to pair and transfer sperm will be the father of about 75 percent of the offspring, thus guaranteeing the continuation of its own genetic line. The females must lay their fertilized eggs within a short time since the feces quickly form an impenetrable crust.

## Variety of maggot diets

The larvae of flies are not as varied in form as the adults. Nevertheless, they develop in a wide range of habitats. Some species—such as the mosquito, midge and gnat larvae—are aquatic. Others are terrestrial and live in a variety of niches. For instance, the larvae of some species are saprophytic, living in decomposing matter; other larvae are phytophagic, feeding on plant tissue; others are zoophagous, eating other animals. Species that feed on excrement are called coprophagous; those that feed off host species are parasitic.

ABOVE A crane fly of the genus *Pachyrina* rests on a leaf where its two small, club-shaped hind wings, or halteres, are visible beneath its transparent forewings. During flight, they act as stabilizers, enabling the insect to control its movements through the air with great precision.

## Crane flies

There are about 13,000 species of crane fly in the family Tipulidae, which is one of the 22 families in the suborder Nematocera. Popularly known as daddy-longlegs, crane flies are familiar summer insects that fly low over the ground with their legs trailing behind them. They have slender bodies and long, thin legs that they are capable of shedding if they are caught by a predator. Their bodies are usually gray or brown, but some species such as *Nephrotoma crocata*, have wasp-like black and yellow stripes.

Although adult crane flies rarely feed, their mouthparts form a fleshy sucking tube through which they are able to drink nectar and water. The sexes are easily distinguished by the shape of their abdomens. The tip of the male's abdomen is swollen, whereas the female's tapers to a point so she can thrust it deep into the ground to lay her eggs.

One of the most common British species is the great crane fly, *Tipula oleracea*, which inhabits damp places with plenty of vegetation. The first adults of the year

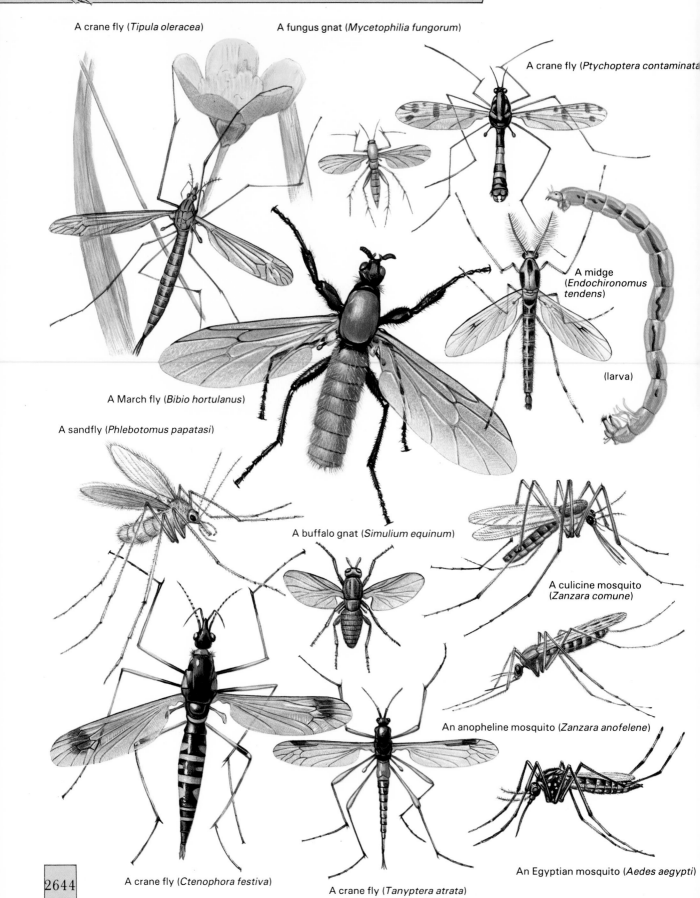

A crane fly (*Tipula oleracea*)

A fungus gnat (*Mycetophilia fungorum*)

A crane fly (*Ptychoptera contaminata*)

A midge (*Endochironomus tendens*)

(larva)

A March fly (*Bibio hortulanus*)

A sandfly (*Phlebotomus papatasi*)

A buffalo gnat (*Simulium equinum*)

A culicine mosquito (*Zanzara comune*)

An anopheline mosquito (*Zanzara anofelene*)

A crane fly (*Ctenophora festiva*)

A crane fly (*Tanyptera atrata*)

An Egyptian mosquito (*Aedes aegypti*)

emerge in the spring. The males hatch before the females, and then wait for the females to emerge from their pupal cases so they can mate. Soon after mating, the male dies. The female lays her fertilized eggs one at a time in damp ground and then she, too, dies.

Larvae of the great crane fly—popularly known as leatherjackets—hatch about two weeks after the female lays her eggs. The larvae are gray-colored, grub-like creatures that dig beneath the surface of the soil and feed on the roots and lower stems of plants, particularly on grasses and food crops. They are voracious eaters and can be serious agricultural pests.

When the larvae are fully grown, they wriggle up to the surface of the soil with the help of the downward-pointing bristles on their backs. There, they pupate before emerging as adults. The newly hatched crane flies produce a second generation of larvae in the same year, but these larvae hibernate in the ground during the winter and become the first adults of the following year.

Not all crane flies lay their eggs in the ground. Some species lay them in water. Aquatic larvae have five pairs of false legs and spend their lives crawling over the bottom, feeding on small worms and insect larvae. They breathe either by absorbing oxygen from the water or by taking in air at the surface.

**ABOVE** With their thin bodies and long legs, crane flies—or "daddy-longlegs"—vaguely resemble large mosquitoes. The largest British species has a wingspan of over 2 in. and inhabits dark woods during the summer. Although adult crane flies are harmless insects, their larvae often cause serious damage to the roots and stems of crop plants. The fat, grub-like larvae live either underwater or in decaying vegetation.

## Gall midges

There are about 4000 species of gall midges in the family Cecidomyiidae. They are tiny, fragile flies, usually measuring 0.04-0.2 in. in length. They generally have orange bodies, long, beaded antennae and grayish wings with few veins.

Gall midges are so called because the larvae of most species live on plants where they produce abnormal swellings—called galls—in response to the larval attack. Every species of gall midge induces its own characteristic type of gall, from which the midge can be identified. For example, a species of gall midge called *Cecidomyia veronica* causes the fluffy white galls found on the tips of speedwell, while the larvae of the species *Taxomyia taxi* attack yew trees and cause the leaves on the tips of their shoots to bunch together tightly so that they resemble buds.

Not all species of gall midge larvae cause galls. Some feed on decaying wood or fungi, and others prey on aphids and mites. One of the best-known species that does not form galls is the Hessian fly (*Mayetiola destructor*). Its larvae cause immense damage to cereal crops by boring into the stems of the young plants and destroying or deforming them. They metamorphose inside a puparium consisting of their last larval skin and, within it, a silken cocoon in which the pupa completes its development. The newly formed adult tears its way out of the puparium and flies off in search of a mate. Up to six generations of gall midge may develop in a year. In all cases, one generation hibernates at the pupal stage and completes its development the following spring.

## Bibionid flies

Bibionid flies—commonly known as hair flies or March flies—belong to the family Bibionidae. There are about 700 species of these stout, hairy flies that have short antennae below their eyes. The adults inhabit areas of open grassland, and are especially common between April and May.

One of the most common species of bibionid flies is the St. Mark's hairfly (*Bibo marci*), which inhabits the outskirts of woods or clearings. It has a characteristic and rather ungainly way of flying, with its legs dangling beneath its body. The males are black, while the females are reddish in color. The larvae live in the ground for two years, where they feed on the decomposing remains of vegetation. However, the larvae of some species such as *Bibio hortulanus*, not only feed on vegetable remains but also attack the roots of many types of vegetable, causing considerable damage.

## Disease and the sandfly

There are some 500 species of sandfly in the family Psychodidae, inhabiting most of the warmer regions of the world. They are tiny, moth-like flies that are rarely more than 0.2 in. in length and have long, slender legs. Their bodies are usually yellow or light brown in color, and both their bodies and their wings are covered with fine hairs. Their mouthparts form piercing, sucking tubes that the females use to feed on the blood of their prey and the males use to feed—if they feed at all—on nectar.

Many species of sandfly are carriers of disease, and although most species feed primarily on the blood of animals, one species in particular—*Phlebotomus papatasi*—feeds on human blood. The female is capable of transmitting to her victim viral diseases such as sandfly fever and protozoan diseases such as skin ulcers and kala-azar (where the protozoa invade the internal organs, causing infection and anemia).

**BELOW Mosquitoes spend their entire preadult lives underwater. The egg contains special air-filled chambers to keep it afloat (A). The newly hatched larva hangs from the water's surface by its breathing tube and feeds on microorganisms. Before developing into a pupa, the growing larva passes through four larval stages (B-E). Air enters the floating pupa through two small breathing tubes attached to the back of its head (F).**

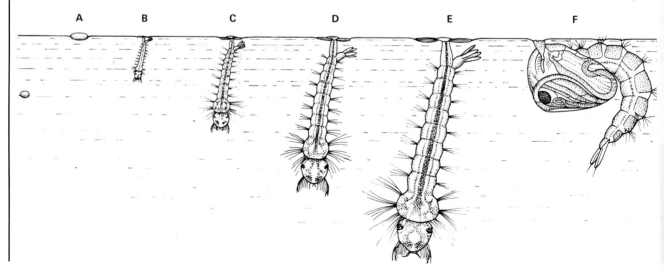

A    B    C    D    E    F

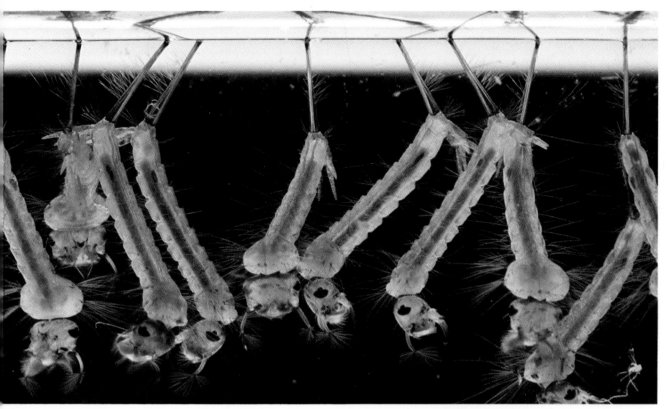

ABOVE **The larvae of the common mosquito hang upside-down in water, attached to the surface film by their** long breathing tubes. **They use their mustache-like mouth brushes to filter food from the water.**

*Phlebotomus papatasi* inhabits many Mediterranean areas. The adults are short-lived and active only at night, when the female flies off in search of suitable victims for her blood meal. Fertilized females require large quantities of blood immediately after mating in order for their eggs to develop. After gorging themselves, they find a damp, dark place in which to lay their eggs. After a few days, the eggs hatch into tiny, hairy, grub-like larvae. The larvae feed on organic debris. When fully grown, about four weeks later, they metamorphose into pupae. Two weeks after that, the adults emerge.

## Mosquitoes

Mosquitoes are found all over the world and form one of the largest families in the entire order Diptera, with about 3000 species in the family Culicidae. They are slender flies with small, spherical heads and long, thin legs. They have a single pair of wings, whose rear edge is usually decorated with small scales. The males have feathery antennae, while those of the females are thread-like.

---

# INSECTS CLASSIFICATION: 26

## *True flies (1)*

The order Diptera contains about 90,000 species of true, or two-winged, flies within the class Insecta. Divided into three suborders and 114 families, they are found in almost every habitat, including deserts, rain forests and subpolar regions.

Twenty-two families of thread-horned flies (those having long, slender antennae) form the first dipteran suborder, the Nematocera. They include such families as the Tipulidae (crane flies or daddy-longlegs) whose approximately 13,000 species include the wasp-like *Nephrotoma crocata* and the great crane fly, *Tipula oleracea*, common in Britain; the Cecidomyiidae (gall midges) containing the species *Taxomyia taxi*, which attacks yew trees, and the Hessian fly, *Mayetiola destructor*, which does not form galls; the Bibionidae (hair flies or March flies) with St. Mark's hair fly, *Bibo marci*; and the Psychodidae (sand flies) including the bloodsucking species *Phlebotomus papatasi* common in some Mediterranean areas.

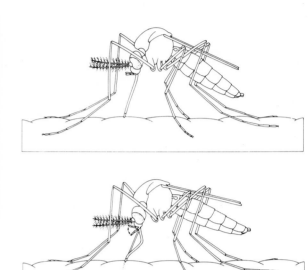

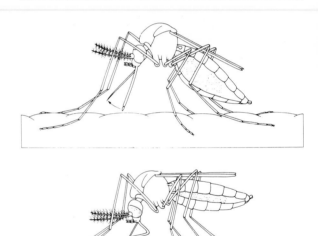

ABOVE **After a blood meal, a female mosquito's body swells so much that her skin stretches; light shining through the thin skin shows the mass of blood inside her stomach.**

RIGHT **A hungry female mosquito alights on her intended victim and pierces its skin with her slender, spear-like mouthparts; a tubular sheath called the labium contains the piercing organs. The labium itself does not penetrate the victim but bends outward, acting as a guide for the piercing mouthparts. A mosquito's saliva contains an anesthetic, which the female injects into her victim, enabling her to feed in peace. After she has gorged herself on blood, the mosquito withdraws her mouthparts and flies away.**

Both male and female mosquitoes have mouthparts modified for piercing and sucking, and both feed on nectar and honeydew as a source of high-energy food for flying. However, the males have small mouthparts; they cannot bite and rely for their nourishment on exposed liquids. The females, by contrast, can also feed on the blood of vertebrates, which they obtain by piercing their victim's skin and sucking its blood through their needle-like mouthparts after first injecting the wound with saliva to prevent the blood from clotting.

Newly emerged adult mosquitoes mate on the wing, close to their breeding site. The males of most species swarm at dusk, and the females are attracted to the males by the sound of their beating wings. As a rule, the females only mate once because the sperm they receive is sufficient to fertilize all their eggs.

## Gorging for the offspring

The female mosquito usually lays her eggs in freshwater, but before doing so she gorges herself with blood to ensure that the eggs receive adequate nourishment to develop properly. Depending on the species of mosquito, the female lays between 30 and 300 eggs. Most are oval-shaped, with air floats to keep them buoyant. Some species of mosquito, such as those of the two genera *Aedes* and *Anopheles,* lay their

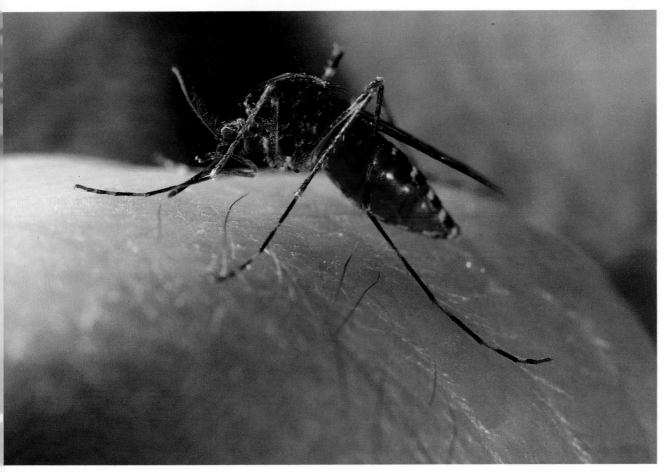

eggs singly. Others, such as the common mosquito, *Culex pipiens,* lay their eggs in batches that float like rafts. Some mosquitoes—notably those of the genus *Aedes*—lay their eggs on the ground above water level, where they remain dormant until they are flooded by rains. The eggs are capable of overwintering in the dried-out state.

Mosquito eggs hatch after only a few days. The larvae are typically aquatic, with long, thin bodies and chewing mouthparts. They have a brush of hairs on either side of their mouthparts, which they use to filter tiny morsels of vegetation and microorganisms out of the water as food. They also feed by rasping or scraping vegetation. Mosquito larvae propel themselves slowly forward through the water by making beating movements with their mouth brushes. They can also swim by jerking their bodies—but only in a backward direction.

Mosquito larvae are air-breathing creatures. At the tip of their abdomens they have a breathing tube, called a siphon, which protrudes above the surface of the water and enables them to breathe. When at rest, the larvae hang in the water with their breathing

ABOVE The *Anopheles maculipennis* mosquito is the main carrier of the malarial parasite. The female lays her eggs in stagnant water; the larvae develop rapidly and the new adults emerge after about 10 days. Since malaria-carrying mosquitoes develop chemical resistance to antimosquito insecticides, malaria infection is widespread among humans. In 1985, for example, it was estimated that there were a hundred million clinical cases of malaria.

siphons exposed at the surface. Larvae of the genus *Anopheles* lie parallel to the water surface, while those of the genus *Culex* hang vertically.

The larval stage of mosquitoes usually lasts for only a few days, except toward winter when the larvae sometimes hibernate. After three or four molts, the larvae pupate in the water.

## Comma-shaped pupae

Mosquito pupae are comma-shaped creatures that move by flexing their abdomens and beating a pair of abdominal paddles. The pupal stage is a short-lived one, and the pupae do not feed. They have float hairs on the front segment of their abdomens, enabling them to float at the surface where they obtain air through two breathing siphons on the back of their heads. The adults emerge from their pupal cases after two or three days. They rest on neighboring vegetation for up to an hour, drying their wings before flying off in search of a mate.

## Malaria-carrying mosquitoes

The most notorious species of mosquito is the *Anopheles* mosquito, *Anopheles maculipennis*, a major carrier of malaria. The first adults of the year appear in the spring, after emerging from hibernation. The females are already fertilized from the previous year, and immediately seek out a blood meal to ensure the complete development of their eggs. They lay their eggs on the surface of stagnant water, either in long chains or in formations that resemble the spokes of a wheel.

The bloodsucking female *A. maculipennis* mosquito transmits the microscopic single-celled animals, or protozoa, that cause malaria. When the mosquito feeds on a person who is already infected with the disease, it swallows the reproductive cells of the malarial protozoan with the blood of its prey. Inside the mosquito, the reproductive cells fuse to form a two-celled stage that bores into the gut wall. Once there, it secretes a protective shell around itself and divides many times to produce thousands of long, slender, free-living cells called sporozoites. Eventually, the shell bursts open, releasing the sporozoites into the body cavity of the mosquito, from where they make their way to its salivary glands.

## Invading red blood cells

When an infected mosquito bites its victim, it injects the sporozoites as well as its saliva into the wound, thereby spreading the malaria. The sporozoites immediately install themselves in the victim's liver, where they divide repeatedly to form thousands of cells called merozoites, which are released into the bloodstream. Some merozoites reinfect liver cells; others enter red blood cells, where they multiply, reenter the blood and seek out a fresh red cell. The attacks of fever that characterize malaria coincide precisely with the release of merozoites into the blood and the subsequent invasion of red blood cells. After a number of generations, the merozoites

produce dormant sexual cells. If they remain in the bloodstream, the sexual cells die. However, if they enter an *A. maculipennis* mosquito, the entire malarial cycle repeats itself. To combat malaria, the carrier—the mosquito—must be destroyed either by the use of insecticides or by draining swamps.

## Threadworm carriers

Another harmful species of mosquito is *Culex fatigans*, which is found in large numbers in most of the tropical regions of the world. It is responsible for transmitting threadworms—tiny, parasitic worms that live on the blood and lymphatic system of humans. When *C. fatigans* bites an infested person, it takes in the threadworm larvae contained in the prey's bloodstream. The larvae grow and develop inside the mosquito's intestine, and finally make their way to its piercing mouthparts. When the mosquito bites again, it transfers the worms to its victim.

## Yellow fever

Not all mosquitoes are harmful. Most species of the genus *Aedes*, for example, are harmless, as is the common mosquito, *Culex pipiens*. An exception is *Aedes aegypti*, which transmits a number of diseases including the yellow fever virus. Unlike the malaria-carrying mosquitoes, *A. aegypti* is a daytime creature that is attracted to its prey by smell, warmth and exhaled breath. It is widespread throughout all tropical regions, and has a painful bite that produces a red swelling. The mosquito spreads disease in much the same way as the malaria-carrying species. When biting someone affected by yellow fever, the mosquito takes in the virus with its blood meal. After a few days, it can spread the disease by biting previously uninfected individuals.

## Midges

There are about 5000 species of midges in the family Chironomidae. They are small flies with long bodies similar to those of common mosquitoes. Unlike mosquitoes, however, midges do not bite; their mouthparts cannot perforate human skin. The larvae are aquatic, worm-like creatures with bodies that are a characteristic red color due to the red, oxygen-carrying pigment (hemoglobin) in their blood.

One of the most common European midges is the feather midge, *Chironomus plumosum*, so called because

the males have bushy, feather-like antennae. On warm summer evenings, feather midges form large swarms in the vicinity of stagnant water. As they dance about in the air, they often mate. The fertilized female immediately flies to the water and lays a large number of eggs on the surface. After a few days, the eggs hatch into tiny, reddish, worm-like larvae.

Feather midge larvae live hidden in the mud at the bottom of the water. Each larva lives inside a small, tubular tunnel consisting of debris that it holds together with its saliva. The larva filters the surrounding water and extracts minute edible particles with a tiny "fishing net" that it makes out of a special secretion from its salivary gland. When the larva is fully grown, it pupates inside the secluded shelter of its tunnel. A few days later, it emerges from the tunnel and swims to the surface. There, the pupal case splits open to let out the newly formed adult.

## Buffalo gnats

Buffalo gnats—also known as blackflies—are members of the family Simuliidae. There are some 1000 species of these tiny, humpbacked flies. They range in length from 0.04 to 0.2 in., and their bodies are usually black in color. They are found worldwide, generally near running water, and they often gather in large swarms.

As the carriers of disease and parasites, buffalo gnats can be harmful to humans. The females have piercing mouthparts with which they suck the blood of vertebrates. Their bite is painful, and the saliva that they inject into their victims' wounds to prevent the blood from clotting can be toxic to small animals. The males, on the other hand, have nonpiercing mouthparts, and feed only on the sweet liquids that exude from plants.

Perhaps the best-known species of buffalo gnat is the horse buffalo gnat, *Simulium equinum*, which is found in all parts of Europe and Africa. The males inhabit areas of vegetation along riverbanks. They are a nuisance, but not dangerous. However, the females are extremely harmful to numerous types of mammal, particularly horses, which may die if attacked by a swarm of buffalo gnats.

## Hundreds of eggs

Fertilized female horse buffalo gnats either lay their eggs on the surface of water or else attach them firmly to a submerged object. They frequently lay batches of

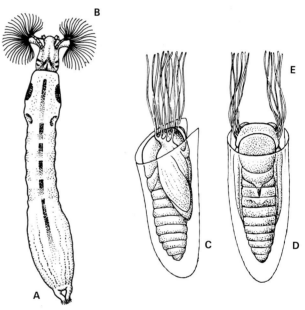

TOP **Buffalo gnats are tiny, stout-bodied flies with short antennae—most species have black coloration. The females are bloodsucking and can carry diseases. In warm countries, buffalo gnats often attack in swarms, and their toxic saliva can cause blood poisoning, killing their large victims.**
ABOVE **The larvae of buffalo gnats are aquatic creatures with cylindrical** bodies. **Each larva possesses a ring of hooks on its abdomen (A), used for holding onto the streambed, and mouth brushes (B) for feeding on suspended particles. When a larva reaches its final stage of development, it prepares for pupation by spinning a silk cocoon (side view (C); back view (D). The pupa absorbs oxygen through branched respiratory organs (E).**

# INSECTS CLASSIFICATION: 27

## True flies (2)

The suborder Nematocera—the first of three suborders in the order Diptera—also contains about 3000 species of mosquitoes in the family Culicidae. These include the common mosquito, *Culex pipiens*; the malaria-carrying *Anopheles maculipennis*; *Aedes aegypti*, which transmits yellow fever; and *Culex fatigans*, which transmits threadworms. Further nempatoceran families include the Chironomidae (midges) with about 5000 species, including the feather midge, *Chironomus plumosum*; and the Simuliidae (buffalo gnats or blackflies, such as the horse buffalo gnat, *Simulium equinum*).

The suborder Brachycera is the second suborder within the order Diptera. It contains 18 families of short-horned flies (those with short antennae) that include the Tabanidae (horseflies and related species, such as the cattle horsefly, *Tabanus bovinus*, of Europe, North Africa and Asia); the Asilidae (robber flies, including *Asilus crabroniformis* of Britain); and the Bombyliidae (bee flies) whose 4000 species live mainly in arid regions and include the giant bee fly, *Bombylius major*.

several hundred eggs, which hatch about two weeks later into tiny, cylindrical larvae. The larvae have hairs on either side of their mouthparts, which they use to filter edible microorganisms from the water.

As soon as each larva emerges, it holds onto its empty egg case with a silk thread produced by its salivary glands. Then, when it can, it uses a ring of hooks on the tip of its abdomen to attach itself to some other object. The larva has a second ring of hooks on the tip of a false leg just behind its head. It loops its body over objects with both sets of hooks in order to move along.

The larval stage of the horse buffalo gnat lasts about a month, during which time it molts six times. When the larva has reached its maximum size, it spins a silken cocoon around itself and turns into a pupa. It attaches the cocoon to a submerged object to prevent it from drifting away with the water current. The pupa breathes by absorbing oxygen from the water through branching respiratory organs that protrude from the cocoon. After about 10 days, the pupa breaks free from the cocoon and rises to the surface of the water, where the adult emerges.

## Horseflies

Horseflies, members of the family Tabanidea, are well known for their painful bite. There are about 3000 species of these large, heavily built flies in the second suborder (Brachycera) of the order Diptera. They have huge, bulging, colorful eyes and mouthparts that are similar to those of a mosquito, but shorter and broader. The males feed on nectar and pollen, while the females suck blood. Horseflies are strong fliers and inhabit most locations, although they prefer damp areas with plenty of livestock.

Female horseflies feed on humans as well as livestock. Their bite produces a large wound, and, like other species of fly, they inject a small amount of their saliva into it to prevent the blood from clotting. Drops of blood often ooze out of the wound, so the fly is able to drink from this in addition to sucking from the wound. Horseflies can transmit disorders that are extremely dangerous to humans—for example, threadworm infestations and sleeping sickness. They also cause a fatal type of anemia (lack of red blood cells) in horses.

A species of horsefly called the cattle horsefly, *Tabanus bovinus*, is found all over Europe and in many parts of North Africa and Asia. It is a large insect—ranging in length from 0.8 to 1 in.—and it has enormous, bright green, compound eyes. Its wings are also large, and it flies quickly, making a continuous noise as it goes. The males are easy to spot as they hover above fields and meadows in search of nectar and pollen. The females, on the other hand, require blood, particularly after they have been fertilized. They obtain it by piercing the skin of their mammal victims with their strong mouthparts. Although their bite is painful, it is harmless—cattle horseflies carry no disease or parasites. When the females have gorged themselves on blood, they settle on a patch of wet ground and lay large numbers of eggs on the stems of plants. After a few days, the eggs hatch into tiny larvae.

Cattle horsefly larvae are caterpillar-like creatures that live in wet soil. They have tough skins decorated with fleshy knobs and large, curved, snapping jaws with which they feed on small insects. They breathe

through a large retractile air tube at the tip of their abdomens. The larvae grow quickly and molt several times. When winter approaches, they hibernate. The following spring, they wake up and complete their development. They have a brief pupal stage and then emerge from their cocoons as adults, ready to repeat the cycle.

## Robber flies

There are about 5000 species of robber fly in the family Asilidae, inhabiting open spaces such as heathlands, fields and forest clearings throughout the world. The adults are 0.8-1.6 in. long, with robust bodies, long, thin legs and large, bulging eyes. Many of them are covered with hair, and some resemble bees or wasps because they have black and yellow stripes on their abdomens.

Robber flies are fierce predators of other insects, and they have dagger-like mouthparts that can pierce the toughest outer body coverings. Excellent fliers, they feed only during the day. They usually seize their prey while it is in flight and kill it by injecting it with poison. Then they carry it to the leaf or branch of a tree and pierce the body again to inject it with a digestive fluid. Finally, they suck out the body fluids and liquefied tissues of their victim, leaving nothing but the hard outer body covering.

## Female cannibal

Although robber flies usually catch their prey on the wing, they also crouch on the ground or on a tree stump and lie in wait for passing insects. When a suitable victim appears, they spring forward and grab it with their front legs. Predatory creatures are often cannibalistic, and the robber fly is no exception. During mating, it is common for female robber flies to seize their mates and subject them to the same fate as their prey.

## Mating in safety

One of the largest British robber flies is *Asilus crabroniformis*. The male usually approaches the female for mating while she is devouring a previously captured victim. As long as the female is eating, the male can mate with her in safety. As soon as she has finished her meal, however, the female turns her attentions to the male, seizing him and killing him with a single jab of her dagger-like mouthparts.

TOP The deer fly is closely related to the horsefly, but is distinguished from it by the brown coloration on its wings. The brilliant colors of its large, compound eyes fade shortly after death.

ABOVE A cattle horsefly rests on a leaf. Females of the species suck the blood of cattle and horses, having a particularly strong appetite after they have been fertilized. Cattle horseflies do not carry disease.

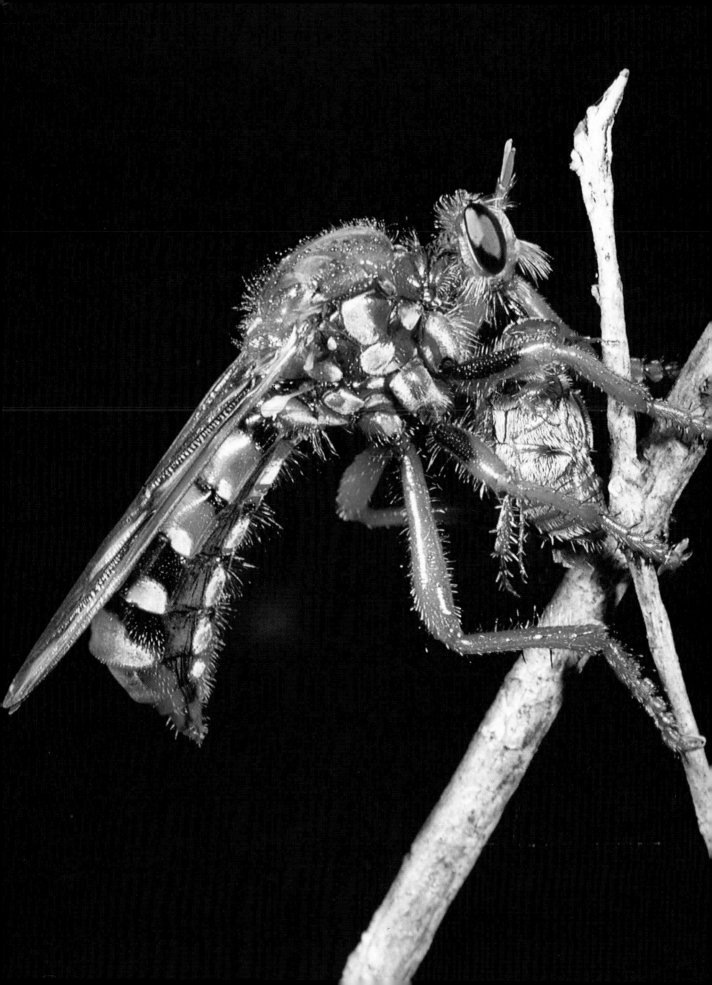

LEFT Robber flies, such as this Australian species *Chrysopogon alba* feeding on a tabanid fly, are the largest of the dipteran or two-winged flies—their bodies are 3 in. long, and their outstretched wings measure 4 in. from tip to tip. (The smallest flies, by contrast, measure just over 0.04 in. long.) Robber flies have enormous appetites and are bold and aggressive hunters of other insects, attacking many that may be even larger than themselves, such as grasshoppers.

The female lays her eggs in rotting vegetation or among decomposing animal matter, both of which provide food for the larvae until they are fully grown. When they are mature, the larvae pupate. After a few days, they emerge from their cocoons as adults and repeat the cycle.

## Bee flies

Bee flies are members of the family Bombyliidae. There are some 4000 species of these insects, which resemble bumblebees in both build and color. They have stout, furry bodies with brown abdomens and long, slender legs. Bee flies are excellent fliers that pursue a meandering path above fields and meadows. In the summer they search for nectar and pollen, and when they feed they appear to hover over the flowers with their wings beating. Close inspection reveals that they do not actually hover but cling to the flowers with their front legs.

Bee fly larvae are strong and mobile. They are all parasitic on other insects, actively searching in the ground for insect eggs or larvae. The female giant bee fly, *Bombylius major*, drops her eggs as she flies over the nesting area of solitary bees. When the larvae hatch, they enter the bee nest and feed on the stored pollen. As the larvae develop, their mouthparts become stronger and they feed on the eggs and larvae of their hosts. Eventually, the bee fly larvae pupate and emerge as adults. Then they fly off in search of pollen and nectar.

## Hover flies

There are some 5000 species of hover fly in the family Syrphidae, one of 74 families in the suborder Cyclorrhapha. They vary in length from 0.2 to 0.8 in. and resemble wasps and bees with their bold black and yellow coloring. Some species are covered with short, dense hairs. Hover flies are skillful fliers, and take their name because they hover over flowers in the

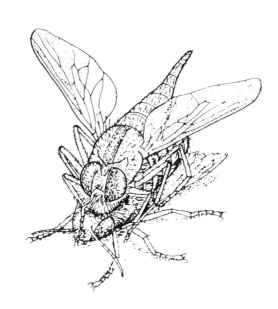

TOP The giant bee fly has a furry, bee-like body and a single pair of half black and half transparent wings. When feeding, it draws nectar and pollen through its unusually long, tubular mouthparts.

ABOVE The robber fly is a fierce and deadly predator of other insects. It usually catches its victims in midair, killing them instantly with a single stab of its dagger-like mouthparts.

**ABOVE The drone fly has evolved so that it bears a remarkable resemblance to the honey-** **bee. Like real bees, it feeds on nectar and pollen, and is an important pollinator. The** **bee-like appearance deceives predators into treating the harmless fly as a dangerous** **stinging insect. The drone fly is an expert flier capable of hovering in one spot.**

summer, searching for pollen and nectar. During their visits to flowers, hover flies unwittingly collect pollen on the undersides of their bodies and thus rival bees in their efficiency as plant pollinators.

Female hover flies lay their eggs in a wide variety of habitats, depending on the species. Their larvae are blind, maggot-like creatures with a diverse range of feeding habits. Some species, such as *Syrphus ribesii*, are extremely useful to agriculture because they feed on sap-sucking aphids, which they locate by touch. Other species are themselves destructive, feeding on living plant material. The narcissus fly, for example, feeds on daffodil bulbs. Yet other species eat decaying organic

matter or waste matter discarded from the nests of ants, wasps or bees. Aquatic species feed on organic sediments on the bottom.

The drone fly, *Eristalis tenax*, is similar to a bee in appearance, and, like a bee, it feeds on pollen as well as nectar. After mating, the fertilized female lays her eggs near mud or muddy water. There, the larvae feed on decaying organic matter until they are fully grown. Their bodies are squat and cylindrical, with a breathing tube at the tips of their abdomens. The breathing tube can extend to a length of 6 in., giving rise to the drone fly larva's popular name—rat-tailed maggot. The tip of the breathing tube protrudes from the surface of the water, enabling the larva to obtain air. During the winter, the larva hibernates and does not complete its transition to adulthood until the following spring.

## Fruit flies

The tiny fruit flies of the family Tephritidae—numbering some 4000 species—are extremely harmful to agriculture. The female has a long, sharp, egg-laying organ called an ovipositor at the tip of her abdomen. With it, she can pierce the toughest plant tissues in order to lay her eggs inside them. The larvae of fruit flies have powerful chewing mouthparts, allowing them to feed on a wide variety of plant material.

The olive fruit fly, *Dacus oleae*, is an important pest of olive groves all over the Mediterranean region. Its entire life cycle lasts little more than 40 days, so it can produce as many as five generations a year. The first generation usually appears in spring, when hibernating pupae wake up and turn into adults. After mating, the fertilized females pierce the skins of young olives and lay their eggs inside them. Each female lays up to 100 eggs, depositing each one in a separate olive.

After a few days, the eggs hatch into tiny larvae that eat the flesh of the olives, digging tunnels in them as they progress. The larvae grow rapidly, reaching their full size within a fortnight. Then they turn into pupae, emerging 10-15 days later as adults ready to begin a new cycle. When it is time for members of the last generation of the year to turn into pupae, they leave their olives and hibernate in the subsoil or in a crevice, emerging to complete their development late the following spring.

The Mediterranean fruit fly, *Ceratitis capitata*, is another agricultural pest. First-generation adult females appear in May. After they mate, the female lays her eggs inside peaches or apricots. The larvae feed on the sweet flesh of the fruits, causing them great damage. Eventually, the affected fruits fall to the ground and the larvae abandon them. The larvae dig themselves into the ground, where they turn into pupae. After a few days they emerge as adults to repeat the entire cycle.

There may be as many as seven generations of Mediterranean fruit fly in a single year, but as the summer passes, the larvae change their source of food according to the fruits that are in season. They finish with citrus fruits—mainly oranges and tangerines. The

ABOVE The Mediterranean fruit fly is a small, yellowish insect with bright red eyes. It is a major pest of fruit crops, feeding on naturally fermenting fallen fruit and tree sap. Fertilized females lay their eggs inside ripe fruits, and the emerging larvae feed on the sweet, rotting flesh. Fruit flies may produce up to seven generations a year, laying their eggs in the various fruits that are in season. They occur as far afield as Europe, Africa and South America.

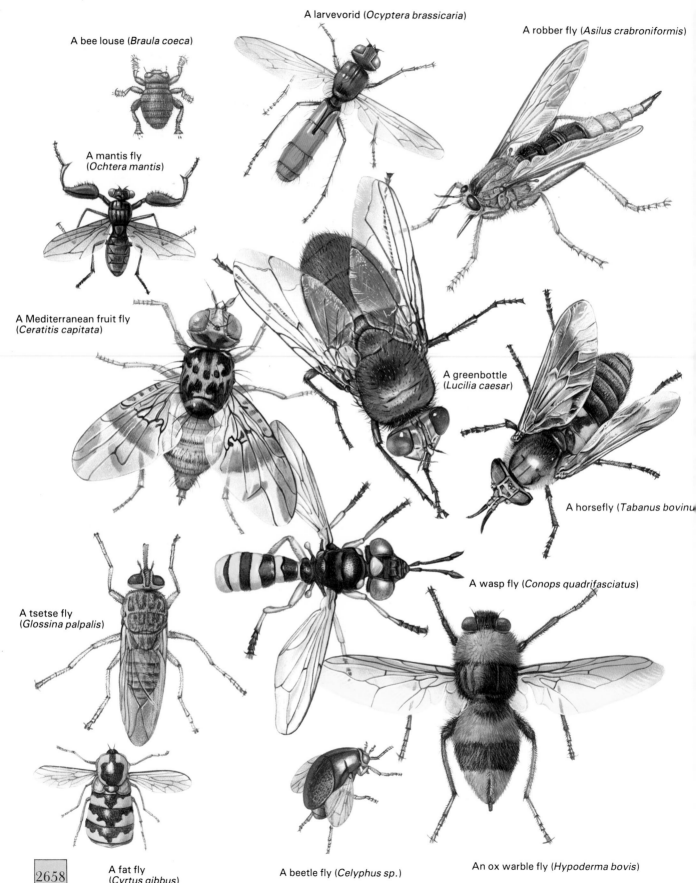

A larvevorid (*Ocyptera brassicaria*)

A robber fly (*Asilus crabroniformis*)

A bee louse (*Braula coeca*)

A mantis fly
(*Ochtera mantis*)

A Mediterranean fruit fly
(*Ceratitis capitata*)

A greenbottle
(*Lucilia caesar*)

A horsefly (*Tabanus bovinu*

A wasp fly (*Conops quadrifasciatus*)

A tsetse fly
(*Glossina palpalis*)

A fat fly
(*Cyrtus gibbus*)

A beetle fly (*Celyphus sp.*)

An ox warble fly (*Hypoderma bovis*)

last larvae of the year hibernate in the pupal stage during the winter and complete their development the following spring.

## Drosophilids

Fruit flies of the family Drosophilidae are small, yellowish flies that have large, bright red eyes, short antennae with sensory bristles, and mouthparts suspended from a forward extension of their heads (the rostrum). Drosophilids usually live in damp, dark places, where they feed and lay their eggs on decaying matter, especially on yeasts that grow in damaged or fermenting fruit.

The fruit fly, *Drosophila melanogaster*, of the genus Drosophila is one of the most common members of the family. The male performs a short courtship dance before mating, gaining a female's attention by beating his wings. After mating, the fertilized female lays batches of 15-20 spindle-shaped eggs in the semi-liquid pulp of fermenting fruit. The eggs have hair-like filaments at one end that float on the surface of the liquid, enabling the eggs to breathe.

The larvae that hatch have 11 segments, each with a ring of hooked spines. They breathe through a telescopic organ at the rear of their bodies that bears spiracles or breathing pores. The larvae raise this organ above the surface of the liquid fruit pulp. They feed on the rotting fruit on which they live. The larvae molt three times before pupating. The pupae do not feed and breathe through feathery organs on their heads. Development from egg to adult takes about 10 days, and in good conditions up to 30 generations may appear in a single year.

## Botflies

Botflies of the family Gasterophilidae are short-lived, large, hairy flies that resemble bees. They have reduced mouthparts and do not feed during their adult lives, although the larvae are parasitic on horses and related animals. Adult botflies lay their eggs on the host animal at the end of the summer. The position of the eggs on the host's body varies according to the species. Female botflies cement their eggs to the hairs of the host animal. Eggs laid near the animal's mouth hatch without any assistance from their host, but eggs laid elsewhere on the host's body, do not hatch until they have been licked.

During bouts of licking, the host animal transports the newly hatched larvae into its mouth. Once in the host's mouth, the larvae burrow into the soft tissues. After two to four weeks, they attach themselves to a region of their host's gut, where they continue to grow

---

## INSECTS
## CLASSIFICATION: 28

### *True flies (3)*

The third and final suborder in the order Diptera is the Cyclorrhapha—the so called "higher flies." They consist of more than 20,000 species in 74 families. The Syrphidae (hover flies) includes *Eristalis tenax*, often called the drone fly because of its resemblance to a male honeybee. Fruit flies belong to two families within the suborder: the Tephritidae contains the larger species, such as the olive fruit fly, *Dacus oleae*, and the Mediterranean fruit fly, *Ceratitis capitata*, which occurs as far afield as Africa, Australia and Hawaii, as well as in the Mediterranean Basin; the Drosophilidae holds much tinier fruit flies such as the species *Drosophila melanogaster* (usually seen hovering over ripe fruit).

Other families of true flies in the suborder Cyclorrhapha include the Gasterophilidae (botflies) whose parasitic larvae infest horses' stomachs; the Oestridae (warble flies, such as the ox warble fly, *Hypoderma bovis*); the Tachinidae (parasitic flies) and the Muscidae (house, stable, and tsetse flies), which contains over 3000 species including the house fly, *Musca domestica*, the stable fly, *Stomoxys calcitrans*, and the tsetse fly, *Glossina palpalis*—one of two tsetse fly species that transmit sleeping sickness in the humid tropical and subtropical regions of Africa. Blowflies belong to the family Calliphoridae and include such species as the bluebottle, *Calliphora erythrocephala*, of Europe, the greenbottles (genus *Lucilia*) and the flesh fly, *Sarcophaga carnaria*, which carries anthrax, a disease of sheep and cattle.

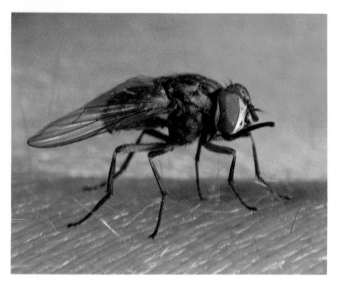

for almost a year, feeding on tissue fluids in the gut wall. When ready to pupate, the larvae release their hold on the gut wall and pass out in the animal's feces. Once outside, they dig themselves into the ground and pupate. They emerge as adults a month or so later. If present in small numbers, botfly larvae do little damage to their host. However, in large numbers, they can cause serious, even fatal, bleeding within their host's intestine.

## Warble flies

Warble flies of the family Oestridae parasitize farm animals. The adults have robust bodies, unobtrusive coloring, and reduced mouthparts—they do not feed. Female warble flies lay their eggs or larvae (some species give birth to live young) in the nostrils of mammals or in the area around their eyes. The larvae enter into the nasal and frontal sinuses, where they feed on mucous secretions and grow. When ready to pupate, the larvae move around, irritating the nasal passages of their host, causing it to sneeze and expel them. They fall to the ground, where they dig themselves in and pupate. The larvae quickly mature into adults, and the whole cycle recommences. Warble flies can be harmful, often fatal, to their unfortunate host.

## Burrowing through skin

The parasitic larvae of the ox warble fly do not enter the gut of the ox, but burrow through its skin. They follow the path of a nerve, until they reach the spinal cord. The larvae bore their way through the back muscles of their host, molting once. Eventually the larvae settle down under the skin of the ox's back, where they continue to grow and develop, feeding on blood and tissue fluids. The larvae can grow up to 1.5 in. long and produce a large swelling on the back of their host. After about a month the larvae crawl out of their host (leaving a hole in the animal's back), fall to the ground, and pupate. The new adults emerge four or five weeks later.

## Tachinid flies

The tachinid flies of the family Tachinidae have squat, bristly bodies and large wings. The adults feed on nectar, while their larvae are internal parasites that feed on the larvae of other insects which, in turn, feed on the tissues of their host. Most species of tachinid flies parasitize a wide range of hosts. The larvae enter their host in a

**TOP** The housefly inhabits human homes and feeds on food, garbage and decaying matter. The germs it carries in and on its body can cause disease.
**ABOVE** The stable fly feeds on the blood of mammals, transmitting diseases such as anthrax.

**FAR RIGHT** The powerful compound eyes of the bluebottle fly give it a wide field of vision. They produce a mosaic of hundreds of tiny visual images, and are acutely sensitive to movement and color in the fly's environment.

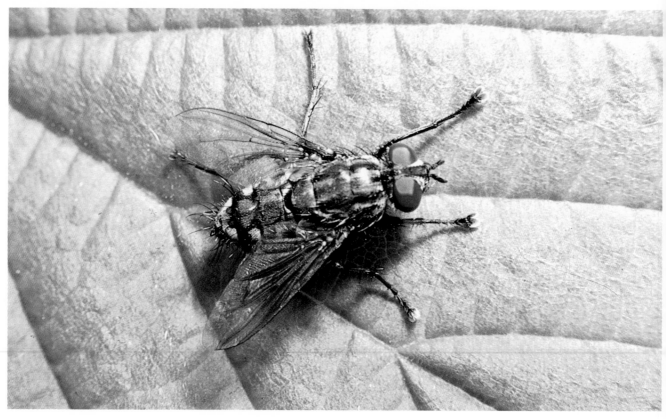

**ABOVE The flesh fly inhabits most regions of the world and feeds on rotting meat. Its larvae break down** decaying animal and vegetable matter and cause serious intestinal disorders in mammals.

variety of ways: the female tachinid fly may lay her eggs inside the host's body; the larvae may bore their way into the host's body; or the host may accidentally eat the tachinid fly's eggs, which hatch internally.

The female tachinid fly of the common European species *Tachina larvarum* attaches her eggs to the skin of a caterpillar. The larvae hatch and enter the caterpillar through the breathing pores in its skin. They feed on the internal organs of their host, attacking the least important organs first and moving on to the rest later. When fully grown, the larvae bore a hole in the caterpillar's skin, killing the caterpillar in the process. They enter a crack in the ground, where they pupate.

## House, stable and tsetse flies

The family Muscidae contains the houseflies, the stable flies and the tsetse flies. Houseflies occur wherever there are human habitations. A housefly's mouthparts form a tubular "tongue" that it folds under its head when not in use, and it does not bite. It has two soft, spongy pads at the tip of its tongue that it places on the food, drawing up fluids through tiny pores leading into its tongue's central collecting channel. The housefly feeds on all types of organic matter, from decaying garbage or feces to human foodstuffs such as jam. While feeding, the fly may pick up living germs from the feces and garbage and transfer them to human food. The germs multiply, spreading diseases such as cholera, dysentery and typhoid.

Fertilized females lay batches of up to 150 tiny white eggs on dung or other decomposing matter. Hatching one to three days later, the newly emerged, white, maggot-like larvae feed on the dung, grow rapidly and molt three times before pupating. The growth of the larvae depends on the temperature; they grow faster in hot weather, although they usually reach full size after about a week. The fully grown larvae bury themselves in the ground and pupate, emerging as adults 3-25 days later. In hot weather, the whole life cycle of a housefly, from egg to adult, takes only three weeks.

During the winter, only flies that live in warm places, such as cattle sheds, continue to breed. Others hibernate as adults or pupae. In the tropics, the flies breed all year round.

## Bloodsucking habits

The stable fly is often mistaken for the housefly because of its similar appearance. But, unlike the

housefly, it has piercing mouthparts and feeds on the blood of mammals. The female lays 25-50 eggs at a time, depositing them on soiled animal bedding. The eggs hatch one to seven days later, and the maggot-like larvae feed on the manure. After two to four weeks, the skin of the larva transforms into a puparial case within which the larva pupates. The adult stable fly emerges a week later.

When feeding, adult stable flies take many small meals from several hosts, rather than one large meal from one individual. Because of this habit, they often spread disease. In man, for example, they may spread anthrax and in horses, a fatal form of anemia.

## Producing live young

The tsetse fly occurs in Africa, where it is the major carrier of a disease known as nagana in cattle and horses, and sleeping sickness in man. Adult tsetse flies have slender bodies with forward-pointing piercing and sucking mouthparts. Both sexes feed exclusively on the blood of a wide variety of animals, including man. The flies hunt by sight. They stay close to the ground and fly quickly. Feeding only twice a week, their meal may last as long as 10 minutes. While feeding, the tsetse fly takes in a lot of unwanted fluid and becomes heavy. After each meal it rests and excretes any excess water.

Newly emerged females mate immediately and give birth to live young. The eggs develop one at a time inside the female's body, and during her short lifetime, about six months, she may only produce 12 offspring. While the larva remains inside its mother, it obtains nourishment from special "milk glands." It breathes through a pair of respiratory lobes on its abdomen that reach the outside via the female's reproductive opening. When the larva has molted twice, the female places it on soft soil where it burrows into the ground. The buried larva becomes immobile, and its skin hardens to form a puparial case. Within the puparium, the larva molts for a third time before turning into a pupa. The adult emerges one to three months later, ready to start the life cycle over again.

## Spreading sleeping sickness

Tsetse flies spread sleeping sickness by biting an uninfected individual. The protozoa that cause this disease, known as trypanosomes, enter the tsetse fly when it feeds on the blood of an infected individual.

**TOP** The flesh fly is one of the few insects that bear live young—the eggs hatch within the female's body.

**ABOVE** Greenbottle flies are metallic-green insects that often rest on rotting meat or feces.

Once inside the tsetse fly, the protozoa enter the fly's intestine where they reproduce. Finally, the protozoa enter the fly's salivary glands. When the tsetse fly bites an uninfected individual, it injects the protozoa along with its saliva. The protozoa reproduce in the bloodstream of the victim before entering its nervous system. Symptoms of sleeping sickness include headache, heart trouble, drowsiness, coma, and often death.

## Blowflies

The family Calliphoridae, or blowflies, consists of medium-sized insects that have metallic-colored

ABOVE **A greenbottle rests on a leaf, its green coloration providing partial camouflage against predators. The female greenbottle frequently lays her eggs in** open wounds, on dead animals or on the soiled wool of sheep. When the larvae hatch, they feed on the body fluids and festering tissues of their host.

bodies. Most species are fast, proficient fliers. They feed on nectar and other sweet liquids, although some species feed on the fluid that oozes from festering wounds or sores. Bluebottle larvae usually live on feces or meat, although some are parasitic on mammals.

The bluebottle, *Calliphora erythrocephala*, is one of the most common species of bluebottle. It occurs in fields and meadows all over Europe, searching for nectar, the juices of rotting flesh and feces on which to feed. It commonly enters human homes. The female bluebottle lays large batches of eggs on raw meat. They hatch after only one day, and the white maggots tunnel into the meat. They liquefy it with their digestive juices in order to feed. A week later, the maggots crawl out of the meat and pupate in a dry place. The skin of the maggot becomes the puparial case, within which the pupa develops. The adult emerges a week later. Bluebottles sometimes transmit the bacteria of serious diseases such as cholera, dysentery and anthrax.

## Carrying anthrax

The closely related flesh fly is also a carrier of disease, notably anthrax. The eggs of this species hatch inside the female, and develop into larvae that enter unclean wounds of humans and other animals, or on decaying organic debris, where they feed on the rotting tissues.

## Fleas

The name "flea" applies to any member of the insect order Siphonaptera, which contains about 1800 species. Fleas are small, bloodsucking insects that live as external parasites on the bodies of warm-blooded hosts. They lack wings as adults, although traces of wings remain in some types of pupae. Rarely more than 0.1-0.2 in. in length, they have laterally compressed bodies (flattened from side to side) that enable them to move more easily through their host's hair or feathers. The tiny claws at the ends of their legs enable them to cling tightly to the body of their host. Fleas have long, powerful back legs and can jump long distances.

Their mouthparts comprise three pointed, needle-like projections called stylets, that form a piercing and sucking apparatus. The stylets have serrated tips enabling the fleas to pierce the skin of their host. They

## INSECTS CLASSIFICATION: 29

### *Fleas*

There are about 1800 species of fleas in the order Siphonaptera (class Insecta). They divide into 200 genera, 16 families and three superfamilies. The two most important are the superfamilies Pulicoidea and Ceratophylloidea.

The superfamily Pulicoidea contains only one family, the Pulicidae, which has 181 species, including the human flea, *Pulex irritans*; the oriental rat flea or plague flea, *Xenopsylla cheopis*, which carries bubonic plague; the cat flea, *Ctenocephalides felis*; *canis*; and the chigoe, *Tunga penetrans*, which occurs mainly in tropical Africa.

The superfamily Ceratophylloidea is divided into 12 families and some 1600 species, including the European rat flea, *Nosopsyllus fasciatus*.

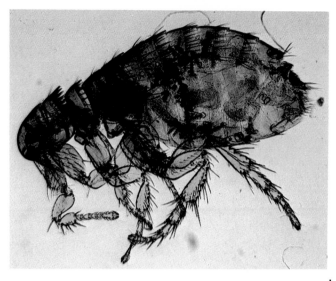

**ABOVE** Fleas are tiny bloodsucking insects that feed on warm-blooded animals. They have a worldwide distribution. Fleas' bodies are flattened sideways to assist easy movement between the feathers or hair of their hosts, and their bodies possess backward-pointing spines that make it difficult for a host to remove the parasites simply by scratching. Fleas use their long, powerful hind legs for jumping.

form a narrow central tube through which the fleas suck up the blood.

### Preparing to attack

When a flea is preparing to bite a victim, it positions its three stylets vertically above the chosen spot—usually where the skin is thin with plenty of blood vessels below the surface. Then, with its head raised slightly, it jabs at the skin several times. The force of the jab causes the stylets to penetrate deeply into the skin of the host, pulling the flea's head down against the skin and forcing its abdomen into the air. Although the bite itself is painless, the saliva, injected into the wound to prevent the blood from clotting, causes a temporary, itchy, red patch around the bite.

### Reproduction

Fleas that spend their lives in the fur of mammals usually breed all the year round, but those that spend most of their lives in the nest of the host (such as bird fleas) time their breeding season to coincide with that of their host. After mating, the fertilized female has a large blood meal before she begins laying her eggs.

Each female flea may lay several hundred eggs in her lifetime. Most fleas either leave their host to drop their eggs on the ground, or else they drop them on the skin of the host, from where many eggs fall onto the ground or into their host's nest. The Tasmanian devil flea cements her eggs to the hair of her host.

The incubation of the eggs usually lasts for one or two weeks. The whitish, worm-like larvae crack open the eggshell by using a small spike on their heads. The larvae are tiny creatures that lack eyes and legs but have biting mandibles. They immediately begin to feed on organic debris, including dried blood excreted by the adult fleas. When fully grown, the larvae spin individual silk cocoons using a secretion from their salivary glands. They camouflage their cocoons with a covering of debris and dust, and pupate.

### A variety of hosts

Adult fleas are bloodsucking parasites that obtain their nourishment from warm-blooded animals. Fleas are divided into two categories: those that remain attached to the outside of the host (epizoic ectoparasites) and those that bury themselves in the skin of their host (endozoic ectoparasites).

Fleas usually parasitize mammals and birds that have a nest in which they live and breed (or that congregate together in large numbers in regular roosts). Most of the known flea species are parasites of rodents, although insectivores and bats are regularly

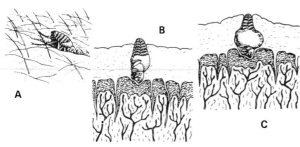

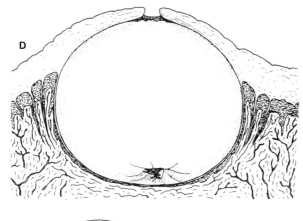

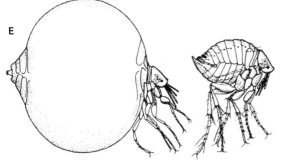

infested. Among birds, fleas are most numerous on the species that nest in holes, such as woodpeckers, tits and sand martins.

## Human fleas

Human fleas, *Pulex irritans*, occur all over the world and flourish in climates with cool, humid summers and mild, wet winters. They have long, stout legs. Their hind legs are adapted for jumping to escape danger or to mount a new host. They have parasitized humans for thousands of years. Always present in houses and dwelling places where conditions are especially damp and unhealthy, their bites were once a source of great discomfort to people. In some parts of the world, the problem is still rife today.

Having first located its prey, a flea chooses the best point of the body to attack, and injects a small amount of saliva into the skin. The saliva contains substances that slow down the clotting of the blood, enabling the flea to drink it. The flea continues to feed in this way for an hour or two, swelling considerably in the process. When it has finished its meal, the flea hides in the victim's clothing, or in some appropriate place nearby, such as a mattress or a crack in the floor. It returns to its victim every time it needs food, but if no prey is available it is able to go without food for long periods.

## A long life

Under favorable conditions, the human flea may live for up to four months, during which time a female is capable of laying between 400 and 500 eggs. She usually deposits her eggs on the ground, in a place where there is plenty of garbage and decaying matter to create a warm, damp environment. After about a month, the eggs hatch into tiny, nonparasitic larvae that feed on the decaying matter.

**TOP LEFT Cat and dog fleas sometimes carry bacteria that cause typhus and bubonic plague.**
**LEFT The chigoe flea is a ground-dwelling tropical insect that feeds on the blood of pigs and humans. A fertilized female chigoe burrows head-first into her victim and sucks its blood (A), (B) and (C). As her eggs develop within her** body, she expands to the size of a pea (D). The fully expanded female is several times larger than her male counterpart (E).
**FAR RIGHT The distribution of the plague flea, *Xenopsylla cheopsis*, which inhabits the warmer areas of the world, and the human flea, *Pulex irritans*, which has a wider distribution.**

## Carriers of disease

The oriental rat flea, commonly known as the plague flea, carries bubonic plague, which it picks up by feeding on infected rats. Inside the flea, the plague bacteria multiply until they completely block the flea's gut. As a result, any subsequent blood meal, unable to pass into the flea's stomach, is regurgitated back into the host, carrying the plague bacteria with it. The flea soon becomes ravenous and begins to bite its host repeatedly in an attempt to feed. As its hunger increases, the flea jumps from victim to victim, spreading the disease with every bite. Usually, the flea feeds only on rats, but, if necessary, it will feed on humans. A tiny creature, it occurs in all regions of the world where there are rats, but especially in the hot, damp environment of the tropics.

Cat fleas, dog fleas and European rat fleas are potential carriers of both the bubonic plague and the typhus bacteria. Cat fleas have bodies covered with backward-pointing bristles that enable them to move forward easily, but prevent them from slipping backward. Sometimes, dog fleas carry tapeworms often resulting in an infestation of the host.

## A tropical African pest

Chigoes are a species of flea that originated in the tropical regions of America and spread to Africa, probably via infested sailors. They are not very common today, mainly as a result of improved living conditions, but they are still a problem in the tropical parts of Africa.

Chigoes are reddish brown in color, and the males and young females are about 0.04 in. long. They live on humans, pigs, dogs, cats and other animals. They have an unpleasant habit of burrowing into the skin of their victims. Males and unfertilized females abandon their victim after they have taken their fill of blood, and hide in the ground. After mating, the fertilized females jump onto a victim and burrow into the skin until they are almost enclosed. Fleas usually infest the lower areas of the host's body first, often underneath toenails, because they are close to the ground, enabling the fleas to leap onto them.

## A painful bite

The chigoe's burrows show up on the surface of the skin where they are each surrounded by a red patch. The body of the flea is often visible at the entrance. Inside its hideaway, the flea continues to suck blood. Within a few days it grows to the size of a pea and begins to lay eggs, dropping them onto the ground.

When the female has laid all her eggs, she leaves the body of the victim, either of her own free will or else in a stream of mucus or pus from the wound. If the victim does not notice the chigoe straightaway, the wound often becomes infected and turns into an abscess. In many cases, bacteria and tetanus attack the wound and gangrene may set in.

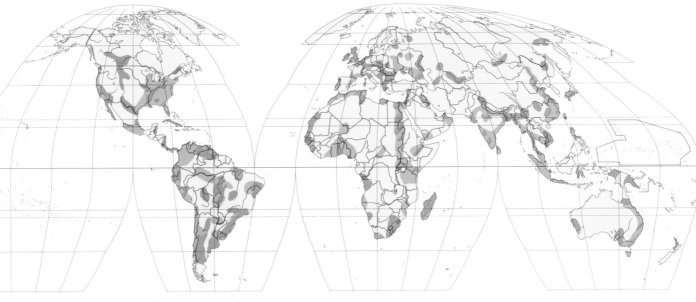

☐ Plague flea          ▨ Human flea

# THE MOLLUSKS

Mollusks form the second-largest group of invertebrates after the arthropods. The phylum contains an estimated 100,000 living species of soft-bodied invertebrates (they derive their name from the Latin *mollis* meaning "soft"). Mollusks occur in a wide range of habitats, and are diverse in body form and life-style. Some of the best-known mollusks are the land-dwelling slugs and snails. But the sea contains a far greater number of mollusk species, such as squids, octopuses, clams and oysters.

The evolutionary success of the mollusks has enabled them to rival the vertebrates in the conquest of territory and the struggle for food.

### The early days

The preservation of mollusk shells in fossil form provides vital information about the age of the sedimentary deposits, and about the environmental conditions that existed at the time. The particular combination of mollusks in a layer of sedimentary rock indicates whether the mollusk lived in a lake, a salty lagoon, a coastal region or a different type of environment.

The study of fossilized mollusk shells has shown that mollusks evolved in the sea more than 570 million years ago. The fossil species of marine mollusks include some of the world's largest invertebrates, such as the giant ammonites, which lived 130 million years ago and grew to nearly 7 ft. in diameter.

No fossil evidence exists to show what the evolutionary ancestor of the first mollusks looked like.

**PAGES 2668–2669 A brightly colored sea slug searches for food on the seabed. The rows of highly decorative and colorful projections along its back act as warning coloration and as camouflage against predators.**

**BELOW Over a period of more than 570 million years, several classes and phyla of insects, mollusks and annelids have evolved from a single class of invertebrate animal — known as the *Protrocophora*.**

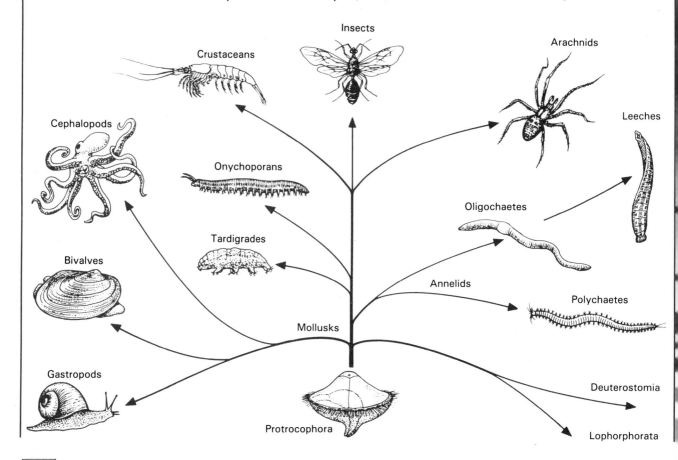

Insects

Crustaceans

Arachnids

Leeches

Cephalopods

Onychoporans

Oligochaetes

Tardigrades

Annelids

Bivalves

Polychaetes

Mollusks

Gastropods

Deuterostomia

Protrocophora

Lophorphorata

However, the study of the larval development of present-day mollusks suggests that the ancestor of both the mollusks and the annelids (segmented worms) was a primitive flatworm that crawled along the seabed.

The earliest mollusk lived in the Precambrian seas, more than 570 million years ago. It probably crawled over the seabed using a wide, muscular foot, and moved in a gliding motion by means of muscular contractions, and by coordinated movements of microscopic hairs on the sole of its foot. Initially its body was covered on top by a protective shell made of organic matter. But, as the mollusks evolved, the shell became reinforced with minerals, particularly calcium carbonate, and assumed the structure of the mollusk shells of today. As in living mollusks, glandular cells along the edge of the underlying skin, called the mantle, secreted the shell. Shell secretion was most active around the edge of the mantle, causing the diameter of the shell to increase in pace with the growth of the animal. In addition, a slow shell secretion by the rest of the mantle caused a gradual increase in the thickness of the shell.

As in the snails of today, one or more pairs of retractile muscles joined the mollusk's shell to its body, enabling the animal to withdraw into its shell. The edge of its shell, and the mantle beneath it, extended over the sides of the mollusk's body and provided protection. At the rear end, the shell and the mantle overhung its body, creating a chamber, known as the mantle cavity, which contained two or more gills and its excretory ducts.

Mollusks' gills were, and still are, formed of thin, blood-filled filaments covered with tiny vibrating hairs called cilia. The vibrations of these hairs created a continuous circulation of water through the mantle cavity, providing the gills with a constant supply of richly oxygenated water for respiration. The water current passed out of the mantle cavity and back into the sea, removing any waste material produced by the mollusk. A similar system exists in all living marine mollusks, though with modifications. When mollusks evolved to live on dry land, their simple gills slowly evolved to become a type of lung. Mollusks discharge their compact, pellet-shaped feces from the same place as they discharge water, preventing the contamination of the flow of water used to oxygenate their gills.

ABOVE The ancient ammonite mollusks lived about 200 million years ago and produced thousands of fossils. All species were sea-dwelling creatures. Their coiled shells were divided internally into several compartments. The only modern relatives of the ammonites are six species of nautiloid mollusks— members of the class Cephalopoda.

## A toothed tongue

Mollusks feed on the algae that cover underwater rocks. In order to remove the algal layer from the rocks, the early mollusks had a special tongue covered with horny teeth, known as the radula. They collected the food scrapings together, mixed them with mucus secreted by their salivary glands, and passed the food to their stomachs.

Many modern rock-dwelling gastropods, such as the limpets, have retained this feature in some form, and feed in a similar manner. They often have several thousand teeth arranged on their radulas. The teeth are replaced as they wear down—the oldest ones pass out in the animals' feces. The shape of the radula and the number of teeth it contains vary according to the feeding habits of the mollusk.

The nervous system of an early mollusk lacked the highly organized brain-like nerve cell clusters of the more advanced mollusks. Instead it consisted of a

ABOVE **Gastropod shells vary greatly in shape, size, thickness and texture. Many species of land-dwelling gastropods have thin shells, while aquatic species often require thick, heavy shells to resist water** **pressure. Most shells consist of a large quantity of calcium and smaller quantities of sodium and carbonate. Snails store calcium salts in their digestive cells for use in shell repair and growth.**

peripheral nerve network and a centralized nervous system formed by a nerve ring around the gut. Two nerves emerged from the ring, connecting it to the mantle and the internal organs.

## Shells galore

As the mollusks diversified, their shells adapted to suit numerous different life-styles—for example, fast burial in the sand or the ability to crawl more rapidly in the pursuit of prey. The basic structure of the gastropod shell consists of a conical spiral made from a series of coils that wind around a central axis. The types of shell that evolved from this basic structure include: the elongate spiral tower shell, which is always buried in the sediment; the large, flat shell of the abalone, formed almost entirely of the last coil; and the thick shell of the spider conch, with its long appendages.

The success of mollusks is due to their adaptability of structure and behavior. Numerous species have flourished because they have evolved a resistant casing that may be used as a refuge or for other purposes, depending on the habits of the species. However, not all mollusks have shells. The shells of some mollusk species have gradually become smaller and in some species, such as slugs, have disappeared completely. The mollusks that lack shells defend themselves by employing mimicry, possessing venomous glands or the ability to move rapidly. Most of the cephalopods (squids and related species), considered to be the most advanced group of mollusks, have smaller or reduced shells. The octopuses lack a shell altogether and have to rely on swimming, mimicry and other strategies for defense.

With the exception of the chitons, mollusks' shells are made from the same compounds—another confirmation of the common origin of the mollusk group. The shells have three identifiable layers: an outer layer, a light-reflecting middle layer and an inner, pearly layer.

Secreted by glandular cells located on the outer edge of the mantle, the outer layer of the shell comprises a thin, tough, organic membrane closely connected to the layer below. In marine species, the

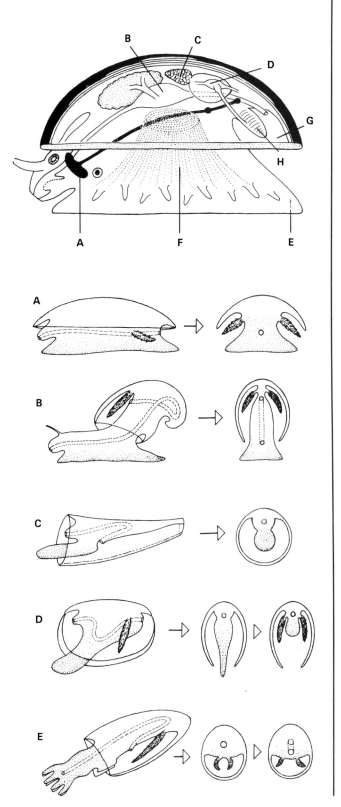

**RIGHT** Most mollusks carry strong protective shells that enclose their delicate body organs: central nerve cluster (A); stomach (B); reproductive organs (C); heart (D); foot (E); foot muscle (F). The shell overhangs the rear end of the body to form a chamber (G) containing the gills (H).

**BELOW RIGHT** All mollusk species share similarities of basic body structure and arrangement of internal organs. The structures of various mollusk classes are shown here longitudinally (left) and in cross-section (right): polyplacophorans (A); gastropods (B); scaphopods (C); bivalves (D); cephalopods (E).

outer layer is often covered with algae and encrusted with numerous species of small marine invertebrates, such as sponges, corals, sea anemones, worms and barnacles. The colonization of the shell provides the mollusk with camouflage, enabling it to blend in with its surroundings.

The shell's middle layer, also produced from the edges of the mantle, contains vertical crystals of calcium carbonate enclosed in an organic membrane. The whole surface of the mantle secretes the inner layer. It consists of thin sheets of crystallized calcium carbonate in the form of calcite or aragonite. The exact composition of the inner layer varies according to the species. Light passing through the fine sheets of the shell gives it a pearly effect.

The shell does not grow continuously—the rate of growth depends on environmental conditions, such as temperature, and on events in the animal's life, such as reproduction. Bivalves of the temperate seas, for example, stop growing during the cold season. The shells of clams reveal concentric "growth" layers, showing where growth stopped during periods of bad weather. Shells do not grow during the mating season, when the mollusks require all their energy for reproduction.

## Internal reorganization

In the earliest mollusk, the primitive arrangement of the mantle cavity at the rear end of the animal did not maximize the circulation of water inside the body. Although this was not a problem for the primitive mollusks, which moved slowly over the rocks, it became a major obstacle for the free-swimming mollusks, such as squids and octopuses, which required an increased supply of oxygen. As the different classes of mollusks evolved, the anatomy of their bodies changed to suit their individual oxygen needs, and

ABOVE Most species of sea slugs, or nudibranchs, possess numerous dorsal appendages called cerata. Nudibranch species that feed on sea anemones transport the stinging cells of their prey to the waxy tips of their cerata and use them to sting attacking predators. The sea slug shown here employs its striking lavender coloration to warn many predatory creatures to steer clear and avoid its painful sting.

## MOLLUSKS CLASSIFICATION: 1

The phylum Mollusca contains approximately 100,000 species divided into seven classes. The most ancient of these classes are the Polyplacophora (chitons); the Aplacophora (solenogasters); the Monoplacophora (monoplacophorans); and the Scaphopoda (tusk shells).

The class Gastropoda contains the greatest number of mollusk species—about 60,000—which occur in three subclasses: Prosobranchia, Opisthobranchia and Pulmonata. They range from the least advanced species, such as the sea-dwelling keyhole limpets and abalones (prosobranchs), through the sea slugs and bubble shells (opisthobranchs), to the most highly evolved gastropods, the land snails and slugs (pulmonates).

The class Bivalvia is the second largest of the mollusk classes with approximately 15,000 species, and includes such familiar marine animals as clams, oysters, scallops and mussels. The seventh class is the Cephalopoda (squids, octopuses, cuttlefishes and the pearly nautilus), whose members are quite different in appearance from other mollusks in the phylum.

each class of mollusk has its own unique arrangement of the mantle cavity.

The gastropods, for example, evolved so that the mantle cavity moved to the front of their bodies; as they move forward, the water passes through their bodies. The bivalves, on the other hand, combined their feeding and breathing functions so that, as well as absorbing oxygen, their gills filter particles of food out of the circulating water and pass them on to their mouths. The squids and octopuses have muscular mantle cavities at the front of their bodies that contract, forcing the water out in a powerful jet that propels them rapidly through the water.

### From nerve cell to brain

The development of a nervous system involves the grouping together of nerve cells into clusters, which gradually accumulate at the front of the animal to form a brain. The structure of the nervous system is, therefore, an excellent indicator of the level of evolution reached by a species. The accumulation of nerve cell clusters at the front of the animal represents an advanced stage of development of the nervous system, and is essential for rapid movement and predatory eating habits.

The evolution of the nervous system of mollusks varies from a primitive, flatworm-like nerve network in the slow-moving mollusks, such as chitons, to a well-developed brain with advanced sensory organs in the fast-moving and predatory species, such as squids and octopuses.

The flatworm-like nervous system of chitons consists of a simple nerve ring around the front end of the gut, connected with two pairs of longitudinal nerve cords. A more complex arrangement has evolved in the gastropods (slugs and snails), which, despite being slow-moving, are actually much faster than chitons. They have a distinct head region, and their nerve cells form definite clusters that may be grouped or fused together in the more highly evolved, air-breathing species.

### Highly developed nervous systems

Cephalopods (squids, octopuses and cuttlefishes) have the most highly developed nervous system of all the mollusks, with a well-developed brain that coordinates all the body's movements. The squid's fast swimming movements and reflexes are controlled by giant nerves that are able to transmit rapid nerve impulses to produce coordinated contractions of the necessary muscles. The complex brain of the octopus consists of many lobes, each of which has its own particular function.

## Sensory systems

Mollusks usually have balance organs embedded in their feet (they each possess one foot), and these consist of a hollow cavity that is lined with sensory cells and contains a hard calcareous granule, called a statocyst. The statocyst always falls to the bottom of the cavity, stimulating the sensory cells there, telling the animal which way up it is.

Mollusks also have chemical-sensitive cells on their bodies. In aquatic species, these are usually inside the mantle cavity. They are grouped on a raised area of skin near the base of the gills and have tiny vibrating hairs, or cilia. The cells monitor the water quality and "taste" the food particles that enter the mantle cavity. Mollusks use their sensory tentacles for feeling and smelling. The number of these varies according to the species. Snails, for example, have a single pair of head tentacles, while scallops have fringes of small tentacles around the edge of their mantle cavities, and squids, cuttlefishes and octopuses have a ring of large, prey-capturing tentacles around their mouths.

Mollusks' eyes show the widest variation of all the sensory organs. In the bivalves, which have no real heads, the eyes are usually situated on the edges of the mantle and at the base of the gills. Shallow-water or burrowing species, such as file shells and dog cockles, have simple light-sensitive eyes, while deepwater species do not have eyes. Species that are able to swim, such as scallops, have slightly more complex eyes with a simple lens, but they can only detect movement and changing light patterns.

## Easily recognizable eyes

Most gastropods, on the other hand, have a pair of easily recognizable eyes on their heads. Exceptions to this are the planktonic violet snails that are blind and float helplessly upside-down, below the surface of warm seas, and species that live in places where there is little light.

Octopuses and squids have the most highly developed eyes. Their eyes are similar to those of humans, and have a movable lens, enabling them to focus on objects.

TOP Bivalves are usually immobile mollusks that remain attached to the seabed or sediment throughout their lives. They feed by filtering organic particles and tiny organisms through the microscopic hairs on their gills.

ABOVE The edible snail, *Helix pomatia*, lives in moist areas on land. Unlike its aquatic relatives, it breathes air with "lungs" in its mantle or shell cavity. Air passes in and out of the cavity through the pneumostome—a flexible breathing pore.

ABOVE The class Cephalopoda (octopuses, squids and their relatives) contains some of the largest and most advanced species of mollusk. All cephalopods have greatly reduced shells and rings of tentacles around their mouths. Octopuses have eight tentacles, each of which is equipped with rows of suckers to aid prey capture. They live sedentary lives, usually only emerging from their rock crevices to pursue prey.

## Adaptation to new environments

Although many present-day mollusks, such as slugs and chitons, have retained a primitive crawling life-style, the flexibility of the basic body plan has allowed the mollusks to conquer new environments. The first bivalves moved around the sandy depths of the sea. However, since they had thin shells, they were easy prey. Natural selection thus favored those species that were able to hide in the sediment, leaving nothing exposed apart from the tips of a pair of tubes for water circulation through the mantle cavity.

Although most bivalves are immobile as adults, some species have developed a rapid escape movement, as a form of defense against predators. The Norwegian cockle, for example, widespread in the cold waters of the north and in the Atlantic, can perform short hops by rapidly bending and extending its foot. Other bivalves, such as the great scallop, have developed a type of swimming ability and can dart forward suddenly if under attack. In order to do this, they seal their water tubes and contract their mantle cavities rapidly, forcing the water out in a powerful jet.

## Free-swimming larvae

Most bivalves are filter feeders and are immobile as adults. To ensure that the various species disperse into new areas, all bivalve larvae are free-swimming. At first, the larvae travel passively, carried along by the water currents, but later they move over the seabed until they find a suitable place in which to transform into an adult. In some species, such as oysters, the larvae are attracted by the presence of individuals of the same species and the young settle on mature individuals, producing irregular piles of many specimens at different stages of growth.

## Gastropod movement

Gastropods, which form the largest class within the mollusks, have adapted the flat, creeping foot of the earliest mollusks for locomotion in a variety of different environments. The animal usually travels over a mucous secretion that it produces from the sole of its foot. Some species, such as the garden snail, move by means of muscular contractions of the whole foot. However, many aquatic species inhabit soft sand and mud bottoms rather than moving over hard surfaces, and the different species have adapted different methods of coping with their particular life-style. A periwinkle, for example, has a shuffling gait because its foot is divided into two halves along its length. Muscular contractions pass along each half of the foot independently, so that the two halves move forward one at a time.

The conch crawls over the sand in a different way. Mollusks have a horny disk on the foot that closes the shell when the foot is withdrawn. In the conch, the horny disk forms a large claw that can be thrust into the sand to anchor the animal, enabling the conch to pull itself forward. Moon shells, on the other hand, crawl below the surface of the seabed using the front part of the foot as a plow.

Other gastropods, such as limpets and slipper shells, are adapted for clinging to hard surfaces. Their shells are low and wide and they can pull them down tightly onto the surface on which they are resting, completely enclosing themselves. Such species have adapted the foot into an adhesive organ that secures the animal to the surface. They also use the foot for locomotion.

## Stationary life-styles

A few species of gastropod, for example the worm shells, have partially abandoned their free-moving life-style. The young worm shell is free-moving and has a tightly coiled shell. However, after a short time, the snail cements its shell to a suitable substrate where it remains for the rest of its life. As the snail grows, it produces a tubular, loosely coiled shell, giving rise to its common name of "worm shell."

Some species of gastropod are free-swimming. The heteropods and sea butterflies, for example, live at the surface of the sea, feeding on the plankton. Their shells are usually reduced in size, or absent, and projections of the foot form fins, or oars, for swimming. Sea slugs are also capable of swimming. Many swim by progressive undulations of the whole body or by snake-like sideways movements. The sea hare spends part of its time crawling over seaweed and part of its time swimming, using flaps on the sides of its foot rather than whole body undulations.

## Feeding habits

The feeding habits of the bivalves are almost the same in all species. They feed mainly on free-living algae, that occur in the upper layers of water. They trap the algae in their gills. However, some species, such as those of the genus *Nucula*, feed on dead cells and other organic particles that settle on the bottom, picking them up with long, finger-like projections. A few deepwater species, known as septibranchs, have a carnivorous diet of worms and crustaceans. Their gills form muscular partitions that they move up and down to suck food into the mantle cavity. Members of the genus *Solemya*, which live on the sea bottom, do not have a stomach digestive apparatus. They obtain their nutrients either by absorption from the water or from bacteria which live in their gills.

## Feeding on algae

Gastropods exhibit many kinds of feeding behavior. The most primitive feed on plant material, which they scrape into their mouths using their toothed tongues. The plant material is then mixed with mucous secretions from the salivary glands and swallowed.

Marine species, such as limpets and sea slugs, graze on algae, while freshwater and land-dwelling snails feed on the tender parts of plants, or on decaying vegetation or fungi. Some land snails, such as the giant African land snail, have become serious agricultural pests, causing immense damage to crops in tropical parts of the world.

Several species of marine gastropod practice suspension feeding. The slipper snail, for example, draws a

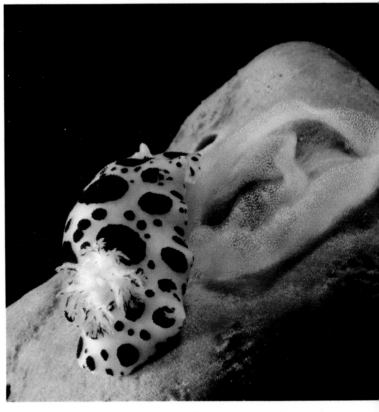

ABOVE Marine mollusks, such as sea slugs, lay several hundred eggs, each of which develops into a free-swimming larva. Many larvae do not reach adulthood, falling prey to other marine animals.

current of water through its mantle cavity, trapping suspended plankton in a mucous layer on the surface of its gills. The worm shells also feed on suspended material, but these snails trail long mucous filaments in the water to trap food, and withdraw them into their mouths when they have caught a sufficient amount.

## Carnivorous gastropods

Some gastropods are carnivores and, although some species, such as those of the genus *Nassarius*, eat dead animal matter (carrion), most carnivorous gastropods are active predators. A few land-dwelling snails feed on earthworms or other snails, but most of the carnivorous species are marine.

Carnivorous gastropods have evolved certain adaptations, such as modifications on their tongues, for cutting or tearing, and the development of a sharp, needle-like, piercing mouthpart called a proboscis. They attack their prey using a variety of methods— they use their powerful muscles to tear them apart, or they inject them with paralyzing liquids and sometimes poisons.

ABOVE Many gastropods hide from predators by burying themselves in sand on the seabed. Certain predatory creatures, however, reach buried gastropods by crawling beneath the surface of the seabed.

The larger bottom-dwelling carnivores feed on other mollusks and echinoderms. The best-known and certainly the most sophisticated gastropod predators are the cone shells that live in tropical and subtropical regions. They impale their prey on a long, sharp tooth that projects from their proboscis and contains a deadly poison. They can release the tooth from the tongue and use it as a poison dart when capturing worms or small gastropods, but when the prey is large, such as a fish, they retain the tooth. The poison quickly kills the victim, enabling the cone shell to feed on the tissues, using its toothed tongue to break them up.

Whelks use a less complicated method to feed on stationary bivalves. The whelk pulls the shells of the bivalve apart using its powerful foot, and wedges them open with its own shell. It then inserts its piercing mouthpart into the victim and feeds at leisure.

## Acidic secretions

Several gastropods, such as moon shells, are able to drill holes in the shells of their prey. The oyster drill, *Urosalpinx*, is particularly well known because of the damage it causes to oyster beds. The animal drills into oysters' shells using an acid secretion from its foot and its narrow tongue. When the oyster drill has made a hole, it pushes its proboscis through and tears at the flesh of the oyster using its tongue.

Many sea slugs are grazing carnivores that feed on stationary creatures, such as sponges and barnacles.

They do not usually have piercing mouthparts, but they often possess cutting jaws. Some sea slugs, such as *Aeolidia papillosa*, prey exclusively on sea anemones by cutting away small pieces of tissue. The sea anemone's stinging cells do not harm the sea slug, even though it swallows them. They become embedded in the sea slug's own body and are used for self-defense against predators.

## Parasitic gastropods

A few gastropods are parasites. Pyramid shell gastropods, such as those of the genus *Pyramidella*, exploit a simple form of parasitism. They live outside their worm or bivalve host and use a hollow, needle-like projection to pierce its tissues and suck its blood. Gastropods of the genus *Entoconcha* display the greatest degree of specialization for parasitism. They lose their shells during their larval stage, and spend the rest of their lives inside the bodies of sea cucumbers, sucking blood with their specially adapted mouthparts.

## Defense and camouflage

Mollusks fall victim to many predators and provide a valuable source of food for birds, fishes and sea mammals. In an attempt to deter predators they have evolved many different defense mechanisms. The mantle, which secretes the shell, also produces slime, acids and ink for defense. Sea squirts and cuttlefishes, for example, squirt poisonous, often blinding substances; the sea hare expels a purple secretion from its purple gland; and several species of dorid sea slugs or sea lemons expel acids. On land, the garlic snails emit a strong aroma of garlic from cells near their breathing glands, and the cone shells have poisonous teeth that they sink into predators.

Some mollusks use camouflage to protect themselves against predators. Mollusks' shells often have protective coloring. The glossy, colored shells of the cowries are usually hidden by a pair of flaps from the mantle. Many species of shell-less mollusks, such as sea slugs, can swim as well as crawl, enabling them to squeeze into small crannies to avoid predators. They have also developed secretions and specialized body colors as a means of defense.

## Monoplacophorans

Mollusks of the genus *Neopilina* caused controversy and excitement when they were discovered in 1952. Initially thought to be limpets belonging to the class

Gastropoda, they were later attributed to a different class, the Monoplacophora, a group of mollusks known only from fossil records and thought to be extinct. They displayed several unusual features, including multiple pairs of organs, such as five or six pairs of gills. Members of the genus *Neopilina* have segmented bodies, a feature that initially led scientists to believe that mollusks were descended from annelids. Today, zoologists believe that the segmented structure of this living fossil developed later. The ancestor of the mollusks may well have been a primitive, unsegmented flatworm from which both annelids and mollusks evolved separately.

Unfortunately, the oldest fossil specimens of the monoplacophorans lie in the most ancient rocks, and all evidence of fossil remains have disappeared. *Neopilina* species appear to have little in common with the chitons—a primitive group of mollusks of the class Polyplacophora. Chitons have remained virtually unchanged since the Cambrian period 570-480 million years ago. The structure of the nervous and digestive systems of both groups of mollusks, their radulas (toothed tongues used for scraping food from

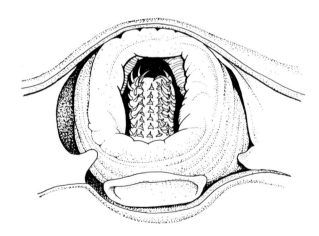

**TOP** The gastropod, *Nassarius reticulatus*, is a member of the dog whelk family. It is a carnivorous scavenger that feeds on carrion, such as the dead, black-eyed shrimp seen here.

**ABOVE** The open mouth of a moon shell gastropod, *Natica sp.*, clearly reveals its toothed tongue (the radula) in the center. The radula has rows of hard, chitinous or horny teeth that scrape away at the food, enabling the animal to swallow only fine and easily digestible pieces of food.

ABOVE Worm shells of the genus *Vermetus* are among the more unusual gastropods, since their shells have been transformed into twisted, chalky tubes, attached to rocks or coral. Many individuals of the species *Vermetus adansoni* live in a cluster, with the animals visible inside their shells.

rocks), and the different shape of their shells suggests that they evolved separately.

## The fossil record

The earliest acknowledged predecessors of the gastropods (snails, limpets and slugs) appeared during the Cambrian period (570-480 million years ago). They had coiled, bilaterally symmetrical, split shells. The Ordovician period (480-435 million years ago) saw the evolution of new families, including some that still exist today, such as the abalones (family Haliotidae) and the keyhole limpets (family Fissurellidae).

The first land mollusks appeared in the Carboniferous period (340-260 million years ago) when the seas retreated. Other groups, such as the worm shells (Turritellidae), appeared later. By the beginning of the Tertiary period (65 million years ago) the major evolutionary branches that make up the mollusks' genealogical tree were established, and there have been no significant changes to them. Many ancient species have disappeared or have not evolved further, and remain confined to limited areas.

## Gastropods

Gastropods (slugs, snails and limpets) comprise the largest class within the mollusk phylum. They have retained most of the basic mollusk features, but have evolved into a wide diversity of shapes and forms and inhabit both land and sea or freshwater. A gastropod has an asymmetrical body, a well-developed head, a broad, muscular foot, and a coiled shell (in varying stages of reduction within the class). There are three subclasses: the Prosobranchia, the Opisthobranchia and the Pulmonata.

The subclass Prosobranchia contains marine gastropods, typically marine snails, that have coiled shells with an operculum or plate that covers the entrance to the shell.

The origins of the subclass Opisthobranchia (sea slugs and bubble shells) derives from anatomical rather than fossil records. The bubble shells of the genus *Acteon*, probably the earliest representatives of the opisthobranchs, are very similar to the more primitive prosobranchs.

The two orders of pteropods in the subclass Opisthobranchia contain the shelled sea butterflies. They are elegant opisthobranchs that swim with the aid of their feet—they each possess a foot that has evolved into a swimming organ. They appeared in the fossil records toward the end of the Cretaceous period (130 million years ago).

The fossil remains of the subclass Pulmonata (land snails) date from the Carboniferous period (340-260 million years ago). Pulmonates are gastropods that lack gills, and superficially differ from prosobranchs in that they lack an operculum. Most live on land, but some are freshwater snails and a few are marine intertidal limpets. Their structural evolution has been slow compared with that of the opisthobranchs. They have evolved special adaptations to life on dry land, to dormancy, to extremes of cold and heat, and they have also developed specialized courtship and reproductive behavior.

## The bivalves

The origins of another common group of mollusks, the bivalves (clams, oysters and their relatives) have not been traced. The oldest fossil remains, dating from 500

million years ago, have provided information on a wide variety of families. They were already highly specialized at this time and cannot be linked to any other class of mollusks. Bivalves have laterally compressed bodies that are covered on the right and left sides by a pair of shell valves.

## The cephalopods

The class Cephalopoda (octopuses, cuttlefishes and squids) are recognizable in the fossil record slightly earlier than the gastropods. Like the gastropods, members of the class have shells in varying degrees of reduction. Some species, like the nautiluses, have large, externally coiled shells, while the squids and octopuses have only vestiges of a shell.

## Distribution

Few species of mollusk occur worldwide; most species are confined to specific geographical areas, although these may be extensive. Many factors determine the distribution of mollusks: different latitudes, which have their own climatic conditions; water temperature; the existence of hot or cold currents; and the presence of deep and extensive rifts in the ocean floor. These features constitute natural boundaries that serve to isolate various populations of

**ABOVE** *Simnia purpurea* is a species of gastropod whose camouflage imitates the color and shape of the colonies of coelenterates (such as jellyfishes and corals) on which it usually lives and feeds. The mantle covering the shell has developed growths that imitate the hydroids (or polyps) of coelenterates.

mollusk. Mollusk populations can evolve independently within these natural boundaries, giving rise to new species that have adapted to specific habitats.

The Indo-Pacific contains the greatest variety of mollusks in any one area. The wide tropical zone has not been affected by major geological or climatic changes, and its fauna has been able to evolve and diversify over thousands of years. The temperature and salinity of the Indo-Pacific waters also remain constant, enabling each species to "specialize." By occupying a precise living space, or biosphere, the mollusk species creates a niche for itself. Such specialization is the first step toward the creation of a new species.

In the temperate zones, the instability of the various environmental factors, especially the temperature, means that fewer new species evolve. Those species that live in temperate zones can, however, adapt to the various environmental conditions.

ABOVE The prosobranch, *Aporrhais serresianus*, is commonly called the burrower because it usually lies buried in firm, muddy gravel. It feeds on algae by grasping the food with its protruded radula teeth.

ABOVE RIGHT The shell of the gastropod *Scala* *communis* has extremely prominent ribbing.

BELOW The main features of a gastropod shell: spiral grooves (A); axial ribs running at right angles to the spiral grooves (B); the columella—the central core of the spiral (C); spiral ribbing (D); a spicule or spine-like structure made from calcium deposits secreted by the mantle (E); a labial tooth, formed by the hardening of the mantle to aid feeding (F); the external lip of the shell (G); digitation or extensions of the shell (H); the siphon, an inhalant tube that can select suitable water to inhale (I); labial folds— parts of the mantle that lie inside the labial tooth (J); center of spiral of shell (K); internal lip of the shell (L); mantle flap (M); extra shell deposits that form tubercles (bumps) (N).

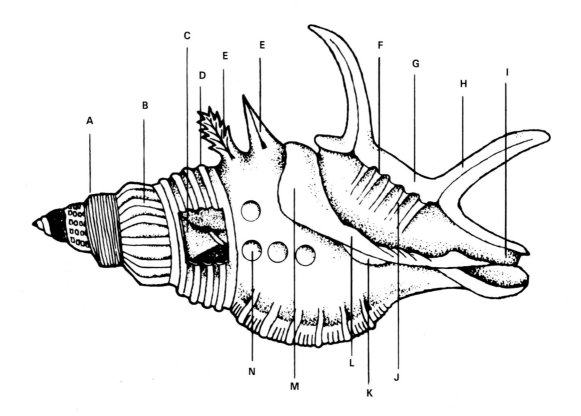

# A PRIMEVAL PEDIGREE

Mollusks such as chitons, tusk shells and worm-shaped solenogasters have remained largely unchanged for hundreds of millions of years, while the limpet-like monoplacophorans stem directly from ancient shelled worms

ABOVE Chitons, such as the species *Tonicella lineata* from the western seaboard of the USA, are small mollusks, whose shells are composed of eight overlapping plates. PAGE 2683 Chitons cling tightly to rocks by creating a vacuum between their broad, flat foot and the rock surface.

The phylum Mollusca (which means "soft-bodied") comprises some 100,000 species grouped into seven classes (see classification box on p. 2674). The first four classes, the more primitive mollusks, are dealt with in this chapter. They are the Polyplacophora (chitons); the Aplacophora (solenogasters); the Monoplacophora (monoplacophorans); and the Scaphophora (tusk shells).

## The chitons

One of the smaller classes of mollusks, the Polyplacophora, contains a group of primitive marine mollusks, known as chitons. They are sedentary or slow-moving animals that graze on algae and on the animals that encrust rocks. Most live in the intertidal zone of rocky shores or in the shallows, but one family has been dredged from depths down to 13,000 ft.

Chitons vary in size from about 0.1 to 12 in., an example being the giant gumshoe chiton that occurs in the Pacific Ocean. Chitons have oval, bilaterally symmetrical bodies. Their backs are covered with a

## MOLLUSKS CLASSIFICATION: 2

### Chitons

The 500 species of marine mollusks known as chitons belong to the class Polyplacophora. They are divided into three orders: the Lepidopleurida; the Ischnochitonida; and the Acanthochitonida. The most primitive, the Lepidopleurida, includes *Lepidopleurus asellus* of Greenland and northern Europe; and *L. intermedius* of the Adriatic Sea. The second order, Ischnochitonida, contains nine families. These include the Mopaliidae (with the species *Placiphorella velata* from the west coast of North America, and *P. atlantica*); and the Chitonidae (with such species as the Caribbean *Chiton tuberculatus* and the Mediterranean *C. olivaceus*). The third order, the Acanthochitonida, has the giant gumshoe, *Cryptochiton stelleri*, of northeast Asia and the North American Pacific coast; the *Cryptoplax larvaeformis* of the Indian Ocean; and *Acanthochitona communis* of the Mediterranean.

### Solenogasters

The class Aplacophora is the second class in the phylum Mollusca. It consists of about 200 species of worm-like marine creatures—the solenogasters and chaetoderms. The solenogasters form the largest group and are subdivided into two superorders: the Aplotegmentaria, which includes the European species *Nematomenia banyulensis* in the order Neomeniamorpha; and the Pachytegmentaria.

shell which is made up of eight shell plates. The shell plates are identical, except for the first and the last. They overlap each other from front to rear. The eight shell plates consist of two layers—all other gastropods have a four-layered shell structure. The mantle forms a tough, thick, skirt-like girdle around the animal. Reinforced with thick, calcareous (chalky) plates, it holds the animal close to the ground.

## Inside the mantle cavity

The bottom surface of a chiton is taken up with a single broad, flat, muscular, creeping foot that contains many mucous glands. A chiton's gills are located inside the mantle cavity and vary in number from 6 to 88 pairs. The gills are called ctenidia and consist of a series of flat, thin-walled leaflets, through which respiratory exchange takes place. Cilia that beat on the gills and on the roof and wall of the mantle groove, create water currents. The water enters the mantle groove, at the point where the chiton lifts its girdle (usually at the front end, either side of its head).

Most species of chiton feed exclusively on the algae that grow on rocks and other hard surfaces. A chiton scrapes its food away from its base using its radula—a chitinous ribbon covered with rows of hard, replaceable teeth. Before feeding, a chiton extends its taste organs, which are contained in a pouch beneath its radula. It moves its teeth over the surface of the rocks or seaweed, rasping off small fragments of food.

The digestive system of a chiton is composed of a tube extending from its mouth to its anus. Glands in its mouth cavity lubricate the food before it passes into the chiton's pharynx and esophagus. The intestine secretes more enzymes to further reduce the food. Compacted pellets of feces pass out through the anus, and are swept away by the water currents leaving the mantle cavity.

## Detecting light and food

Chitons do not have distinct heads, eyes or other sensory organs. Instead, they possess special cells, known as aesthetes. Sensitive to their surroundings and sometimes to light, these cells enable the chitons to detect food. The aesthetes are embedded individually or in large clusters—some species have thousands of them—in their shell plates and in their girdles.

Most chitons have separate sexes (dioecious). When a male detects the presence of a female, he releases sperm into the water surrounding his mantle cavity. The water current carries the sperm into the female's mantle cavity, where fertilization takes place.

## Clinging tightly to rocks

Chitons are all marine mollusks, generally living on rocky substrates and on the upper parts of reefs. They cling tightly to the rocks or corals, moving little and hiding in cracks to escape predators. Some species live among underwater plants that grow inshore. Only a few species of chiton, for example some members of the order Lepidopleurida, live in deeper waters.

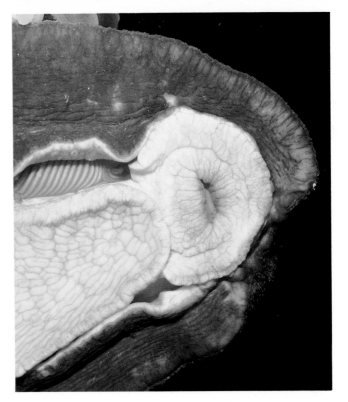

TOP An underside view of *Chryptochiton stelleri*, the largest of the chitons, shows the animal's gills— the striped feature within the protective mantle— and its mouth. Called the giant gumshoe, this chiton measures up to 13 in. long.

ABOVE *Lepidopleurus asellus* lives on the sandy bottom near northern European coasts, where it feeds on silica-rich algae. The species is a primitive member of the class of chitons, lacking muscles between the plates on its back.

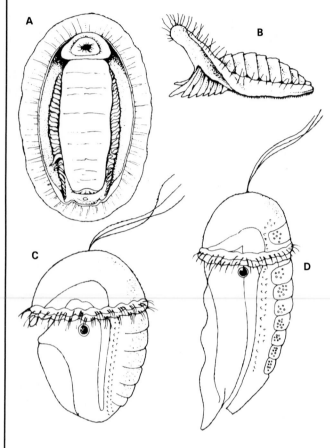

LEFT **The underside of a *Chiton tuberculatus* (A) shows the animal's open mouth at the top, the large central area of the foot, and the gills (striped) along the foot's margins. To capture prey, such as small crustaceans, the chiton raises the large mantle area or "veil" at its front end (B), then swiftly brings it down as soon as the victim passes underneath. The lower drawings (C and D) show two stages in the development of a chiton** larva (or trocophore). **Initially only about 0.02 in. in length and roughly egg-shaped (C), the trocophore gradually develops the plates on its back that are the main features of the adult chiton (D).**
RIGHT **These chitons clinging to rocks on a West Indian beach are almost impossible to dislodge and so insulated that they are safe from predators, rough waves and the drying heat of the sun.**

The class Polyplacophora is divided into three orders: the Lepidopleurida, Ischnochitonida and the Acanthochitonida. The order Lepidopleurida contains the most primitive species of the class. Their shell plates are not connected and have no muscles between them. The order Lepidopleurida comprises species that are no more than 0.8 in. in length. It includes many deepwater species, such as *Lepidopleurus belknapi*, which occurs at a depth of 5000-10,000 ft. *L. asellus*, a native of Greenland and the northern European coasts, does not live on rocks but on the sandy seabed. It feeds on algae rich in silica. *L. cajetanus* occurs throughout the Mediterranean Basin. It lives on rocks at depths of less than 130 ft. *L. intermedius*, a native of the Adriatic, lives on "sand" made up of broken mollusk shells.

### Free-swimming larvae

The order Ischnochitonida contains nine families, including the family Chitonidae. The tips of chitonids' aesthetes, or sensory cells, are often visible on their body surface as dark spots. Female chitonids expel their fertilized eggs into the sea either individually or in groups. The eggs are usually sealed in a spiny envelope. The fertilized eggs develop into free-swimming larvae, or trocophores. Usually shaped like a spinning top, they have a band of cilia around their middles that serves as a locomotor organ and also brings food to their mouths. As the larvae settle on rocks or coral, the band of cilia disappears. The larvae gradually become flattened in shape and take up their creeping way of life. Some species, such as *Chiton barnesi*, incubate their eggs, and others, such as *C. viviparus*, produce live young.

Most chitons have retained their primitive feeding habits and feed on microscopic organisms, such as algae. Some species, such as *Placiphorella velata* of the family Mopaliidae, feed on worms and small crustaceans. *P. velata* lives on the west coast of North America and has a yellowish girdle that is flattened in front. Its shell plates are green or brown in color with blue or brown flecks. Keeping the front part of its girdle raised, it waits for prey to pass beneath it. Using a minimum of movement, it suddenly closes the girdle, trapping the prey, which it slowly absorbs.

### Spines for protection

The best-known member of the family Mopaliidae is *C. tuberculatus*. It lives in the Caribbean Sea and measures approximately 2 in. in length. It can live for as long as 12 years. The top of its body is rounded with eight or nine dark projections. It has five dark brown, knobby spines on its sides,

ABOVE *Acanthochitona communis* is a species of Mediterranean chiton that measures about 1.2 in. long. Its nine pairs of whitish, silky bristles, located on the sides between each plate, function as touch-sensitive organs that enable the animal to feel its way along the bottom.

and its girdle has alternating white, green and black areas.

*Chiton olivaceus* is the most common European species. It lives beneath stones at depths of less than 17 ft. Its coloring ranges from yellow to blue. It is the largest Mediterranean species, growing up to 2 in. in length. Its front and back shell plates are semicircular in shape and are decorated with sharp spines, arranged in a sunburst pattern. The six intermediate plates have a smooth central area with between four and six raised spines on the sides. The Mediterranean species *Ischnochiton rissoi* is much rarer. Its back plate, which varies greatly in color, is decorated with concentric grooves, while the front plate has longitudinal grooves.

## Hiding in their shells

Chitons cling so tightly to rocks with their sucker-like feet and girdles that potential predators have great difficulty in prying them off. A series of muscles causes the chiton's body to contract, creating a "sucker" effect similar to that used by limpets. Chitons' shell plates are flexible and movable, and this articulation, combined with the powerful foot muscle, enables them to curl up on their underside to protect themselves from predators. Because of their tough, outer shell, chitons have very few predators, but they are eaten by a few fishes, such as cod and sole.

Members of the order Acanthochitonida have mantles that cover most of the shell plates on their backs. Covered with red spines, the yellow and brown mantle of the giant gumshoe chiton completely sheathes its butterfly-shaped white plates. It lives among the rocks of the intertidal zones of northeast Asia (where it originated), Alaska and the Pacific coast of America as far south as California. It reaches a maximum length of 12 in., making it the largest species in the class.

## Reduced shell plates

Within the order Acanthochitonida, the plates on the backs of the animals progressively reduce in size. *Cryptoplax larvaeformis*, a species of chiton that lives in the Indian Ocean, has eight small shell plates. Its gills are limited to the rear and sides of its mantle cavity. Its foot is elongated and narrow, barely protruding from

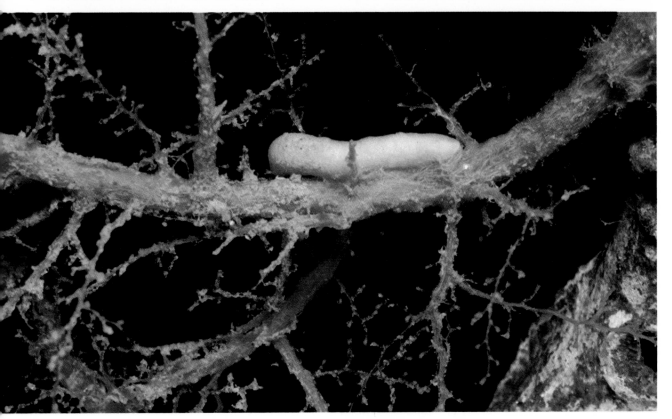

the mantle cavity. It has a habit of penetrating cracks and crevices in the rocks, which it is able to do because of its flexible and elongated body. Chitons have nine pairs of white, bristly tufts, positioned laterally between their plates, that serve a tactile function.

## Primitive relations

Chitons were once classed in the same group as solenogasters—another group of primitive mollusks, now in a separate class. It was once thought that chitons of the genus *Cryptoplax* might be a transitional stage between chitons and solenogasters, a theory reinforced by various physical similarities. Today, however, the similarity is thought to be simply a case of convergent evolution, due to similar life-styles and habitats.

## Mollusks without shells

The class Aplacophora, containing the solenogasters, is the least known of all the mollusks. It contains about 200 species of worm-shaped, bilaterally symmetrical creatures that live in the mud of offshore marine deposits. They do not have shells, but their skins contain tiny, pointed calcareous spicules that give them a silvery, fur-like appearance.

Solenogasters are subdivided into two superorders—the Pachytegmentaria and the Aplotegmentaria. They

**ABOVE** Solenogasters are a small class of mollusks that resemble worms. The upper layer of their skin covers the body either partially or completely, forming a thick cuticle.

The animal takes its name from a groove that runs along the length of its undersurface—hence the Greek *solen*, a tube or channel, and *gaster*, a stomach.

evolved from similar groups but followed different evolutionary paths. Like all solenogasters, creatures in the superorder Aplotegmentaria are widespread throughout the world, including the Arctic and Antarctic oceans. They inhabit ocean waters that vary in depth from several yards to 30,000 ft.

## Making waves

Solenogasters in the superorder Aplotegmentaria have a foot that is reduced to a central furrow and a mantle cavity confined to the rear of their bodies. They move by creating waves of contractions along their hair-like cilia, a process that they facilitate by secreting a lubricating mucous substance from glands behind their mouths. They live in contact with the seabed, but almost always on top of the sediment, and they do not need gills in order to breathe. Their gills have disappeared and been replaced by folds, or lamellae, that serve the same function.

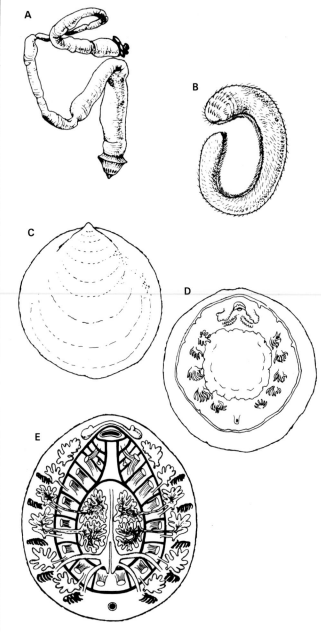

ABOVE The top drawings show two species of solenogaster: *Crystallophrisson indicum* (A) and an immature *Proneomenia aglaopheniae* (B). Both display the worm-like, rather than molluscan, appearance, since the common mollusk features of shell, mantle and foot are absent. Three views of the minute, cap-shaped monoplacophoran *Neopilina galatheae* show it from above (C); from below (D) revealing the paired gills around the foot; and from within, showing its internal structure (E).

## Unsheathing for mating

Some species in the superorder Aplotegmentaria, such as those of the genus *Nierstraszia*, have calcareous spicules inside special sacs that they unsheathe during mating. The species range in length from only 0.1 in. up to 12 in., and they live on algae or coral. Like all mollusks, including the solenogasters, they have a toothed tongue called a radula. The radula is sometimes similar to that of the gastropods, but is often shaped like pincers and used for grasping prey.

The radula has completely disappeared in some species, such as *Nematomenia banyulensis*, a European species that lives exclusively on certain jellyfishes. Instead, it uses its enzyme-rich secretions to digest prey. The stinging cells of the jellyfish, feared by many marine animals, somehow manage to pass through the digestive system of *N. banyulensis* without emitting their toxins. It is not known how this is achieved, and a similar phenomenon takes place among the opisthobranchs. The stinging capsules of the jellyfish remain attached to the spicules on the mantle of some species of solenogaster, and it is likely that they deter predators.

## Tunnel diggers

Among solenogasters in the superorder Pachytegmentaria, the foot has almost completely disappeared, and is restricted to a dorsal shield located near the mouth. The animals live in tunnels under the sand or in the ooze of the seabed, and their shields enable them to dig into the substrate.

Solenogasters in the superorder Pachytegmentaria have respiratory organs modified to suit the group's habitat. The mantle cavity is restricted to the rear of their bodies, where there are two gills. When the creatures bury themselves, the cavity protrudes from the entrance to the hole and is protected by long stings located all around the mantle groove. The solenogasters are either hermaphroditic or have separate sexes, and their feeding tends to be microphagous (the food they eat is minute in relation to their own size). Most feed on algae, protozoa and other microorganisms on the seabed.

## A class thought to be extinct

The class Monoplacophora is a small group of primitive, limpet-like marine creatures that were thought to have become extinct 400 million years ago.

ABOVE Like all the species in its class (Scaphopoda), the tusk shell *Dentalium senegalensis* is an elongated marine mollusk that lives on and in the seabed. Tusk shell species vary in length from 0.2 to 6 in.

RIGHT The tusk shell digs itself into the seabed by extending a muscular foot from its broad end and pushing it into the sand. Repeated extensions and contractions of the foot pull the animal deeper into the sand, while foot lobes help to anchor it. Long tentacles tipped with sensory receptors gather food particles in the sand and pass them into the tiny mouth hidden within the broad end of the shell.

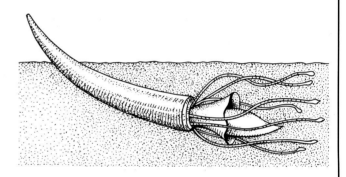

Examples of one of the five species in the class, *Neopilina galatheae*, have been discovered off the coast of Mexico, dredged up from a depth of 12,000 ft.

All species of the genus *Neopilina* have a pale, thin dorsal shell in the shape of a flattened cone, with the tip pointing forward. The shell, which consists of three layers, resembles that of a limpet, which is why the group used to be classified with the gastropods. If the shell is viewed from below, the almost circular foot, with its eight pairs of retractable muscles, is visible. The foot is surrounded by the mantle cavity, in which there are five pairs of gills. To oxygenate the gills, water circulates in a manner similar to that of present-day chitons. The water enters from the front, at the sides of the animal's head, and leaves near its anus.

Species of *Neopilina* possess two unique features. The larvae (called veliger-type larvae) have a foot and a shell, and the adults have a crystalline stylus in their stomach cavities, which releases digestive enzymes.

## Tusk-shelled mollusks

There are about 350 species of tusk- or tooth-shelled mollusks in the class Scaphopoda. Known as tusk shells, they live exclusively on sand and sediment, burrowing into it at an angle and keeping the hind part of their shells outside the substrate by extending their large, club-shaped foot and sinking it over an inch into the sediment. The foot swells when blood pumps into the end part of it, thereby anchoring the mollusk into the substrate. Then, when the foot contracts, the animal is drawn down. The scaphopod repeats the cycle until it is almost completely buried.

All tusk shells have shells that resemble an elephant's tusk. They vary in length from 0.08 in. to 6 in. and are always open at both ends. As the animal grows, new matter is deposited near the larger opening, while the smaller hole gradually widens as the calcium already deposited there dissolves.

The mantle of the tusk shell larva is formed from two lobes that join, forming a tube open at both ends. In some species, such as *Dentalium stenoschizum*, the fusion is not complete. One or more holes or a long slit appear in the shell. The circulation of water within the mantle cavity is not continuous; it is aided by the movement of countless hair-like structures, called

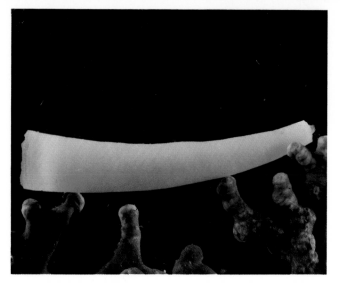

ABOVE Green tusk shells of the genus *Dentalium* occur in the seas off the eastern coast of India. Lacking gills, tusk shells breathe by absorbing oxygen from water that passes into the body through the narrowest (rear) end of the shell.

## MOLLUSKS CLASSIFICATION: 3

### Monoplacophorans

The four or five species of limpet-shaped mollusks known as monoplacophorans belong to the class Monoplacophora, and include the deep-sea species *Neopilina galatheae* taken from the Pacific Ocean off the coast of Central America. Monoplacophorans measure about an inch long and have been found in deepwater trenches around the world.

### Tusk shells

About 350 species of tusk shells constitute the class Scaphopoda. These marine mollusks, with shells shaped like elephants' tusks, are divided into eight families. They include the Dentaliidae (containing the species *Dentalium texasianum* of the North American Pacific coast, *D. vulgare* of European waters, and *D. senegalensis*); and the Siphonodentaiidae (with the species *Cadulus quadridentatus*).

cilia. A tusk shell larva has no gills, and the exchange of respiratory gases takes place over the entire surface of the mantle.

Adult tusk shells have an unusual feeding technique. Around their mouths, they have numerous filaments with broad tips known as captacula. The captacula search for food in the spaces between the grains of sand, where there is considerable animal and plant life, such as diatoms. They capture minute prey with their tentacles—helped by sticky secretions from their glands—and carry the food to their mouths, where a radula crushes it before it is ingested. Once a tusk shell has exhausted one area of its food supplies, it moves on and burrows elsewhere.

Tusk shells have separate sexes. The eggs, which the female expels one by one, are planktonic. Surprisingly, tusk shells are anatomically related to bivalves. They are similar in their body symmetry, the structure of their nervous systems, and the fact that their mantles are divided into two lobes in the larval stage. However, scaphopods probably broke away from the bivalves at an early stage. Today, there are about 350 species of tusk shells distributed throughout the world, including the two poles, at depths varying from 20 to 6000 ft.

### Varied tusk shells

Tusk shells are subdivided into eight families, although in the past only two were recognized. Members of the family Dentaliidae have a conical

shell. In section, it may be circular, hexagonal or octagonal, and its surface can be smooth, ribbed or decorated. *Dentalium texasianum*, a species from the Pacific coast of North America, has a hexagonal, narrow section with an intermediary wall toward the opposite end. *D. vulgare* is perhaps the most common European species, and is found throughout the Mediterranean Basin and in northern Europe. It has a transparent or opaque white shell that is sometimes pinkish toward the tip and can grow up to 3 in. in length. It is textured only at the tip, which is covered in thick, pale grooves. The rest of the shell is smooth. Other species commonly found in the Mediterranean are *D. dentalis*, *D. rossati* and *D. inaequicostatum*.

There are three species in the family Siphonodentaiidae that never exceed 0.4 in. in length in the Mediterranean Sea. Inadequately protected by their shells, members of the group are attacked by a large number of predators. One opisthobranch mollusk, *Scaphander lignarius*, feeds exclusively on these creatures.